Complementary medicine
and health psychology

Health Psychology

Series editors:
Sheila Payne and Sandra Horn

Complementary medicine and health psychology

Anna van Wersch,
Mark Forshaw and
Tina Cartwright

 Open University Press

Open University Press
McGraw-Hill Education
McGraw-Hill House
Shoppenhangers Road
Maidenhead
Berkshire
England
SL6 2QL

email: enquiries@openup.co.uk
world wide web: www.openup.co.uk

and Two Penn Plaza, New York, NY 10121-2289, USA

First published 2009

A catalogue record of this book is available from the British Library

ISBN–10 0335 22011 8 (pb)   0335 22012 6 (hb)
ISBN–13 978 0335 22011 3 (pb)   978 0335 22012 0 (hb)

Library of Congress Cataloging-in-Publication Data
CIP data applied for

Typeset by RefineCatch Limited, Bungay, Suffolk
Printed in the UK by Bell and Bain Ltd, Glasgow

Fictitious names of companies, products, people, characters and/or data that may be
used herein (in case studies or in examples) are not intended to represent any real
individual, company, product or event.

Mixed Sources

Product group from well-managed
forests and other controlled sources
www.fsc.org Cert no. TT-COC-002769
© 1996 Forest Stewardship Council

FSC

The *McGraw-Hill* Companies

Contents

List of tables and figures

Series editors' foreword

This series of books in health psychology has been in progress for over a decade. It is quite remarkable that in so short a period we have seen health psychology change from a marginal topic to a much more mainstream position. This has been a time of rapid growth in the popularity of health psychology as a taught subject at undergraduate and postgraduate level in universities around the world. In addition, health psychology is also emerging strongly as an important 'voice' in psychology with influential things to say about health promotion, health care services and health experiences for those with acute and chronic conditions. Concerned as it is with the application of psychological theories and models to the promotion and maintenance of health and the individual and interpersonal aspects of adaptive behaviour in illness and disability, health psychology has a wide remit. Health psychologists are working in many areas including influencing health care policies at national level, investigating new interventions and health behaviours and working directly with clients or in multidisciplinary teams to deliver good psychological care for those facing illness and impairment. Our book series was designed to support postgraduate and post-qualification studies in psychology, nursing, medicine and paramedical sciences and health psychology units in the undergraduate curriculum.

We are delighted to have Anna van Wersch, Mark Forshaw and Tina Cartwright's book on Complementary and Alternative Medicine (CAM) in this health psychology series. That the book has been commissioned reflects the significant increase in the number of people seeking alternative ways of addressing health and illness issues, beyond what is available to them via conventional medicine and health care. There has been a limited acceptance of some forms of CAM, for example acupuncture, in certain areas of mainstream health care, but considerable scepticism remains. This is very largely because of the lack of sound, empirical evidence of efficacy for many forms of CAM. The result is a mismatch between what many people perceive they need for their health care and what is on offer from conventional health services. This issue can only be resolved by the generation of empirical evidence of the mechanisms and outcomes of CAM. The authors argue that health psychology is uniquely placed to facilitate the development and evaluation of such evidence, through its wide range of theoretical approaches and research methods.

This book, therefore, provides a long-overdue, thorough and critical evaluation of the range of complementary therapies and their place in the health care system. In a clear and accessible way, the authors have addressed these contemporary issues in health and illness. They have taken a wide-ranging look at theories, belief systems, approaches, research findings and developments in the fields of complementary and alternative therapies, in relation to health psychology. In this book they have considered meanings and contexts of health; illness and health care decisions; models of the person and how they relate to health care in different cultures; beliefs and explanations in experimental and non-experimental psychology; research and research methods in CAM; stress and psychoneuroimmunology; pain and anxiety; the management of chronic illness; interactions in health care and challenges for health psychology in future health care. Finally and most importantly, the authors have offered a theoretical framework for future research in CAM therapies, so that findings can be made more comparable to and compatible with those from conventional health sciences. We believe this book to be the first in its field to offer so wide and deep a consideration of this increasingly important aspect of wellness and health care.

Sheila Payne and Sandra Horn
Series Editors

Acknowledgements

The authors wish to thank the series editors, Sheila Payne and Sandra Horn, for their considerable patience and encouragement. In addition, we are grateful to Monika Lee for taking over our project with such professionalism and vigour.

Anna van Wersch
To my children Maartje (Emma) and Ric Stringer – some of the chapters will always remind me of Italy and Spain –, my sisters Marijke and Elsa – other chapters of Mykonos, the 'green table', and restaurant Lotus –, my brother Huub – for visiting me three times in 2008 –, to Mark Forshaw – for our very often late-night discussions on science, physics, mysticism, CAM and health psychology on our BPS accreditation visits throughout the country, and your constant encouragement to get this text in print –, to Tina Cartwright – for always believing in me –, to Darren Flynn – for listening, believing, encouraging, and proofreading with the hat on of an MSc Health Psychology graduate –, to all the students at the University of Teesside who since 1997 up till recently have followed my modules on 'A Critical Psychology of New Age and Alternative Medicine', and 'Health Psychology and Complementary Medicine' – for their debates, insights, and above all enthusiasm, and their continuous requests for 'a book' helping them in their struggle to link psychology to CAM –, to my late mum – who took us all to Tandarts Fred Neelissen, who practised acupuncture and kept us healthy when our GP and hospital doctors were left with their hands in their hair –, for Theo de Boer, Professor of Philosophy, University of Amsterdam – for admitting me as the only psychology student to his modules on Levinas in 1984, and for submitting my essay for publication –, to the Social Futures Institute at the University of Teesside – for giving me a sabbatical and the financial support to go on a medical tour in China, which enabled me to visit over 20 hospitals, community centres and barefoot doctors, and having discussions

via Tjong, our group leader, with Chinese doctors, nurses, patients and Public Health directors in Shanghai, Beijing, Xian, Guilin and Hong Kong in order to understand their different belief system and their harmonious way of integrating both science with Confucianism, and western medicine with traditional Chinese practices –, and last but not least, to Bert-Jan Heijmans, my dearest husband – for carrying around my laptop, books and papers wherever we went – with love.

Mark Forshaw
For her support and love, my thanks to the genuinely unique Amanda Crowfoot, en voor jullie uitstekende vriendschap, Anneke en Bert-Jan, eindeloos bedankt.

Tina Cartwright
To my boys, Tom and Rowan, and to Chris for his love and infinite patience – thank you. Thanks also to Anna, for inviting me to join the team and for her lessons in quantum mechanics!

 Introduction

Health psychology is a relatively new area of the discipline of psychology, and has made significant headway in the last 20 years or so in departing from clinical psychology, which, historically, it is arguably an offshoot from. While CAM (complementary and alternative medicine) is not new, it is only more recently that it has begun to attract significant attention, and begun to rise in popularity, and become something more than a set of 'fringe' practices. Of course, the history of CAM, in general, is such that orthodox medicine is, one could argue, the child of CAM. Orthodox practice is actually the more recently introduced alternative, since systems of CAM such as Ayurveda and Chinese medicine are thousands of years old, as opposed to modern medicine, which in its recognizable form of clinical practice backed up by scientific laboratory assays and the like, has been around a matter of a couple of centuries (Porter, 1997). Complementary approaches represent an interesting psychological and cultural phenomenon alone, regardless of their actual diagnostic or therapeutic value. They are part of the world's heritage, and contentiously, one could argue that they will be part of its future too.

In many ways, health psychologists are best placed to understand and investigate CAM. First, we pride ourselves on our research base and training, which ideally equips us to take an empirical and evidential approach, which in many ways has been lacking in CAM until recently. Health psychology is, in essence, a good bridge between theory and practice, passing over the 'river island' of research on the way. Second, we are, as psychologists, human behaviour experts, which allows us to understand CAM from all angles, both in terms of the therapist and their motivations and those of the client, and to fully comprehend the nature of the interactions between both in the therapeutic context. Third, as a relatively new branch of psychology, we understand what it is like to have to justify what we do, to debate with the powerbase over our practices, and to struggle against misunderstandings. In many ways, this means that we have certain insights into the nature of the attempts by CAM practitioners to be accepted by the proponents of the orthodox.

Here, we try to apply health psychology, as we understand it, to CAM in the important contexts as we see them. We explore the models of the person, and how views of who we are and what we are interact with medicine, CAM and allopathy. We interrogate the literature pertaining to the popularity and individual choices to use CAM. We look at ways in which CAM can be investigated, through a number of research modalities and consider the political and social milieu in which CAM practitioners ply their trade. Since stress and stress management are key issues for health psychologists, we consider the ways in which complementary approaches can legitimately or otherwise claim to be helpful tools in creating a calmer, more rational and happier individual. Similarly, we take a look at chronic illness, where often orthodox medicine has been able to achieve only a limited amelioration of a health condition, leaving room for other approaches, with a greater or lesser degree of success, dependent upon the particular CAM being considered.

In this volume, the reader will *not* find a wholeheartedly supportive approach to complementary and alternative medicine, *nor* will they encounter a vehement attack on CAM in all its diversity. Rather, the most productive way to address CAM in the context of health psychology is to accept that negative research findings are indicative of a 'problem' of sorts, but that there are still things that remain to be learned and discovered. All things have the potential for good and bad, and what is needed is a thorough, open-minded look at what is a substantial phenomenon. Only through a balanced and fair approach can all interests be properly represented. If progress is to be achieved, of whatever sort, it is achieved through rational conversation, not through clamour.

In this book, we refer to certain CAMs specifically, and others are not mentioned. It is important to note that inclusion in this book does not constitute an endorsement, nor does exclusion necessarily imply criticism of any particular approach. Specific CAMs are referred to where they are particularly useful examples to illustrate a point, but we are aware of the vast range of CAMs, which could never all be discussed and debated neither equally nor fully in a work of this length. The idea is to provide a flavour, rather than the whole banquet. Our overarching aim in writing this book is to provide a central point of reference for health psychologists (and to a certain extent other health professionals) learning about or researching CAM, and to generate a debate around the place of CAM in health psychology *and* the place of health psychology in CAM. In so doing, we hope that we have also created a work that will be of use to CAM practitioners who wish to understand a little more about what health psychologists do. To return to an earlier analogy, we are bridge builders.

Complementary medicine in context

Things fall apart; the centre cannot hold.

(W.B. Yeats)

Introduction

Complementary and alternative medicine (CAM) refers to a diverse range of therapeutic practices and systems of healing that are primarily defined by their relationship (or opposition) to mainstream conventional medicine. For example, the Cochrane Collaboration define CAM as 'a broad domain of healing resources that encompasses all health systems, modalities, and practices and their accompanying theories and beliefs, other than those intrinsic to the politically dominant health system of a particular society or culture in a given historical period' (Zollman and Vickers, 1999). Originally, 'alternative medicine' was used to define therapeutic approaches that were incompatible with and replaced conventional medicine, but over time, the definition has broadened as many therapies and systems of healing are seen to 'complement' rather than oppose conventional medical care. Defining CAM is an inherently complex process, since it incorporates such a wide range of therapies (from complete systems of healing such as Traditional Chinese Medicine (TCM) to over-the-counter herbal remedies) and what is considered to be CAM changes as some modalities become absorbed into mainstream practice and new therapies emerge.

Irrespective of definitional issues, it is generally agreed that CAM use is increasing exponentially in western countries. This raises a number of issues central to health psychology. What are the explanations for the trend towards more pluralistic healthcare? What does it tell us about patients' expectations and health needs? What are the implications for patients' experiences of illness and treatment, both allopathic and complementary?

Psychological research remains relatively limited in this multi-disciplinary field, predominantly focusing on the reasons why people turn to CAM and psychological aspects of the treatment. However, many of the theoretical approaches within psychology can be applied to this area to better understand the motivations underlying people's treatment decisions as well as attitudes within orthodox medicine. In order to understand the context of changes in health care decision making, we can also draw on anthropological and sociological data to understand the impact of wider social and cultural factors on our beliefs about health, and the relationship between CAM and established orthodox systems.

The relationship between complementary and orthodox medicine

The fundamental approaches of complementary and conventional medicine are frequently contrasted, in which the former is seen to adopt a biopsychosocial approach, the latter a reductionist biomedical perspective. Although it includes a diverse spectrum of therapeutic systems, the discourse of complementary medicine emphasizes the health-promoting ability of the body and the importance of aligning physical, social and environmental factors in a holistic, integrative approach. In contrast, the biomedical model has traditionally focused on the treatment of disease and is highly interventionist, treating the individual parts of the body that are not functioning correctly. Critics of the biomedical model thus have argued that the patient has become increasingly marginalized from medicine through this 'spatialization' of illness (Foucault, 1976), which not only separates the person from their body but also disempowers the patient and discourages their active participation. Parallels can be drawn with Mischler's discussion of the struggle between the 'voice of lifeworld' and the 'voice of medicine' in the medical consultation, causing fragmentation and ineffective communication:

> the voice of the lifeworld refers to the patient's contextually-grounded experiences of events and problems in her life . . . In contrast the voice of medicine reflects a technical interest and expresses a 'scientific attitude'.
> (1984, p. 104)

Certainly there is evidence from the satisfaction literature that patients want more personal relationships with their practitioners and greater attention placed on psychosocial issues (Bertakis et al., 1991; Greene et al., 1994). In CAM consultations, particularly during initial history taking, greater time and attention is given over to the context of the patient's illness and life history. It has therefore been suggested that this greater congruency with the patient's lifeworld is one reason why people are increasingly turning to complementary health care (Busby, 1999).

'Holism' is another well-used term to characterize complementary therapies and differentiate them from the reductionism of conventional medicine. Indeed, the holistic nature of CAM is frequently cited by users of CAM as an important component of their experience of the treatment process, both in terms of uncovering and explaining causal patterns and in treating illness using a range of strategies (Gould and MacPherson, 2001; Paterson, 2004; Richardson, 2004; Cartwright and Torr, 2005). However, there is some debate about the meaning of 'holistic' and the extent to which it can be applied to any therapeutic approach. 'Holistic' is defined as diagnosing and treating the individual within their wider environment, using complex interventions and involving the patient in the treatment process (Pietroni, 1987). Thus, despite the strong association between holistic practice and CAM, holism is the goal of all therapeutic practice. As Fulder (2005, p. 775) points out, 'the holistic approach is simply good medicine, and it cuts across all modalities and techniques, whether alternative or conventional'.

Indeed, we must be wary of an overly simplistic view of biomedicine. Sharma (2000, p. 214) argues that biomedicine is not 'the monolithic entity which it so often appears to be from the perspective of patients'. She suggests that we understand the recent rise of CAM within the context of a 'wider web of relationships' characterized by medical pluralism. Several theorists link such pluralistic practice with the fragmentation indicative of post-modernism. For example, Bakx (1991) argues that the increasing separation and alienation of consumers from biomedicine has resulted in a new culture of medical pluralism in which conventional medicine is losing its ideological hegemony while complementary and folk therapies thrive. The failure of medicine to reflect wider cultural shifts has resulted in it becoming 'politically and culturally out of "synch" with a growing section of the population' (1991, p. 25). However, in the majority of cases, orthodox or allopathic medicine is not rejected but rather supplemented with complementary healthcare (Eisenberg et al., 1993; Astin, 1998; Thomas, Nicholl, and Coleman, 2001).

A change in attitudes towards health and illness has certainly been linked with the increasingly consumerist health culture prevalent in the West. For example, Kelner and Wellman (1997) argue that the popularity of CAM reflects the increase in 'smart consumers' who are more proactive and informed in health matters. The majority of studies have shown that users of CAM meet their health needs by 'shopping around' for treatments and using both orthodox and complementary medicine (Sharma, 1994). Indeed, health information is more widely available through the internet, media and illness-specific support groups encouraging greater involvement in one's health. Such shifts are also evident within medicine, with increasing attention on patient-centred care and patient participation, particularly in the area of chronic illness. In the UK, the Department of Health has invested £18 million in the expert patient education programme, which aims to help

100,000 people with chronic illnesses manage their conditions better through a lay-led self-management programme. This has been linked with a 'new era of opportunity for the NHS' (Donaldson, 2003, p. 1279), although findings regarding its success are mixed (Griffiths et al. 2007).

The meaning of health and illness: lay beliefs

Research into people's beliefs about health and illness and their relationship to behaviour is a key focus of health psychology and one which overlaps with the related disciplines of medical sociology and anthropology. Our conceptions of health and illness vary according to our socio-cultural background and are a strong determinant of our health-seeking behaviour. It has therefore been suggested that one explanation for the popularity of CAM lies in the congruence between patient and practitioner models of health and illness (e.g. Astin, 1998).

So how do people conceptualize their health? Studies show that lay beliefs about health are multi-faceted, reflecting medical (absence of disease), psychological (vitality and well-being), and social perspectives (social relationships) (Blaxter, 1990). Herzlich's (1973) classic study of lay beliefs in France highlighted the importance of harmony or balance and capacity for activity. Such beliefs are congruent with the philosophy and language of CAM, users of which are predominantly from the middle classes, like the majority of Herzlich's sample. A more recent review of qualitative studies exploring perceptions of health and illness revealed interesting class differences in beliefs (Chamberlain, 1997). While working-class people tended to see health in functional terms, namely the absence of disease and the ability to carry out daily activities, those of higher socio-economic status (SES) placed more emphasis on the positive qualities of health such as vitality and well-being. Chamberlain (1997) differentiated four further groups which represented differing views of health in terms of complexity and integration as well as reflecting broad socio-economic trends. The *solitary view* held by lower SES participants perceived health as purely physical while the *dualistic view* incorporated both physical and mental aspects but saw them as operating independently. The two remaining groups were predominantly of higher SES, in which the *complementary view* perceived mental and physical aspects as forming an integrated whole, while the *multiple view* saw health as an interdependent balance of physical, emotional, social and spiritual elements. Linking this with the use of CAM, it might be surmised that the integrated approach characteristic of most complementary therapies is particularly congruent with the beliefs of those from higher SES groups, who are also more able to purchase private CAM care.

Beliefs about underlying aetiology are also central to our understanding of health and illness. In a British Q-sort study, Stainton-Rogers (1991) found seven key explanations of health/illness, ranging from the biomedical perspective of 'body as machine' to a sociological 'cultural critique' in which illness is a consequence of exploitation and oppression. People also develop theories about specific illness episodes in order to make sense of their condition and to decide on appropriate action. Indeed there is an abundant literature on the importance of causal beliefs in people's understanding and adaptation to illness (Benyamini et al., 1997; Turnquist et al., 1988; Roesch and Weiner, 2001). Reflecting on its impact on evaluations of care, adequate explanation is frequently cited as an area of dissatisfaction with the medical consultation (Greenberg et al., 1984; Williams et al., 1995). Looking at congruence between patients' expectations and outcomes in primary care, Williams et al. (1995) found that 'explanation of the problem' (of the course, cause and prognosis) was central to patients' expectations and was also the area of greatest discrepancies between expressed need and actual outcome. The failure to get at the 'root cause' of a condition and provide adequate explanation has been cited as a reason for turning to CAM (Kelner and Wellman, 2001; Sharma, 2001). For example, a qualitative study with frequent users of CAM found that the integrative explanatory frameworks provided by CAM contributed to their understanding and adaptation to illness as well as their understanding of the treatment itself (Cartwright and Torr, 2005). This suggests that CAM offers a more congruent biopsychosocial framework to incorporate lay people's beliefs about health and illness (Astin, 1998).

The context of health care decisions

Decisions concerning the treatment of illness are strongly influenced by our beliefs, prior experiences and availability of health care. Using a cross-cultural perspective, cognitive anthropologist Arthur Kleinman (1980) divides the health care system into three sectors: popular, folk, and professional. The balance and relationships between the sectors differ according to cultural norms and historical changes in beliefs and institutional power. The popular or lay sector is where illness is typically first defined and initial health care decisions made, such as whether to self-treat or refer to one of the other sectors. This non-specialist sector includes a broad range of sources, including friends and family, colleagues, church members and any other lay person with relevant illness experience. Studies in the UK suggest that the most symptoms are initially treated within this sector (Verbrugge and Ascione, 1989), and the majority of visits to both complementary and orthodox practitioners involve lay referral (Scambler et al., 1981; Sharma, 2001). The folk sector incorporates both sacred and secular healing and is characterized as non-bureaucratic and non-professional in contrast with the organized and regulated professional sector exemplified by the western medical system.

The positioning of complementary medicine in this typology is somewhat problematic due to the great diversity of therapeutic modalities encompassed within the umbrella term 'complementary and alternative medicine'. Thus, therapeutic systems that have formalized training and regulatory bodies (e.g. osteopathy, chiropractic, acupuncture and homeopathy) are more 'professionalized' than therapies without such formal guidelines and standards. Additionally, conventional medicine is not the dominant system in all cultures; in countries such as China, traditional Chinese medicine (TCM) is equally mainstream and institutionalized. Moreover, folk medicine is characterized as being embedded within a particular culture, yet many complementary therapies are not indigenous healing systems but rather relatively recent adoptions from other cultures. Clearly, there is considerable cross-over between the sectors and health care decisions are iterative, often involving movement between the different sectors, both to inform understanding of somatic symptoms and facilitate adequate treatment for the evolving illness experience.

Use of CAM

The increase in the popularity and use of CAM has been widely documented both in research and the media. Estimates of use vary according to the inclusiveness of the criteria used. For example whereas some studies focus solely on consultations with complementary practitioners (Thomas, Nicholl and Coleman, 2001), others include the use of over-the-counter remedies (Ernst and White, 2000). Additionally, surveys vary in the use of checklists of specific complementary therapies versus open questions which allow greater inclusivity of 'fringe' therapies. This lack of standardization in both the definitional umbrella of CAM and the study methodology makes temporal and cross-cultural comparisons problematic.

Two surveys have attempted to provide population estimates of CAM use in the UK population, postulating that between 20 and 28% of the population use CAM each year, when including both consultations and over-the-counter remedies (Ernst and White, 2000; Thomas, Nicholl and Coleman, 2001). In the BBC survey (Ernst and White, 2000), telephone interviews were conducted with 1204 randomly selected participants of which 20% reported using 'any alternative or complementary medicines or therapies' in the previous 12 months. The most popular therapies were herbalism, aromatherapy, homeopathy, acupuncture/acupressure, massage and reflexology. Based on average monthly estimates of spending, Ernst and White (2000) extrapolate that 1.6 billion is spent per year on complementary health care in the UK. The larger of the two studies favoured a narrower definition of CAM and focused primarily on consultations with practitioners of six of the more established therapies (acupuncture, chiropractic, homeopathy, hypnotherapy, medical herbalism, and osteopathy), with additional questions about two further therapies (reflexology and aromatherapy) and over-the-counter remedies (Thomas, Nicholl and Coleman, 2001). From 2669 respondents to a postal questionnaire, they estimated that 10.6% of the population in England used one of the above six therapies in 1998, rising to 13.6% with the inclusion of the additional two therapies, and 28.3% with the inclusion of over-the-counter remedies. When lifetime use is considered, estimates increase to 46.6% using the most inclusive definition of CAM. From this data they extrapolate that 22 million visits were made to the six key therapies in 1998, at a cost of £450 million, since 90% of consultations are made outside the NHS. Comparisons with a pilot study conducted five years previously indicate an increase of around 2% in the number of CAM consultations per annum. A more recent Omnibus survey conducted in 2001 estimated that 10% of the population had used one of 23 named CAM therapies in the past 12 months, slightly lower than previous estimates (Thomas and Coleman, 2004). However, this may reflect differences in methodology and the fact that the survey was conducted across the UK rather than just England.

Figures of CAM use are similar or higher in the USA and Continental Europe where therapies such as homeopathy and acupuncture are often included in medical insurance. In the USA, it has been estimated that the number of consultations with complementary practitioners is higher than the number of visits to primary care physicians (Eisenberg et al., 1993). For comparison with the UK, Thomas, Fall and Nicholl (2001) estimated 1 CAM consultation for every 9 GP visits. Two large scale studies estimate that 40% of people use CAM each year in the USA (Astin, 1998; Eisenberg et al., 1998). However, the definition of 'unconventional health care' used in both studies was very broad to incorporate practices 'neither taught widely in the U.S. medical schools nor generally available in U.S hospitals', including megavitamins and lifestyle factors providing they were outside of standard medical care. Thus, such statistics are likely to over-estimate the usage of more narrowly defined complementary medicine. For example, a more recent large-scale US survey reported that 62% of adults had used some form of CAM in the previous 12 months, which dropped to 36% when prayer specifically for health reasons was excluded (Barnes et al., 2004). Eisenberg et al. (1998) noted a substantial increase in use from 33.8% in 1990 to 42.1% in 1997, again considerably higher than that estimated by Thomas, Fall and Nicholl (2001) in the UK, although this may largely reflect the measurement differences between the two studies.

Virtually all studies, irrespective of country and methodology, indicate that users of CAM are more likely to be female, younger, educated to a higher level, and of higher social class and income. This is likely to indicate differential access to CAM; those of higher income and education have greater access to information about health care options and the disposable income to afford private therapy. It has also been suggested that those from higher social groups are more likely to be self-directed and willing to explore non-conventional health care options as well as consuming all kinds of culture at higher rates (Kelner and Wellman, 2001). Unfortunately, this may perpetuate health inequalities in which those from higher socio-economic groups have access to a wider range of health resources. In terms of gender, women are also higher users of allopathic primary care (Bradlow et al., 1992) and it has been suggested that they are more likely to seek medical care when suffering from psychological complaints (Verbrugge and Ascione, 1989; McIntyre et al., 1996).

Reasons for using CAM

Clearly the demand for CAM has increased substantially and much of the psychological research has focused on delineating the factors associated with CAM use. First, a number of studies have compared users of various complementary therapies (generally homeopathy, acupuncture and osteopathy) with patients of conventional medicine to provide a 'CAM user' profile (e.g. Vincent and Furnham, 1997). Such studies indicate that compared with patients of conventional medicine, CAM users are more critical of orthodox medicine (Furnham and Smith, 1988; Furnham and Bhagrath, 1993; Furnham and Kirkcaldy, 1996; Vincent and Furnham, 1996), place greater emphasis on psychological factors in illness (Furnham et al., 1995), are more likely to have holistic health beliefs (Astin, 1998; Furnham and Smith, 1988), and are more concerned with environmental issues and preventative health practices (Furnham and Forey, 1994; Furnham et al., 1995; Furnham and Kirkcaldy, 1996; Kelner and Wellman, 1997). These findings are consistent with the argument that complementary therapies are attractive because they are more congruent with patients' philosophical and health beliefs compared with the biomedical perspective (Furnham and Beard, 1995; Vincent and Furnham, 1996; Astin, 1998). However, we should be wary of treating all CAM users as a homogenous group with similar health beliefs and attitudes (Furnham et al., 1995). There is evidence that those seeking a more spiritual focus are more likely to choose less mainstream therapies such as Reiki (Kelner & Wellman, 2001). While the above surveys offer a descriptive profile of the typical user, they tell us little about people's underlying motivations to use CAM. Additionally, the notion that CAM users are somehow 'different' from non-users is perhaps less relevant as more people are using CAM.

A second related area of research has thus focused more specifically on the reasons why people are choosing to use CAM. The findings from such research are typically categorized into 'push' and 'pull' factors, namely those factors which push people away from conventional medicine and which attract people to look for alternatives (Vincent and Furnham, 1996). For example, in a questionnaire study with 250 patients of acupuncture, osteopathy and homeopathy, Vincent and Furnham (1996) identified five factors describing reasons for using CAM: perceiving CAM as valuable, perceiving conventional medicine as ineffective, concerns about the side-effects of conventional medicine, poor doctor–patient communication in conventional medicine, and the availability of CAM. Bishop et al. (2007) recently synthesized studies exploring beliefs associated with CAM use in a systematic review. They concluded that 'CAM users want to participate in treatment decisions, are likely to have active coping styles and *might* believe that they can control their health.[1] They value non-toxic, holistic approaches to health and hold "postmodern belief systems" while viewing themselves as unconventional and spiritual' (2007, p. 862).

However, we also need to view the motivations for using CAM within the wider context of health needs and attitudes towards health care. First, concerns about conventional medicine are in part likely to reflect the greater prevalence of CAM use in people with chronic diseases (Vincent and Furnham, 1996; Kelner and Wellman, 1997; Eisenberg et al., 1998), which tend to be difficult to treat successfully within the orthodox medical system. Several studies have shown that users of CAM tend to have poorer health than non-users (Astin, 1998; Eisenberg et al., 1998; Sirois and Gick, 2002) suggesting a pragmatic use of CAM based on health need.

Decisions to seek alternatives to conventional care is frequently indicative of wider concerns with medical treatment, particularly regarding side-effects and worries about medication dependency (Conrad, 1985; Donovan and Blake, 1992; Horne, 1997; Horne et al., 1999). In developing a questionnaire to assess people's beliefs about medicine, Horne et al. (1999) found that those attending a complementary medicine clinic (homeopath/herbalist) were more likely to perceive medicine as harmful and over-used than those presenting a prescription at a pharmacy. In-depth studies with users of CAM reflect these wider concerns over long-term medication and invasive treatments, whereas CAM is valued for providing 'natural' treatments that work in harmony with the body and which are therefore perceived as safer and more desirable (Sharma, 1994; Cartwright and Torr, 2005).

Additional attractions of CAM include the nature of the consultation itself (good communication, lengthy consultations, attention to psychosocial factors) and the role of the patient in the treatment process (greater autonomy and control over health, more patient-centred/egalitarian). It has been suggested that communication within medicine has lagged behind scientific developments, resulting in a lack of attention to the emotional needs of patients (Willison and Andrews, 2004). In contrast CAM provides longer consultations with in-depth history taking and highly individualized treatments. Additionally, a more collaborative and egalitarian relationship with the practitioner may be particularly attractive to those seeking a more proactive role in their health (Kelner and Wellman, 1997). The nature of the patient–practitioner relationship has received much attention within the literature of both complementary and conventional medicine, linking it with patient satisfaction, adherence to treatment recommendations and better health outcomes (Noble, 1998; Ong et al., 1995; Beck et al., 2002). Certainly a host of studies show that CAM users highly rate the therapeutic relationship and recognize the role it plays in the healing process (Luff and Thomas, 2000; Sharma, 2001; Scott et al., 2003; Cartwright and Torr, 2005).

We have already considered the role of people's beliefs in their care-seeking decisions. Astin (1998) found that concordance with spiritual and philosophical orientations was a more important predictor of CAM use than dissatisfaction with conventional medicine. Others have attempted to understand CAM use through the framework of post-modern values, arguing that the philosophy of CAM is consistent with cultural changes indicative of the post-modern era (Bakx, 1991; Siapush, 1999). Such attitudes have been characterized as: the rejection of authority, consumerism, individual responsibility for health (Coward, 1989; Bakx, 1991; Siapush, 1999) and also having a holistic outlook, viewing nature as benevolent and holding anti-science sentiments (Siapush, 1999). Two Australian studies have attempted to map such beliefs onto people's attitudes towards and use of CAM, providing some support for the role of post-modern values in treatment choices and reinforcing previous research regarding the precedence given to 'natural' remedies (Siapush, 1998; Callaghan and Jordan, 2003). However, there is little evidence that people are sceptical of science (Siapush, 1999) nor that use of CAM is a 'flight from science'; instead people are making treatment decisions on the basis of personal rather than institutional legitimacy (Haug and Lavin, 1983).

It seems likely that multiple factors, both pragmatic and ideological, influence initial and subsequent decisions to use complementary therapies and that the relative emphasis of these factors change over time. For example, dissatisfaction with conventional medicine is likely to be particularly salient in initial decisions to turn to CAM, while positive experiences with CAM are more important in subsequent motivations (Luff and Thomas, 2000; Sharma, 2001). Indeed, many of the 'pull' factors are experiential and emerge as individuals use alternative practices. Similarly, beliefs in holism and preferences for natural treatments may reflect individuals' acceptance of beliefs represented by practitioners rather than ideological orientations towards CAM. Cross-sectional studies looking at CAM users at one point in time do not differentiate between types of user (e.g. committed or one-off) or indicate whether different health beliefs lead to health care choices or whether the treatment itself results in changes to patients' beliefs and attitudes. For example, Yardley et al. (2001) observed reciprocal interactions between people's illness and treatment beliefs and their experiences of chiropractic therapy and suggest that the therapeutic relationship plays a significant role in this process. Qualitative studies have been valuable in providing greater insight into this complexity and suggesting how the meaning of CAM changes over time. However, there is a need to explore motivations at different stages of CAM use and to follow up patients longitudinally.

Sirois and Gick (2002) attempted to distinguish between new/infrequent and established users of CAM, alongside non-users in a cross-sectional questionnaire study. Both the CAM groups reported more health-aware behaviours, openness to new experiences and dissatisfaction with conventional medicine, which they suggest are important factors in initial treatment decisions. However, the best predictor of committed CAM use was health need (number of health problems). They interpret their findings using a socio-behavioural framework, which suggests that CAM use reflects three factors: predisposing (e.g. beliefs), enabling (e.g. financial resources) and need (e.g. health problems). Very few studies, however, have explored the process of using CAM longitudinally. One such study interviewed 23 new users of acupuncture on three occasions over a six-month period (Paterson and Britten, 2003). Their findings supported other single-account qualitative studies as to the evolving nature of CAM use (Sharma, 1992; Cassidy, 1998; Luff and Thomas, 2000; Gould and MacPherson, 2001). Dissatisfaction with conventional medicine was central to initial decisions, with other factors such as a desire for more holistic care and a concern with maintaining health and well-being, featuring in later accounts.

Surprisingly few studies have utilized psychological models to understand and predict the use of CAM. Despite the extensive use of the Theory of Planned Behaviour (TPB) to predict a host of behaviours in health and social psychology, only one published study has applied it to the prediction of CAM use, specifically the self-reported use of homeopathy (Furnham and Lovett, 2001). This prospective study found that attitudes, subjective norms and perceived behavioural control predicted 49% of the variance in intention to use homeopathy, while intention predicted 56% of the variance in behaviour (frequency of homeopathy use).

Another psychological model that has been under-utilized in CAM research is Leventhal's self-regulation model which posits that people's perceptions of their illness help them to make sense of their condition and guide their coping responses, such as the decision to use CAM or take medication (Leventhal et al., 1980, 1984). Illness perceptions consist of beliefs about symptoms, aetiology, illness duration, consequences and potential for cure or control (Leventhal et al., 1980; Lau and Hartman, 1983). Also relevant to treatment decisions are beliefs about the treatment itself, such as whether it is harmful or necessary (Horne, 1997, 1999). Although this model suggests a useful framework for understanding CAM use within the wider context of the illness experience, its application to CAM use has been limited. A small longitudinal study ($N = 30$) with users of homeopathy found causal beliefs to be most predictive of understanding and adherence to homeopathy (Searle and Murphy, 2000). A larger cross-sectional online survey found that illness (beliefs in serious consequences, emotional causation and illness coherence) and treatment beliefs (holistic health beliefs) were predictive of current CAM use (Bishop et al., 2006). Additionally, different beliefs were associated with the use of different CAM therapies. The sample was however, biased towards those with favourable attitudes towards CAM, with the majority having used at least one therapy in the past. Further work is warranted in this area, not simply to predict CAM use but to better understand the role of CAM in how people interpret and respond to the changing trajectory of illness.

Locus of control (Rotter, 1966) has been extensively studied within psychology and linked to a variety of health-related beliefs and behaviours (Norman and Bennett, 1996). It assumes that people have generalized expectancies regarding their control over their environment. Individuals with high internal control interpret events as resulting from their own behaviour, while those with external control attribute events to factors outside their control such as luck, chance, fate and the impact of powerful others. While having control over one's health and treatment is a significant factor in people's decisions to use CAM (Kelner and Wellman, 1997), findings regarding the more general concept of locus of control are rather mixed. Several studies using Lau's (1982) health locus of control scale found that users of CAM reported higher self-control over health (Furnham and Bhagrath, 1993) and lower provider control over health (Furnham and Smith, 1988; Furnham and Kirkcaldy, 1996). However, this latter finding may simply reflect a scepticism of conventional medicine, since the provider control sub-scale referred specifically to 'doctors' rather than health professionals more generally. A more recent study using the multi-dimensional health locus of control scale found no differences in control beliefs between non-users, new users and committed users of CAM (Sirois and Gick, 2002).

Although we have discussed in some depth the beliefs of CAM users, it should be reiterated that the strength and prevalence of such beliefs are likely to vary according to the modality preferences of individuals. Some therapies have greater legitimacy, regulation and integration with conventional practices (e.g. osteopathy, acupuncture), while others remain on the 'fringes' (e.g. Reiki). The beliefs and motivations underlying such choices are therefore likely to vary considerably. A related issue is the impact of different institutional contexts on beliefs and expectancies. The majority of research has been conducted with users of privately funded CAM, but as CAM becomes increasingly available of the NHS, there is a need to explore pathways to publicly funded CAM and its relationship with experiences of care. Several previous qualitative studies with both homeopathy (Barry, 2002) and acupuncture (Paterson, 2004), have suggested that there may be differences in outcome according to the way in which the therapy is practised, namely the utilization of a traditional vs. medical approach. The relationships between beliefs, treatment context and outcomes have not, however, been explored systematically. The impact of cultural factors on decisions to use CAM is also an under-researched area, with the majority of studies being conducted with predominantly white, middle-class participants. Considering the importance of cultural factors to the development of health and illness beliefs, it is somewhat surprising that there is such a paucity of research into ethnic differences in attitudes and use of complementary therapies.

Attitudes within conventional medicine

In conjunction with the increasing popularity of CAM among patients, a growing number of studies have explored the attitudes and behaviours of health professionals towards CAM with several reviews of the literature in the UK (Botting and Cook, 2000) and internationally (Ernst et al., 1995; Astin et al., 1998; Hirschkorn and Bourgeault, 2005). Broadly speaking, these studies indicate an interest and acceptance of CAM within conventional medicine but also concerns about the evidence base for complementary therapies. One of the first UK studies was conducted over two decades ago with a small sample of GP trainees attending a training conference (Reilly, 1983). It found that over 80% viewed acupuncture as useful, and 50% considered homeopathy and osteopathy useful. Additionally, 20% reported using CAM therapies and a third had made referrals. Although this was a small unrepresentative study ($N = 86$), it revealed a positive attitude towards CAM that is mirrored in larger more recent studies in the UK and elsewhere. One such study (van Wersch et al., 2003) found a positive attitude towards CAM in 87% of the 84 practising GPs in the Northeast of England. However, 37% of these took the opportunity to vent their concerns in the open-ended final question, by indicating the lack of evidence of these therapies, and the uncertainty of these practitioners' qualifications. Several referred to the possibilities of 'dubious practitioners', 'quacks' and 'mumbo jumbo'.

Various methodological limitations have hampered drawing conclusions in this area, in which most studies remain small scale, unrepresentative and lacking questionnaire standardization or validation. Moreover, definitional variations of what constitutes CAM once again raise difficulties of equivalence and hamper cross-cultural comparisons. Despite such methodological variability between studies, Ernst et al. (1995) conducted a meta-analysis with 12 studies using an expert grading system to evaluate perceived physician effectiveness of CAM. They conclude that doctors perceived CAM as 'moderately effective', which they contrast with the actual evidence of efficacy from randomised controlled trials. In a later review of 25 international studies, Astin et al. (1998) argued that a meta-analysis was inappropriate given the variability in the methodology of the studies. They found that half of physicians believed in the efficacy of at least one CAM modality, with 43% referring for acupuncture, 40% for chiropractic and 21% for massage. Both studies found that manipulative therapies (e.g. osteopathy and chiropractice) followed by acupuncture are commonly viewed as among the most effective therapies. Indeed, these therapeutic systems are the most easily incorporated into the biomedical framework.

The majority of surveys have been carried out with general practitioners or medical students. It might be surmised that GPs are more holistic in their approach to medicine and therefore more open to CAM. Indeed, Thomas, Fall, & Nicholl (2001) estimate that 40% of GPs are involved in the provision of CAM in the UK. In a comparative study, Perkin et al. (1994) investigated the attitudes of hospital doctors ($N = 81$), GPs ($N = 87$) and medical students ($N = 237$). The latter were the most enthusiastic about CAM but the least informed. This supports a number of findings that student and younger doctors are more favourable towards CAM (White et al., 1997; Botting and Cook, 2000; Easthope et al., 2000). Twenty per cent of GPs and 12% of consultants were practising CAM, with the majority of both groups (93 and 70% respectively) having made at least one referral to an external CAM practitioner. In a national study focusing on the attitudes of hospital physicians towards CAM, Lewith et al. (2001) sent questionnaires to all members of the Royal College of Physicians in the UK. Although the response rate was low (23%), the sample included 2748 physicians from a range of specialities. They found that 41% of doctors referred patients to CAM, although referral rates were low with the majority referring 0–1 patients per month. Using a conservative estimate by assuming that all non-responders had no involvement with CAM, they suggest that at least 1 in 10 specialists are using or referring to complementary therapies in the UK. Rather worryingly, only 13% of those using CAM had any specific training, which echoes previous findings (Botting and Cook, 2000). This raises serious issues regarding both safety and appropriateness of CAM use by physicians.

Despite the lack of large representative national studies on health professionals use of CAM, the available evidence suggests that patient demand influences health-provider behaviour (Astin et al., 1998) and that attitude, together with training, is the strongest predictor of use of CAM (Hirschkorn and Bourgeault, 2005). In a critical review, Hirschkorn and Bourgeault (2005) argue that the literature is primarily descriptive and lacks 'adequate theorization of constructs' in explaining provider attitudes and behaviour. Despite apparently positive attitudes, evidence suggests that this is not necessarily put into practice, thus 'a substantial degree of slippage exists between attitudes and behaviour, whereby an expressed positive or negative attitude does not easily equate with positively or negatively orientated professional behaviour towards CAM' (Hirschkorn and Bourgeault, 2005, p. 157). For example, while younger doctors report more favourable attitudes towards CAM, they are less likely to refer patients (Lewith et al., 2001). Of course the attitude–behaviour gap is a well-observed phenomenon in health psychology and has received considerable attention by theorists using a social cognition framework. It is therefore rather surprising that no studies have been conducted using psychological models to predict physician behaviour.

Using a sociological framework, Hirschkorn and Bourgeault (2005) propose a comparative conceptual model (see Figure 1.1) that attempts to contextualize health providers' decisions and highlight areas that might account for conflicting findings in the literature. Provider factors include personal characteristics such as age and sex, and professional characteristics such as consultation style and CAM training. They point out that despite discrepancies between personal and professional viewpoints, they are not

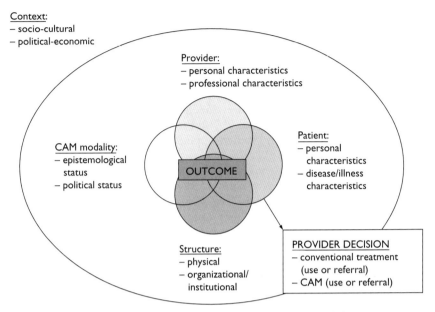

Figure 1.1 A conceptual framework of health care providers' attitudes/behaviours regarding CAM

Source: Hirschkorn and Bourgeault (2005).

always fully differentiated in the literature. In terms of patient characteristics, research indicates that practitioners are more likely to use/refer patients to CAM for certain conditions or illness states such as palliation (Lewith et al., 2001), but beyond this we know little about how the practitioners' attitude towards patients impacts on their behaviour. Modality factors particularly relate to the degree of epistemological 'fit' between specific complementary therapies and biomedicine. This may explain why some therapeutic systems are more acceptable to orthodox practitioners, since their mechanisms can be interpreted within a biomedical explanatory framework (e.g. acupuncture and chiropractic). Since this in turn influences status and referral rates, it again highlights the professional hegemony of biomedicine. Structural factors are primarily framed in terms of barriers to CAM use, such as lack of time, potential for liability, and financial constraints, although exactly how practitioners negotiate such factors is under-researched. Finally, Hirschkorn and Bourgeault highlight the under-development of research into contextual factors which incorporate socio-cultural and political-economic influences and impact upon how CAM is viewed within a society. Indeed, such criticisms are levelled more generally at health psychology and its neglect of wider socio-cultural and political influences on health (Marks, 1996; Murray and Campbell, 2003).

Despite a lack of theorization in this area, surveys consistently highlight several issues which act as barriers to a more extensive integration of CAM: lack of information about the effectiveness of therapies, lack of health professional knowledge about CAM, lack of statutory regulation, and concerns about the possible harmful effects of treatment (BMA, 1993; Botting and Cook, 2000). It has been suggested that the spread of CAM within conventional medicine reflects public need/demand rather than evidence-based practice (Botting and Cook, 2000). Personal endorsement by patients appears to be a key factor in predicting positive attitudes of health professionals (Easthope et al., 2000). Certainly, the use of CAM by orthodox practitioners without sufficient knowledge or training highlights the importance of adequate regulation within conventional medicine (Botting and Cook, 2000; Lewith et al., 2001; Owen et al., 2001). It is therefore of no surprise that CAM practitioners have concerns that their expertise and the effectiveness of their therapies may be under-valued by the practice of orthodox practitioners.

In summary, while studies suggest that health care professionals hold favourable attitudes towards CAM with considerable numbers either practising or referring patients, methodological and theoretical shortfalls limit the generalizability of the findings. Additionally, discrepancies appear to exist between doctors' attitudes towards CAM and (a) their actual behaviour and (b) patients' perceptions of doctors' attitudes. A number of studies have pointed to the fact that the majority of CAM users do not disclose this to their doctors (Sharma, 2001; Robinson and McGrail, 2004). The primary reason given is the perception that their doctors are not supportive of their CAM use (Williamson et al., 2003; Robinson and McGrail, 2004). Further theory-based research is necessary to disentangle the complexities of health care providers' attitudes towards and use of CAM in their clinical practice.

Well-being: a new direction for health care?

It has been suggested that conceptions of health have moved beyond the narrow definitions espoused by biomedicine to a much broader view of health as a 'state of well-being' which entails the individual assuming greater responsibility for their health (Coward, 1989). This search for well-being may be a key factor in explaining the popularity of CAM, since its holistic approach is perceived as better able to address the needs of the 'whole' individual. Certainly, as we have seen, users of CAM are more health conscious, more concerned with the prevention of ill-health and more likely to adopt healthy behaviours (Furnham and Kirkcaldy, 1996; Kelner and Wellman, 1997)

However, well-being remains a nebulous concept that *may* include health but also goes beyond it to include vitality, happiness, creativity and fulfillment (Huppert et al., 2005). From a psychological perspective, well-being is generally equated with life satisfaction and happiness (Kahneman et al., 1999), factors that are associated with better health but are not typically incorporated within the treatment goals of health care. Despite the broad nature of well-being, there is frequently little differentiation between health and well-being in the literature. In contrast, a phenomenological study specifically explored the meaning of well-being for lay people, using a range of methods including multiple interviews with participants (Schickler, 2005). Schickler (2005) identified three key themes: energy and vitality, 'to enable one to do all that one wanted to do'; being in control of one's life, including decision making and independence; and ethical congruity, living in accordance with one's values and beliefs. Such themes resonate with qualitative studies that have identified 'expanded effects' of CAM which relate to wider psycho-social improvements in people's lives beyond specific health problems (Cassidy, 1998; Paterson and Britten, 2003; Cartwright, 2007). In Schickler's study, consulting a conventional or complementary practitioner was seen as one means of either restoring or maintaining well-being, although lifestyle factors such as diet and stress reduction were most commonly reported. Additionally, health practitioners were rated as a source of loss of well-being when experiences were negative.

This has several implications for health care practice. First, CAM is inherently more orientated towards the broader concept of well-being (as opposed to health) with greater time and focus on the consultation process, individualized treatments and greater attention to the active participation of the patient through lifestyle change. Traditionally, many complementary therapies such as acupuncture have focused on the maintenance of health and energy rather than the treatment of illness. Additionally, the goal of treatment for many people using CAM, particularly long-term users, is to enhance well-being rather than to simply address illness (Gould and MacPherson, 2001; Paterson, 2004; Verhoef et al., 2005). However, looking at well-being in its wider context, to what extent does it reflect middle-class beliefs and access to resources? Research considered earlier (e.g. Chamberlain, 1997) suggested significant class differences in perceptions of health, with a middle-class focus on vitality and well-being compared with the utilitarian focus of lower SES groups. Since the majority of complementary therapies are purchased privately at considerable cost, the prevalence of CAM use in higher SES groups reflects wider inequalities, in which individuals from lower SES groups have poorer health but are less likely to use health care (Carroll, et al., 1993; Wilkinson, 1996; Marmot, 2001).

To what extent has conventional medicine taken on board the concept of well-being? While its focus remains on the biomedical, it has arguably responded to the shift in attitudes by moving towards a more participatory patient role (Coulter, 1999; Say and Thomson, 2003; Haywood, et al. 2006), in discourse if not always in practice. Similarly, the increasing 'problem' of chronic illness requires greater attention to quality of life issues and acknowledgment of the central role the patient plays in managing their own condition, hence the attention given to the expert patient programme. According to Kelner and Wellman (2001) 'well-being is a state which can only be achieved if the individual is prepared to work at it through exercise, diet and other kinds of self-discipline', suggesting that an active role in one's health care in crucial to this state. However, despite all the rhetoric around patient-centred care and active engagement of the patient, not everyone desires a more participatory role in health care decisions. Indeed, many patients fear making the wrong decision and prefer the more traditional directive approach (Savage and Armstrong, 1990; Lupton, 1997). As we have seen, complementary medicine particularly appeals to those who want to have more control over their health and treatment decisions. Both conventional and complementary medicine have the potential to facilitate well-being through the control of symptoms and empowerment of patients. However, the particular focus of CAM on a holistic, individualized approach to diagnosis and treatment and the precedence on the therapeutic relationship suggest an approach that is particularly congruent with the wider concept of well-being.

Summary and implications

> With the current policy emphasis on patients as "partners" in health care, able and expected to make informed decisions about the treatment they receive, it is no longer tenable to ignore this clearly stated demand for CAM health care.
>
> (Thomas, Nicholl and Coleman 2001, p. 10)

This chapter has explored the context in which health care decisions are made and looked at the reasons why increasing numbers of people are choosing to use CAM, often at considerable financial cost. Research presents a picture of CAM users as *critical* 'smart consumers' for whom decisions about using CAM are based on personal models of health and illness, experiences of medical care, health need and access to services. Although often dissatisfied with conventional medicine, the majority of people are not rejecting this approach to treating illness, but rather supplementing it with alternative practices. This therefore reflects wider cultural changes in which people are more informed about health matters and willing to meet their health needs by adopting more pluralistic health practices.

While 90% of CAM remains in the private sector (Thomas, Nicholl and Coleman, 2001), there is increasing pressure from patients for CAM to be made more widely available on the NHS. Research with health professionals, mainly doctors, demonstrates generally positive attitudes towards complementary therapies, particularly those that are more congruent with a biomedical framework, such as manipulative therapies and acupuncture. However, such attitudes are not always translated into referral behaviours and, more worryingly, there is evidence that a minority of health professionals are using CAM without sufficient training (Botting and Cook, 2000; Lewith et al., 2001). For health professionals, any further integration of CAM into mainstream health care requires evidence-based research, adopting a biomedical methodological framework. The tensions and applicability of such methods to CAM are discussed elsewhere (see Chapters 2 and 4). For patients however, personal legitimacy based on factors personally relevant to the individual such as treatment effectiveness, is likely to take greater precedence than scientific evidence in treatment decisions:

> for many patients the question of scientific proof is equally irrelevant. They have already tried orthodox remedies which are supposed to have been subjected to rigorous testing but which have not worked for them.
>
> (Sharma, 1992, p. 206)

Research in this multi-disciplinary area has been somewhat piecemeal, and frequently descriptive rather than analytical or theoretical in focus. Additionally, the huge range of complementary therapies subsumed under the umbrella of CAM make generalizations about 'CAM users' problematic. Therapies vary in their epistemology, application, degree of regulation, evidence base and acceptability within the biomedical paradigm, all of which are likely to impact on their appeal to both consumers and health professionals. The majority of research also provides a 'snapshot' of CAM users at a single point in time and does not distinguish between different types of user (e.g. committed vs occasional user). Consequently it is difficult to determine if people's beliefs about health and illness underlie motivations for using CAM or whether such beliefs are a product of the treatment itself. In order to unravel the complexities in this area, there is a need for prospective and longitudinal research together with theory-based and inquiry-focused methodological approaches.

Note

1. Findings regarding control beliefs are inconclusive – this is discussed further later in this section.

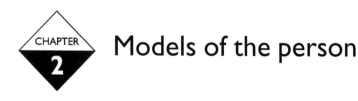

Models of the person

CHAPTER
2

Le soi même est l'irrémissible identité, sans nul besoin de justifier, ou de thématiser, son identité. Le soi même est 'en soi' comme dans sa peau.
(Levinas, 1968, p. 494)

Introduction

Health psychology and complementary and alternative medicine (CAM) both have health, illness and well-being as their major concerns, however, thus far not much on CAM has been reported in health psychology textbooks or in taught health psychology curricula. One might wonder why this is. Motivations for and attitudes towards CAM use have been studied but issues such as furthering the understanding of its functioning, examining alternative models of the body, or exploring the benefits of a different communication pattern (Watt, 1988), have so far been ignored. The omission of CAM from mainstream health psychology raises several pertinent questions. Do health psychologists uncritically follow the claims of biomedicine that CAM practice equals quackery? Or is it assumed that CAM's 'unproven' practice is explained by the placebo effect? Since health psychologists are social scientists interested in the contribution of psychology to the treatment of illness or the identification of its aetiologic and diagnostic correlates (Matarazzo, 1982), more attention to this alternative and popular form of health care would have been expected. Drawing upon cultural differences, historical developments in psychology, and both philosophy of science and science perspectives, explanations will be sought for this gap in the health psychology literature. Will the favoured biopsychosocial model of health psychology be sufficient in the study of CAM? Or will a biophysics-psychosocial model do more justice to both the models of the body and the workings of CAM within the origins of its social-cultural heritage? In that case, will a biophysics-psychosocial model be the way forward to enhance our knowledge and understanding of CAM? And, could health psychology play an important role in this area?

CAM and health psychology: differences in epistemology

Complementary versus mainstream medicine

Complementary health care is, as Conner (2004, p. 1695) stated, 'post-institutional care', meaning 'the proliferation of non-biomedical therapies that are mostly unsupported by government-authorised systems of medicine, such as hospitals, medical training schools and health insurance schemes'. Complementary therapies are seen as something 'extra' or 'additional' (Murray and Shepherd, 1993), which is not part of the core curriculum of medical university education. It was not until 1998 that intentions to include CAM in the education of physicians were documented in both Britain (Rampes et al., 1997, 1998) and the USA (Wetzel, et al., 1998). Since then, additional teaching seem to have happened at some, but not all, medical schools in various countries in different forms, such as 'taster sessions' in Britain (Greenfield et al., 2002), options in The Netherlands (Visser, 2006), or as a selection of lectures in the undergraduate programme in both the USA (Forjuoh et al., 2003; Wahner-Roedler et al., 2005) and Germany (Hahn et al., 2005). Initiatives for *postgraduate* curriculum development in medical schools have also been documented, but thus far only for the USA (Wahner-Roedler et al., 2005).

As main reasons for the categorization of CAM into 'complementary or alternative' medicine, the following two main points have been identified: (i) non-compatibility with current scientific understandings and nomenclature in bio-medicine (Lewith and Chan, 2002; Barrett et al., 2003; Oberbaum et al., 2003; Cohen, 2005; Walach, 2005; Westerman, 2006); and (ii) difference in philosophy of care (Watt, 1988; Cohen, 2005; Geller and Francomano, 2005). The latter has been specified as *holistic* versus *positivistic* (Marian et al., 2006) or, *intuitive* versus *deductive* (Barrett et al., 2003). Other factors include: (a) distinctive credentialling and regulation of practitioners (Cohen, 2005; Curtis and Gaylord, 2005); (b) unequal status and access to public funding (Bennet, 1987; Cohen, 2005); and (c) various governmental arrangements regarding the Medicine Act to guarantee both safety (Trumpington, 1987; Ernst, 1995; Jonas, 1997) and effectiveness of medication (Watt, 1988; Mills, 2001; Cohen, 2005; Curtis and Gaylord, 2005).

Health psychology versus conventional medicine

Health psychology is taught either as one of the sub-disciplines of an undergraduate academic psychology programme, or as a masters or professional doctorate/PhD course. As such, health psychology is focused on the empirical understanding and explanation of health and illness behaviour at micro (personal), meso (social context) and macro (government/cultural)-level. Health psychology mirrors conventional medicine in several ways, such as in the scientific epistemology of rationalism and empiricism, the Cartesian split of body and mind and in its understanding of health and illness. As Stam (2004) argued, health psychology has uncritically followed the aims and institutional priorities of biomedicine. Crossley (2000) distinguished this 'uncritical' view from 'critical' health psychology and named it 'mainstream health psychology'. Mainstream health psychology is what is most often taught in universities and practised by clinicians, researchers and consultants (Crossley, 2000). Health in mainstream health psychology is, according to Stam (2004), just taken as a functional entity; a healthy person is the one who has, or has regained the ability to perform, also following the single simplified model of biomedicine.

Health psychology versus complementary medicine

From this derivation of biomedicine, it is not surprising that mainstream health psychology thus far has shown limited interest in complementary medicine, but nor has critical health psychology. The most obvious reasons for this are the incompatibility of various basic thoughts, such as the epistemology models of the person, methods of inquiry and critical descriptions of its practices.

Mainstream health psychology as an academic discipline falls within the traditions of the search for knowledge, the search for 'truth', based on the assumptions of realism and rationalism (Feyerabend, 1981; Dancy, 1985; Audi, 2004), that there is a real world out there which can be 'objectively' known. As a social science, it has followed the laws of classical natural science, the methodologies of which are based on the processes of induction and deduction, of model and theory building, and hypothesis testing. The discipline derives its knowledge, as applications to the health and illness domains, from other 'sister disciplines', such as biopsychology, developmental psychology, cognitive psychology, personality psychology and social psychology. Its claims for knowledge are based on the positivistic assumptions of 'prediction', 'replication' and 'control'. Hence the over-domination of social cognition models (St Claire, 2003) or models including systems theory, self-regulatory theories or biopsychosocial theory, which according to Stam (2004), are all variants of functionalism.

Complementary medicine on the other hand is not based on a positivistic understanding of the world, but in the majority of its cases on an intuitive 'knowing' by eastern 'mystics'. The claims of its workings and successes are hard to control, predict and especially to replicate – the evidence is seen as anecdotal storytelling and its effects characterized as placebo (Kaptchuk, 1996; Kaptchuk et al., 1997; Graham, 1999; Peters, 2001). CAM has been criticized for a lack of objectivity of its results, and a non–generalization of its findings.

It is precisely this 'scientific knowledge' which is the crux of the discussion regarding the relationship between complementary therapies, western bio-medicine and health psychology. Because, what is 'scientific knowledge'? How can we know the world and what distinguishes knowledge from beliefs and religion?

Scientific knowledge

Many ideas have been proposed as to what constitutes knowledge, and what represents its valid methods. Historically, two main streams can be distinguished, one based on intuition, the other on scientific enquiry. Capra (1990) explored the parallels between modern physics and eastern mysti-cism, and showed that the eastern way to understand life in the fullest is not by scientific empirical enquiry, but by the spiritual faculty of intuition as one of the postulates of mysticism. It was the mystics, who through the stage of enlightenment (also called 'peak experience' or 'cosmic con-sciousness'), obtained such wisdom that this was seen as knowledge and the ultimate truth (Capra, 1990; McTaggert, 2001): 'When the psyche is in darkness one needs the light of reason to see his or her way through life, but when the psyche is illuminated, no one needs reason's candle' (Arasteh and Sheikh, 1989, pp. 151–2). Described in ancient books of various eastern philosophies, such as the *Avatamsaka of Buddhism*, the *Vedas of Hinduism*, and the *Tao Te Ching* and the writings of Chuang-tzu of Taoism, this knowledge formed the basis of intellectual life in eastern countries such as China, Japan and India, and formed the basis for understanding all aspects of life including healing and communication (Marsella et al., 1985; Capra, 1990; McTaggert, 2001).

These belief systems are not seen as *knowledge* in western intellectual thinking (e.g. Marks, 2000; Schwartz and Schloss, 2006), which has followed a different historical path, based on reason and the 'scientific method'. Positivism, as the philosophy of science, starting with Auguste Comte (1798–1857) in France with his publication, *Cours de philosophie positive* (or, *Course of Positive Philosophy*) (1842, in Störig, 1979), rejected any form of metaphysics or phenomena which could not be explained. John Stuart Mill (1806–73) gave psychology a role on the basis of this rationalist phil-osophy by describing in his main work, *System of the Inductive and Deductive Logic* (1843, in Störig, 1979), how philosophical 'truth' should be tested in empiricism. Reality in that sense could be 'known' by developing and testing models of both observations and intuitive ideas in order to deter-mine 'true' from 'false', following the laws of the natural sciences such as physics.

The domination of positivism as the *only* epistemology leading to the truth has recently lost its ground in the social sciences, as in health psychology, but not in western biomedicine. Epistemologies such as constructivism and subjectivism were gradually accepted as different, but equally valid, ways of understanding human reality, and have been further explored by critical health psychologists (Crossley, 2000; Marks, 2002; Stainton Rogers, 1996; Chamberlain, 2004; Murray, 2004). This has led to the use of various methodologies in obtaining scientific knowledge, also for health psychology.

Five research strands in health psychology

Wilkinson (2004) provided a clear overview of different research strands applied to health psychology, in which experiential, interpretative and discursive methods are distinguished from the 'objective' positivist methods. In addition to her classification, participatory research, in which the researcher works together with the participants in an applied research setting, has also received more academic credit (Brydon-Miller, 2004; Campbell, 2004). Fox (1999) goes even further than these post-modernist methods by introducing a new framework for action research in health care ('beyond health') based on 'nomadology'. In this approach, a researcher not only collaborates with an disempowered group with the aim to improve their situation and to disseminate the results to others, but they also 'care' as a human for these people by being both fully engaged with the participants in the project, and by acknowledging difference (instead of 'grasping' experiences of the participants in pre-set categories). Further discussions on research methods are to be found in Chapter 4.

Scientific criteria

If this subjective epistemology is the emerging picture on 'scientific' research in health psychology, then why is the vast amount of literature on complementary medicine still not included in health psychology textbooks or peer-reviewed journals? Vickers (1998, p. 2) described this issue well as the absence of critical self-analysis: 'Turn to just about any book on complementary medicine and you will usually be hard pressed to find even a single statement that criticises any theoretical or practical aspect of the therapy concerned. Most books are characterised by long lists of claims, stated baldly as matter of fact'. The majority of popular CAM publications do not conform to current ideas in philosophy of science, social science or psychology. (Nonetheless, the body of 'scientific' research in complementary medicine is growing and attempts to use scientific frameworks, for better or worse.)

Feyerabend (1981, p. ix) in his dismissal of positivism and the idea of an ultimate and only truth, emphasized the importance of science in being critical by 'not simply accepting the phenomena, processes, institutions that surround us'. Haack (2003), who is sceptical of both positivistic deterministic research and constructionist research, identified the scientific enterprise as a systematic, logical and honest enquiry, which is different from journalism and propagandistic research. In her philosophy, the scientist has been compared to a detective. Rosenberg (1980), who struggled with what social science is, acknowledged that it will never be able to reach a truth as the natural sciences do. This is because of the complexity of its subject, as acknowledged by Mill: 'Individuals and social groups are just more complicated than moving bodies, chemical reagents and ocean tides' (in Störig, 1979, p. 10). However, he does state what social science cannot be: 'it cannot be the same as an interesting novel or an exciting film' (1980, p. 22), nor can it be just giving an account of an actual conceptual situation such as phrenology or astrology, which is 'hollow and unconvincing' (1980, p. 18).

What else it can be, has in particular been expressed by psychologists working from subjective epistemologies (Smith et al., 1995). For example, Giorgi (1995) in his justification of phenomenology as a subjective scientific method, distinguished four characteristics of scientific knowledge which are arguably absent in popular complementary publications (e.g. Vickers, 1998), such as (i) a systematic presentation related to previous knowledge; (ii) the use of a method which is replicable; (iii) critical interpretations instead of accepting phenomena at face value; and (iv) generalizability of the findings in the sense of indicating applications beyond the context of the research.

Conventional medicine and randomized controlled trials (RCTs)

For conventional biomedicine, an alternative epistemology to positivism is still unconvincing. In its objective epistemology, the randomized control trials (RCTs) are not only the preferred methodology but set as the gold standard (Crossman and Mackenzie, 2005), a standard which is used as the basis for evidence-based medicine and clinical guidelines (van Wersch and Eccles, 1999, 2001; Walji and Boon, 2006).

However, the exclusiveness of RCTs as methodology has been criticized for its limitations in conventional medical care as, for example, Kienle (2005) demonstrated by highlighting its commercial bias, career bias, bias of large numbers, and bureaucratic misuse. Nonetheless, its elite status is even more serious for research on complementary medicine. For example, Milgrom (2005) has shown how ignoring the entanglement between patient, practitioner and remedy in research on the effectiveness of homeopathy, results in unreliable outcomes. Similarly, Walji and Boon (2006) demonstrated how randomization based on western science's diagnostic criteria in acupuncture research leads to a non-effective comparison of the two groups. Kaptchuk (2000) illustrated with an example of six different case studies, in which patients suffered the same physical complaints of stomach pain, how Traditional Chinese Medicine (TCM) differed from western medicine. In conventional medicine these patients were all examined similarly with upper-gastrointestinal x-rays or endoscopy by means of a fibroscope, and diagnosed as having peptic ulcer disease. In Chinese medicine there was a difference in examination, diagnosis and treatment for all six patients, depending on their physical appearances, life stories and bodily reactions. An RCT showing the effectiveness of TCM used for this condition cannot be a valid comparison. A combination of methods would provide a fuller picture, especially if one compares the outcomes of both the health status and the quality of life after the patient has been treated.

Nonetheless, by western biomedicine claiming the gold standard of research methodology, it will remain ignorant of the possible value of complementary therapies. It is as Marks et al. (2000), following the thoughts of Leslie and Young, said: 'Being based on a positivistic perspective, the practitioners of biomedicine believed that they had access to a reality that exists prior to and independent of people's attempts to understand and control it. As such, alternative perspectives were seen as basically wrong' (2000, p. 63).

As an alternative to RCTs, different frameworks for evaluating CAM have been suggested. Verhoef et al. (2005) proposed the whole systems research (WSR) approach as more applicable to health care provision. It includes a wide range of modalities to provide individual treatment, while at the same time remaining scientific. Working from this model, scope is provided to effectively capture the important components of the research process: a unique healing theory, treatment individualization, problems of diagnosis, patient–practitioner interaction, varying therapeutic contexts, patient-determined outcome values, and a mixed method approach (Ritenbaugh et al., 2003; Verhoef et al., 2005).

So far, this is all theory. It gives the impression of a research framework in which everything is possible. Boon et al. (2006) compared WSR with three other models from the UK, USA as well as Finland, and concluded that not much variation was found. Interestingly, one of the reported differences was the extent to which the framework was applicable to conventional as well as alternative medicine. If the models of the person of both these health care systems could be similar, comparison would not be a problem. However, it will be argued in the following sections that these models diverge. Question marks will be placed on the application of research designs not recognizing these differences. A comprehensive person model is what is missing from the whole system research framework. Could health psychology play a role in contributing to the knowledge base by exploring the validity of a distinct model of the person?

The energy model in non-western medicine

The body as matter in western medicine

The model of the body in conventional western medicine is different from the body model used in CAM in several ways: (i) it is based on biochemistry, anatomy and physiology rather than physics; (ii) the bodily structures (bones, muscles, cells and organs) are part of the real world: they can be touched and made visible; (iii) structures can be photographed; (iv) structures can be analysed in labs; and, (v) separate functions of the structures have been established.

More concretely, this means that in western medicine a heart failure patient will be treated by thorough examination of the heart and related vascular system. Similar procedures apply to the assessments of other ailments such as stomach, pancreas or kidney problems. Even though there is current recognition of the relationships between health behaviours and functional disorders (e.g. cigarette smoking and lung cancer), the idea that gallbladder problems can be related to an old scar on the skull, will be condemned as 'not making any sense'.

The body in complementary medicine as energy

The model of the human body underlying complementary medicine is of a different order from the physiology and anatomy of western understandings. It is based on an idealistic rather than a rationalist epistemology. The body is constructed as 'energy' rather than 'matter' (Jacobs, 1989; Kenyon, 1989; Heelas, 1996; Westerman, 2006). Traditionally, this bodily energy was recognized under different names in different cultures such as Ptah in Ancient Egypt, vis medicatrix naturae (healing energy) (Hippocrates) in ancient Greece, qi (chi) in China, ki in Japan and prana in Hindu beliefs (Wood, 1998). Contemporarily, this energy model is constructed as 'bio-energy' (Westerman, 2006). The idea is that this bodily energy is connected with the energy of the cosmos, the latter named as Brahman in Indian Philosophy, Tao in Chinese Philosophies (Marsella et al., 1985; Graham, 1999), and 'the field' in contemporary physics (McTaggert, 2001).

In this philosophy, the body is believed to be surrounded with more bodies, the so called 'aura' (comparable to the visible light surrounding the moon), and considered to be connected to the universal energy. Only clairvoyants, such as the physicist Brennan (1988), seem to be able to see these light particles, which she distinguished in three bodies: etherical, astral and spiritual. However, inconsistencies exist: Tiller (1979) described four, by differentiating the spiritual layer in a mental and causal body; and the physician Gerber (2001) believed that there are even higher-frequency subtle energy dimensions beyond the causal form.

No scientific evidence has been reported on the existence of these bodies. The Kirlian Camera, developed to photograph these auras, seems to be detecting no more than a transformation of energy into colour from the galvanic skin response (Jessel-Kenyon, et al., 1998). However, interesting claims have been made that these energy bodies can explain and treat phantom limb pain. When the material body has disappeared, the energy body will remain, and will be treatable (Mason, 2001) with a complementary therapy such as radionics, a therapy well explained by Fulder (1996) in his handbook of alternative and complementary medicine. These postulations may be seen as similar to the notion of 'memory-like' processes in the nervous system of the gate control theory of pain, as proposed by Melzack and Wall (1965). To research these claims could be an interesting new field of study for health psychologists.

Meridians, acupressure points, nadis and chakras

The main images of the body in CAM are illustrated as an outer body shape, filled with meridians, acupressure points and/or chakras, irrespective of organs, bones, muscles, and a neurological network. Traditionally, the chakras and nadis are based on Indian, Tibetan or Asian philosophy, the meridians and acupressure points on TCM. However, contemporary complementary therapies tend to have a combined model (e.g. Brennan, 1988).

The existence of acupuncture points and meridians, the latter as virtual channels (Idou, 2001) through which the qi or ki (life-giving and sustaining energy) flows into specific body organs, has been challenged by rationalists' scientists. Researchers such as Kim (1964), Darras (1977) and de Vernejoul et al. (1984; see also de Vernejoul, 1985) did find in the body, after injecting identifiable chemicals in the acupuncture points, a duct-like system of about 0.5–1.5 microns in diameter in coherence with the meridians. Additional support for these ducts, called 'bonghan' in Korean medicine (Kim, 1964), was found when the chemical could not be retrieved when injected in places other than the acupuncture points. Researchers looked also for electrical conductance in the meridians and seem to have verified a similar existence (Reichmanis, et al., 1975; Becker et al., 1976; Nordenstrom, 1983). These findings raise questions as to why conventional medicine has not been able to accept these empirical studies as an addition to their biological paradigm. Could this be another worthwhile research topic for health psychology?

There is some evidence that the meridians are morphologically developed in embryos *before* the neurological and vascular systems, and that the meridians are connected to the DNA in the nuclei of the cells (Kim, 1964; Shang 2000, 2001). Rao and Motoyama (1993) did not measure the connection between meridians and the DNA, but repeatedly found, with an electronically developed device called AMI, a connection between the meridians and the organs as described in eastern literature. Gallo (2002) stated that it is possible that light is part of qi, as it is well known that light carries enormous amounts of information, which should be necessary for morphological development. Could it be that there is light between the phosphor structures of Tymine and Adenine in DNA? Kim (1964) discovered high concentrations of DNA running through the meridians (bonghan ducts), the light of which, called 'biophotons' has been studied extensively by Popp and his colleagues (Popp, 1998; van Wijk and van Wijk, 2005; van Wijk et al., 2005, 2006). Could there be an anatomical-histological system other than the vascular and nervous systems known to our understanding of physiology and anatomy? And if yes, what does it look like; how does it work; and, could health psychologists contribute to its study?

Confusion seems to be the results of the use of different terminology for perhaps the same system. The Korean biologist Kim (1964) has described his discovery of new bodily structures in his book on the 'kyungrak system', on the basis of experiments on human and animal bodies. These structures appear to overlap with both the Chinese meridians and the Indian nadis. The Chinese system seems more structured and compact; only 12 meridians have been identified, named and numbered. In Indian Aryuvedic philosophy, up to 72,000 nadis have been described. These seem to represent an extensive network of fluid-like energies linking the chakras with the body, which are believed to be connected to the brain, spinal cord and nervous system (Gerber, 2001). The Dutch physician Westerman explained in his book, *Bioenergy* (2006), that another system, such as the kyungrak or meridian system, *has* to exist because the workings of acupuncture cannot be understood in relation to the central nervous system.

However, there are conflicting results in the literature. Idou (2001) indeed showed that the meridians were not directly related to the nervous system, but Kido and Sato (2001) in Japan showed effects in the electroconductivity of the meridians on the parasympathetic nervous system after sessions of ki healing. Similarly, Roney-Dougal (1999) claimed that the autonomic nervous system can be equated with the yogic nadis. However, Westerman's (2006) defence of neural independence might be applicable to the acupressure points only, but not to the nadis, or kyungrak system as a whole. He argued that if all of the more than 1000 acupressure points had their own viscerocutane reflexes, the central nervous system would have to be much larger. Also, parts of the skin are connected to similar neurons, and as such, should give an equal neurological response, independent of the place of pressure. In studies comparing activation of the acupressure and sham points, results were reported in favour of the first (Wu et al., 2004; He et al., 2005; Ezzo, et al., 2006).

Perhaps the process of inner and outer energy connection in the body has not been established as yet. Could this be another interesting area to be explored by health psychologists? To compare differences in people's perceptions of energy transference through acupressure points, chakras, or other parts of the body should be a fascinating topic.

In the body model of complementary medicine, seven major chakras have been recognized, descending in a vertical line from the top of the head to the bottom of the spine: crown, forehead (third eye: spot between the eyes), throat, heart, plexus solaris (underneath breast bone), gut and root (e.g. Gallegos, 2002; Gallo, 2002; McArthur, 2003). However, some literature reports more chakras (from 12 up to 360 minor chakras; Gerber, 2001). Healers claim that the chakras correspond with the colours of the rainbow (or spectrum) with the crown chakra being violet light, the third eye being purple, the throat blue, the heart green, the plexus solaris yellow, gut orange and the root chakra being red (Brennan, 1988).

Some research has been generated to support the eastern ideas of chakras. Gould's (1992) study with 81 university students found, after watching commercial and music videos, a relationship between perceived affective symptoms and emotions, and the chakra theory. Motoyama and Brown (1978) created a special lead-lined recording booth that was shielded from outside electromagnetic disturbance to measure the claimed chakra energy which was going in and out of the body. They carried out several studies, and found consistently with people who meditate and individuals with a previous history of psychic experience, that the amplitude and frequency of the electric field over the chakra being concentrated upon, was significantly higher than those of control subjects.

Shang's (2000, 2001) work has been showing links with modern science, based on the morphogenetic singularity theory, in which meridians and chakras are related to the undifferentiated, interconnected cellular network that regulates growth and physiological processes. This theory successfully predicted several findings in conventional biomedical science. In line with this, Roney-Dougal (1999) also found support for the chakras from a bio-physiological framework. He observed the importance of melatonin as the off-switch for the endocrine glands' output of hormones and this was working together with the pituitary gland (the on-switch). By this he concluded that both the positioning and functioning of endocrine glands were related to the traditional points and functions of the chakras. However, Robins (2000) did not replicate these findings. In her study with 27 males living with HIV, she did not find significant effects of Healing Touch on their well-being and neuroendocrine and immune function.

One possible explanation for these contradictory results could be linked to differences in epistemologies of the research, and, non-transparency of the body–mind and spiritual belief systems of both participants and researchers. Both Harari (2003) and Schneider (2005) acknowledged these issues and designed their PhD research accordingly. Harari developed the Energy Anatomy Questionnaire (EAQ) and tested this unilaterally and cross-culturally with 30 Tibetans and 30 Caucasian-Americans. Unilaterally, some tentative evidence was found for the chakra model, however, incongruent worldviews were among one of the factors disturbing cross-cultural comparisons. Schneider developed a diagnostic tool to assess the chakras through qualitative written responses (ACT-QR), in order to identify dominant chakras for a person, and to assess relationships with supposed psychological characteristics and experienced emotions. Reliability for her scale was found with a Cronbach's α of .84 for the first part and .76 for the second, but it is in need of further testing. Health psychologists could replicate these studies in different samples and validate these scales.

Psychological qualities have been associated (but not tested) with the seven chakras, such as from the root to the crown being security, sensation, power, love, creativity and receptivity, integration and mindfulness, and fulfilment and enlightenment. All chakras but the crown and root seem to have two connection points with the body: at the front being responsible for feelings; at the back being responsible for the will (Brennan, 1988). Jung (1976) was the first psychologist in the west who explored and described various modes of consciousness associated with each chakra from a cosmic standpoint, believing in chakras as universally human and not specific to a culture such as India. Bittlinger (1998) discussed these in more detail in relation to Jung's different stages of individuation. Gilchrist and Mikulas (1993) integrated the chakra model in the developmental theory of Maslow (1954/1987), and discussed how most successful groups passed through the first four stages but that it was rare to enter the fulfilment stage. Further applications in psychology of chakra theory have been carried out in the following domains: cognitive psychology in the sense of thought and altered states of consciousness (Hunt, 1985) and on psychotherapy (Gallegos, 2002; Gallo, 2002; Hover-Kramer, 2002). The exploration of these psychological qualities in relation to the chakras and health and well-being could be appealing to psychologists interested in health.

Quantum mechanics: a new physics explaining the energy model of the person?

Western-trained scholars are not familiar with the energy model of the body, because it is not part of mainstream education. Western scientific models are based on a reality as understood by physics, still heavily relying on Newtonian mechanics, with differences between energy and matter and causal relationships between phenomena. Einstein believed in a positivistic science in which processes can be determined and understood by models and theories to determine the truth. His identification of photons started the new physics known as 'quantum mechanics'. Up till his death in 1955, however, he had problems accepting the probabilistic models of quantum mechanics as presented by Bohr regarding the universe as a hologram and Heisenberg's uncertainty principle with respect to the wave/particle duality. The idea that particles and waves can never be simultaneously measured with precision was unacceptable for Einstein. Together with Podolsky and Rosen he carried out his famous EPR thought experiments (Einstein et al., 1935), to prove Heisenberg wrong. Now, half a century later quantum mechanics has been accepted as a new paradigm in physics.

This new physics is relevant for the understanding of recent postmodernist epistemologies and methodologies, as well as the model of the person underlying complementary medicine. First, a changing self-concept related to its context is more in line with probabilistic than deterministic science. Second, the acceptance and use of qualitative research methods as a valid way of scientific enquiry also recognizes individual perceptions and change. Third, it offers an explanation of the mystery of the connection between universe, other people and the self.

Among the theories trying to explain human life through energy paradigms, such as Sheldrake's (1988) theory of morphogenetic fields and morphic resonance, or McCutcheon's (2002) 'final' theory, it is Laszlo's (2003) connectivity hypothesis that seems to be more applicable to complementary medicine and health psychology. Quantum mechanics, the cosmos, human and animal life, as well as consciousness lie at the basis of this non-materialist and non-reductionist paradigm. His hypotheses are possible explanations for a connection between the energies of the universe, and the chakra and meridian ideas of the organism. He postulated coherence between the macro-domain of cosmos, the meso-domain of quantum and the micro-domain of life and mind, and showed how space is an energy-filled plenum, full of restless and sub-atomic particles actively entangled with organisms, also called 'the field' by McTaggert (2001). Laszlo (2003, p. 10) concluded from reported experiments that 'it is not necessary that the particles should have originated in the same quantum state . . . any two particles, whether electrons, neutrons or photons, can originate at different points in space and time – they remain correlated as long as they had once assumed the same quantum state, that is, were part of the same coordinate system'. From this, he hypothesized how people's bodily energies are connected through electromagnetic fields in space and time, within their own bodily selves as well as transpersonally with other people. Explanations are assumed for the workings of healing energy with meditation, telesomatic action or remote healing, psionic medicine, and the often anecdotal reports of energetic connections between identical twins and mothers and sons. The only condition is that that the receiver of these energies should be in a relaxed and attentive state – open for the energy to flow freely through the body. In that sense the body can be seen as one major variable resistance device as used in electronic apparatus to regulate the flow of current (e.g. volume control on a television).

Although not explicitly discussed by Laszlo, the connectivity hypothesis could be a possible explanation of the process of radionics (Fulder, 1996; Mason, 2001). In radionics, healing energy is sent by means of a witness – a bit of hair or blood from the patient which the practitioners use to diagnose patients' health and to correct their flow of energy. In previous understandings of the relationships between two particles as shown by Einstein and his colleagues (1935) in the EPR-experiments, what Einstein called the 'ghostly action at a distance', this phenomenon could be explained through the connection of the DNA in the hair and in the patient. If the particles in the hair were measured with a specific technical device, there was instant reversal effect in the particles of the patient. However, newer explanations as shown in the earlier quote by Laszlo (2003) state that the connection between particles is intrinsic to the particles, and is not due to signals transmitted by the measuring apparatus. This may also explain how radionics' healing energy can be sent remotely with a photo or name of the patient, for example through a computer rather than as a 'witness' derived from the body, because they are part of the same coordinate system.

The connectivity hypothesis could also be construed as the basis of Energy Psychology (Gallo, 2002), a new field in psychology claiming that psychopathology can be treated by addressing subtle energy systems in the body. Gallo says: 'Because energy is not highly inertia laden, if thought and psychological problems exist in energy-field form, then these problems can be resolved much more easily than one might assume, based on other paradigms. It would then merely be a matter of altering or collapsing the energy field' (2002, p. 15).

But these are all new speculations which need further verification in research. However, much of the workings in complementary medicine seem to be better understood from the perspectives and concepts of the energy model from physics, than the chemistry-based biology as part of the 'bio'medical and 'bio'psychosocial model. More effects of CAM could arguably be measured and explained. As social scientists interested in the human aspects of health and illness, health psychologists could examine the claims made by the biophysics model on the understandings of the workings of complementary medicine.

Self theories

'Holistic' self

Biomedicine does not recognize the uniqueness of a person. In the context of evidence-based medicine, patients are grouped according to averages, and as a result their commonality, not their uniqueness, is acknowledged. This is similar for mainstream health psychology research with its functional orientation and use of social-cognition models, which ignores the individual or unique self in the experiences of health and illness.

As one of the attractions of complementary medicine, the 'holistic' approach has been identified (Dunfield, 1996; Peters, 1998; Shankar and Liao, 2004; Smith, 2006). As such, the idea is that a person's body, mind and spirit (Shankar and Liao, 2004) are seen as an integrated whole, promoting harmony in the person's whole self (Kutlenios, 1987), rather than as a reductionist part of that whole, as applied to biomedicine (Pietroni, 1997). In that sense the holistic self is perceived as equivalent to the eastern ideas of self, and the unique self is presented as the soul or the spirit of the person (Marsella et al., 1985; Shankar and Liao, 2004). Peters (1998, p. 141) critically describes the effects of CAM on this holistic model because it assumes to 'unify mind and body, and is able to treat the body through soul and spirit'. He warns against the pseudo-psychological claims it makes because these seem 'simplistic, prescriptive, a-theoretical and overly-reliant on the poorly articulated insights of charismatic founder figures' (1998, p. 141), such as, for example, Louise Hay.

This leaves us with, on the one hand, an alternative health approach which makes pseudo-psychological claims about the workings of CAM on a holistic person model and, on the other hand, both a conventional health approach and mainstream psychology discipline applied to health, which operates from a reductionist mind–body model of the person. Why is it that psychology cannot form the bridge between complementary and conventional person models? Why is the unique inner self of the person ignored in psychology? What is it about psychology, the social science of human beings, that it operates from a reductionist model of the person? Has this always been the case, or have different models, including more holistic models, been applied in psychology?

Self models in psychology related to complementary medicine

In complementary medicine, dysfunction of the body is not construed at the level of the organs or connected tissue, but as a blockage of energy. For Chinese medicine, this is alongside any one of the meridians, which are all numbered, named and described in books from 'medical' systems that are much older than the books of modern medicine (Brennan, 1988; Gerber, 2001; Gallo, 2002). In the history of psychology, equivalent models of the person have been applied.

William James (1890/1950), seen as the father of American psychology, developed a model of the person similar to the 'holistic' model of complementary medicine, and to post-modernism. The self according to James is the personal continuity that is recognized every time one wakens; the self is the conscious experience of many selves in a constantly fluctuating field, made out of biological, material, social and spiritual layers. James (1897/1956, 1902/1982), originally trained as a physician, believed that human beings had an underlying drive to increase their own health, and that blocked or bottled up emotion, positive or negative, can lead to mental and physical illness. James (1907/1982) worked from 'pragmatism' as epistemology, and developed 'pluralistic thinking' as his method. He used stories of people (anecdotes), employed himself as subject of his experiments, worked in labs, travelled the world, listened to influential people, had been depressed, had been happy, lectured and wrote up his thoughts in journal articles and in line with CAM and health psychology, he wrote about meditation, relaxation, mystical experiences, hypnosis, deep prayer, sensory deprivation, and the onset of acute psychosis.

The European father of psychology, Wilhelm Wundt worked most of his working life in labs, trying to establish the structures of the mind through 'introspection'. However, he also showed later in his life an interest in eastern mysticism. He published work on spirituality and science (1879; cited in Rieber and Robinson, 2001) and on hypnosis and suggestion (1892; cited in Rieber and Robinson, 2001). After Wundt's death, Titchener and his other students called his approach 'Ganzheit Psychologie' which, also in line with complementary medicine, has been translated into English as 'holistic psychology' (Plotkin, 2004).

Freud (1901, 1911) structured the self in terms of an Id, Ego and Superego and saw human behaviour as the result of the processes between the energy flow which he called libido, and a blockage of this energy in cathexis. Jung (1965/1982, 1969), with his Analytic Psychology, had a more elaborated structure of the person than his fellow psycho-analysts Freud and Adler. His idea of the inner self of the person was similar to that of James (1902/1982) and Laszlo (2003), in the sense of it being connected with a greater whole, a greater energy which was described in philosophy and in primitive cultures before physics tried to 'prove' it (Jung, 1969): 'Instead of enjoying the apparent certainty of a single, simple truth, we feel ourselves castaways on a boundless sea of ever-changing conditions, helplessly tossed from one vagary to the next' (Jung, 1965/1982, p. 83).

Energy was also an important concept for Reich (1961), as formulated in his Somatic Psychology. According to his model, bioenergy (orgone energy) flows through the body and is connected with the psychological state of the person, which can be measured through the muscular armour, and treated by loosening the armour segments (Reich, 1973). As with the complementary medicine model, mental as well as physical illness is constructed as a blockage of energy in the human body. Reich's model of the person, was criticized for his 'fantasy' model and his 'dangerous' practice derived from it. Several times he had to leave his own country, and in the USA he was even imprisoned for his ideas.

Another development in self theory, was 'symbolic interactionism', pioneered by George Herbert Mead (1934) in the 1930s. This school of thought was inspired by Buber's philosophy of *I and Thou* (1922) and William James's (1890/1950, 1897/1956) ideas of the multifaceted self, both claiming that the 'I' grows, develops and exists through the relations with other people. This idea reflected a rejection of a static individual personality, determined by personality characteristics, and welcomed the idea of changing social self. Mead (1934, p. 135) stated:

> The self is something which has a development; it is not initially there, at birth, but arises in the process of social experience and activity, that is, develops in a given individual as a result of his relations to that process as a whole and to other individuals within that process . . . The self . . . is essentially a social structure, and it arises in social experience.

Interesting questions arise. Is there a relationship between Laszlo's connectivity hypothesis and Mead's symbolic interactionism? The interaction between health practitioner and patient is supposed to be different between CAM and western medicine. Could symbolic interactionism in relation to Laszlo's model offer explanations? Could health psychologists contribute possible answers to these questions?

Death of the self

Eventually, these psychologists were all criticized for their anecdotal evidence and the use of unscientific methods by fellow academic psychologists (Skinner, 1953, 1984). For Skinner (1953, 1984), behaviourism was the new philosophy of science, inspired by Comte's positivism and the methods of research as used in the natural sciences such as biology, physics and chemistry. Skinner (1953, pp. 12–13) stated:

> Science is a disposition to deal with the facts rather than what someone has said about them . . . It is a search for order, for uniformities, for lawful relations among the events in nature. It begins, as we all begin, by observing single episodes, but it quickly passes on the general rule, to scientific law.

For behaviourism, the self and the idea of personality were reduced to observable behaviour. The self, the person, which one would expect to be the subject of psychology as the science of people, died. An individualistic experimental psychology was the outcome, in which various aspects of the self were studied in sub-disciplines of psychology such as cognitive psychology, biopsychology and social psychology.

Does this mean that the work of the psychological scholars, James, Wundt, Freud, Jung and Reich, can be equated with popular publications on complementary medicine which are criticised by Vickers (1998) as bold uncritical statements, and by Peters (1998) as pseudo-psychological, simplistic, a-theoretical understanding of the human being?

There is a difference here. First, these psychological scholars were not charismatic founder figures but well educated and respectable intellectual thinkers of their time. Their work, unlike popular complementary books, does adhere to scientific criteria as set by Feyerabend (1981), Haack (2003), Giorgi (1995), and Rosenberg (1980). Their writings were systematically structured in a logical and analytical way, and expressed as a constant debate with scholars of and before their time. They worked from a well developed epistemology, model of the person, and a critical method of inquiry, not accepting phenomena at face value. Their work cannot be compared to 'propagandism'.

Both James and Jung's psychological enquiry was in line with Feyerabend's (1981, p. ix) concept of 'proliferation' meaning that 'we do not work with a single theory, system of thought, institutional framework . . . we use a plurality of theories'. Jung criticized both Freud and Adler for their simple model as though there is only one truth, 'of assuming the continuous operation of one and the same instinct . . . If that were the case, man would be mainly sexual according to Freud, and mainly self assertive, according to Adler' (1965/1982, p. 82). The way these psychologists went about searching for the truth about human existence, thought, and behaviour, was similar to Haack's (2003) idea of the scientist as a detective trying to solve a mystery;

and was not the same as writing a novel (Rosenberg, 1980). Their publications were presented in such a way that future research could progress.

Revival of the self

In the 1950 and 1960s a reaction came to the death of the person in psychology and a movement reviving the human subjective experience was born in humanistic psychology. More models of the person were developed by psychologists to provide an understanding of people's selves, their experiences, their emotions, their cognitions, their perceptions of themselves and the world. Abraham Maslow (1954/1987) construed the human being in terms of needs progression in five stages: from physiological needs related to survival, to needs for safety, love and belonging, esteem and the highest, the need for self-actualization. Carl Rogers (1959) viewed the self as a personal development journey whose main goal is to express and get in touch with one's feelings and whose path will be happy and healthy when guided with love and positive feedback. These models are more in line with the 'holistic' person model of complementary medicine (Kutlenios, 1987; Shankar and Liao, 2004). However, again, these humanistic models of the person were seen as subjective and non-testable. Marsella et al. (1985) acknowledged that humanistic psychology became more a social movement than an academic field.

In most cases these models were assumed to be the true reflection of the nature of the human being without questioning its structure, or with no discussion or comparisons with other models. The models of the person were the social constructions of the psychologists who invented them. Their model of the person worked for their construction of what a person is, the way they saw it, the way they could deal with it in their own understanding of themselves and the world around them. Psychological scholars who could understand both themselves and other people through the same looking glass, used and applied these models in their own work with human beings, and helped verify and/or amend the models.

It is precisely for that reason that these structuralistic epistemologies have been criticized by post-modernist thinkers such as Bernard Iddings Bell, Michel Foucault, Gilles Deleuze, Jean-Francois Lyotard, Fredric Jameson, Luce Irigaray and many others (Drolet, 2004). In line with post-modernist thinkers, the self as typified in these models, is seen as the construction of the reality of the developer or user of the model. The other person, the self in that sense, is nothing more than a social construction without 'knowing' who these people really are, where they come from and how they have grown to be who they are now. This criticism has been applied to all psychological models of the person. Hampson (1992, p. 160) concluded in her review of the construction of personality that 'not one absolute, definitive, personality structure will emerge and will be shown to be the best', and Johnson (1985) criticized the western concept of self as individualistic, materialistic and rationalistic. Omission of the social and cultural context of the person, and the idea of a dynamic context-dependent changing self as opposed to a static constant idea of the self, led post-modernist thinkers (e.g. Potter et al., 1984; Shotter, 1984; Gergen, 1985; Harré, 1995) to conclude that there is no such thing as personality, as earlier said by Mead (1934) and Mischel (1968, 1969). However, post-modernists have been criticized (e.g. Fox, 1999) for not believing in any self. In that sense are we just chameleons, changing colours with our social environments? And if so, what is the reason for this?

The remaining question is then, can there be a self which is not a social constructed self? Is there an I, an inner self as opposed to the social self which is the subject of investigation in psychology?

Inner self

The problems are related to the use of language. Because psychology is a social science, and science is communicated in language, the self will always be trapped within the boundaries of this language. Even the recent developments in psychology, in which qualitative methods have been developed to understand the human person in their uniqueness, in their own meanings, away from the positivistic generalized self, with no pre-perceptions but as a person derived from a *tabula rasa* mind, will still have to capture the observations of this person in language. This is illustrated in the application of, for example, interpretive methods such as 'interpretative phenomenological analysis' (Smith and Osborn, 2003), 'grounded theory' (Strauss and Corbin, 1990) or, discursive understandings such as both 'discourse analysis' (Potter and Whetherell, 1987) and 'Foucauldian discourse analysis' (Parker, 1997; Willig, 2004).

Language is in principle social, so even the qualitative perception of the unique individual person and their feelings, cognitions and behaviour will still be social. This means that the experience of the true inner self will come before or during the use of language. The inner self is the whole of sensations which predispose the perceptions. In philosophy these are called proprioceptions (e.g. Harré, 1998). The sensations are purely me/I ('le soi même'; Levinas, 1968, p. 494). In Levinas's sense, they are an 'en-soi' (Levinas, 1968, p. 494) (inner self) as opposed to a 'pour-soi' (consciousness/social self; Levinas, 1968, p. 490). The inner self as 'la contraction même du sentiment' (Levinas, 1971, p. 123), such as the heartbeat when excited or anxious (Levinas, 1968, p. 492), the thrills when enjoying oneself (Levinas, 1971, p. 124), the pain of suffering and grief (Levinas, 1979, p. 55). They are the bodily unintended movements. They are as James (1890/1950, p. 296) called it, 'the most enduring and intimate part of the self', which affects pleasure and pain.

The inner self, in this sense, links in with contemporary theorizing of embodiment as 'being the body' as opposed to the body as 'having the body'. MacLachlan (2004, p. 180) showed this throughout his book as a new way of experiencing the self as not via cognition only: 'the mind is not only of the brain; I believe that the essence of embodiment implies that it is also of the body. Organs are emotional'. Furthermore, he quoted Carey (2000) to the effect that 'because the cells of the body, not just the brain, receive and secrete information-bearing chemicals, the whole body is an intelligent-bearing organism' (MacLachlan, 2004, p. 38), in which the heart 'as it beats with excitement, passion or anxiety, is not only providing signals to a cerebral relay station, it is also living a meaning. How my heart reacts tells me how I feel about things, just as my eyes and ears tell me how things look and sound' (2004, p. 180).

These ideas of the inner self bear resemblance with the area of the body in non-western medicine which is the focus of meditation, relaxation, visualization, healing (and arguably also with homeopathy, acupuncture and massage in connection with the placebo response, as will be discussed in Chapter 3). However, this leads us to the topic of the next section, what the self models in biomedicine and in health psychology are, and whether they suffice for research in complementary medicine.

The biomedical model and biopsychosocial model

Biomedical model

The biomedical model can be seen to have parted from a holistic view of the person since the time of Descartes and the idea that the body was a separate entity from the mind. Health, illness and disease became the topics of the biomedical sciences, and any social, cultural, or psychological influence was denied (Mayr, 1998; Alonso, 2004). This was partly because of the great discoveries in the sciences due to the invention of technologies such as the microscope and the change in the law regarding dissection of cadavers, which until the Renaissance, were forbidden by the church. Anatomy and physiology were the new ways of discovering the structure and function of the human body. The rapid developments of molecular biology and genetics, and the sophisticated medical technology which was developed in the 20th century led to a convincing idea that the ultimate explanation for human illnesses lies in the elementary cellular structures and their dysfunctions (Puustinen et al., 2003).

Because of the basics of medicine in science, knowledge and its progression were only possible with the use of the positivistic scientific method. Up until today the medical curriculum is mainly formed by the science subjects; in Britain the entrance criteria for medical school are in line with that. As said previously, medical practice is based on evidence-based guidelines, which are still mainly focused on the bodily processes only. Any plea for multi-disciplinary guidelines has thus far been ignored (van Wersch and Eccles, 1999, 2001).

Biopsychosocial model

Since the publication of Engel in 1977, in which he proposed the biopsychosocial model as a more comprehensive model of medicine, the biomedical model has received considerable criticism because of its narrow definition of health (e.g. Alonso, 2004), its exclusion of psychological and social factors (e.g. Engel, 1977; Greaves, 2002), its priority of facts over values (e.g. Greaves, 2002), and its primary reliance on positivism as its epistemology (e.g. Gilet, 2003).

According to Engel (1977, p. 132),

> the existing biomedical model does not suffice. To provide a basis for understanding the determinants of disease and arriving at rational treatments and patterns of health care, a medical model must also take into account the patient, the social context in which he lives, and the complementary system devised by society to deal with disruptive effects of illness, that is, the physician role and the health care system. This requires a biopsychosocial model.

For Engel the proposition of the biopsychosocial model is to offer 'a blueprint for research, a framework for teaching, and a design for action in the real world of health care' (1977, p. 136).

Biopsychosocial model and health psychology

The biopsychosocial model has been welcomed by health psychology (e.g. Sheridan and Radmacher, 1991; Ogden, 1996; Sarafino, 1998; Marks et al., 2000; Forshaw, 2002; Lyons and Chamberlain, 2006) for the recognition of the influence of other factors on health and illness than the isolated deterministic idea of the workings of the body on its own. Both Ogden (1996) and Marks et al. (2000) acknowledge the influence of this model on the redefinition of health related to a broader psychosocial meaning than solely the absence of illness. Marks et al. also highlight the influence of this model on the inclusion of Quality of Life assessments in medical care. Although the biopsychosocial model has been applied in health psychology to topics such as cancer (e.g. Baltrusch and Walt, 1985), pain (e.g. Gatchel, 2004), adolescent health (e.g. Williams et al., 2002) and ageing (e.g. Lutgendorf and Costanzo, 2003), its scope as a model for research, teaching and practice has been criticized by the many scholars and practitioners who have tried to use it.

Questioning the biopsychosocial model as 'model'

At a theoretical research level, the biopsychosocial model has been disapproved of for not being a model in the scientific sense of a framework derived from inductive observations or deductions from a theory or hypothetical model, the components of which are displayed in a relational network (McLaren, 1998, 2002). Stam (2000, p. 275) argued: 'The "model" has simply been taken for granted and, remarkably, there is absolutely no discussion of what this term could mean other than the "interplay" or "interaction" of biological, psychological and social factors'. This problem was discussed ten years earlier by Themoshok (1990), who struggled to fit her data on AIDS and cancer in the biopsychosocial framework, and argued for a further articulation of the model. Epstein and Borrell-Carrio (2005) also expressed their views that the model is more an approach for practice than an empirically verifiable theory. Muir (1998) on the other hand indicated that he believed that the term 'model' was used by Engel in a metaphorical sense, in a way that was an analogy with the hard sciences but clearly not homologous with it. Support for this view can be given, because the same can be said about the use of the word 'model' in this chapter. The term is derived from philosophy and resembles a greater meaning than the words 'ideas' or 'views'. In that philosophical sense, it has a different connotation than the scientific explanatory framework of interrelated variables.

The biopsychosocial model in practice

The application of the biopsychosocial model in practice has been positively and negatively evaluated. Cohen and Alfonso (1997) used the framework in a positive way by applying its components as the basis for the development of guidelines for sexual history taking. Epstein and Borrell-Carrio (2005) valued the model as a teachable model for practice, not in an imagined static state, but in the sense of an ongoing process of 'becoming biopsychosocial' through habits of mind such as attentiveness, peripheral vision, curiosity and informed flexibility. In his examination of the application of the biopsychosocial model by an experienced physician, Bartz (1999) concluded that this model fell short in the patient-centred approaches to communication. The physician felt that value judgements about the patients such as 'feeling manipulated, disbelieving statements, distrusting information, despairing over differences, and even detaching from any expectation of helping a patient she could never trust' (1999, p. 602) got in the way of a biopsychosocial approach to her clinical practice. Brody (1999) did not see this as a conflicting situation, but as complementary. He valued the biopsychosocial model as a theoretical framework which could be underpinned by patient-illness narratives, physician–patient interactions, physician self-awareness and the organization of primary care practices.

Together, these approaches to practice will help to develop new strategies for reconstructing problematic interactions in health care practices. Sadler and Hulgus (1992) proposed a similar solution to the gap between the model and its clinical application and proposed a clinical decision-making model that directed the clinician's attention to three core aspects of the clinical encounter: (i) problems of knowledge; (ii) ethics; and (iii) pragmatics, that complemented the biopsychosocial model.

Connection between biopsychosocial model and complementary medicine

Borrell-Carrio et al. (2004) acknowledged the problems in fitting observations of patient–doctor communication into the biopsychosocial model. In answer to that, they developed a biopsychosocial-oriented clinical practice with seven basic aspects, leading almost to a practitioner–patient model close to that of complementary medicine, namely: (1) self-awareness; (2) active cultivation of trust; (3) an emotional style characterized by empathic curiosity; (4) self-calibration as a way to reduce bias; (5) educating emotions to assist with diagnosis and forming therapeutic relationships; (6) using informed intuition; and (7) communicating clinical evidence to foster dialogue, not just mechanical application of protocol. For these authors 'George Engel's most enduring contribution was to broaden the scope of the clinician's gaze. His biopsychosocial model was a call to change our way of understanding the patient and to expand the domain of medical knowledge to address the needs of each patient' (2004, p. 581). They concluded by saying that 'It is perhaps the transformation of the way illness, suffering, and healing are viewed that may be Engel's most durable contribution' (2004, p. 581).

Not only the practitioners developed new models inspired by the biopsychosocial model for a more elaborate health and medical care, based on suffering and healing. For example, Greaves (2002) proposed a 'Medical Cosmology', as a reaction, as he sees it, to the failure of the biopsychosocial model to harmonise the scientific and humanistic aspects of medicine. His health philosophy was based on five pillars: (1) goals and values; (2) definitions and boundaries of medicine and health care; (3) the reconfiguration of medical knowledge; (4) healing and the healer; (5) medical education; and (6) collective responsibility; all derived from the underlying idea that healing has a spiritual and mysterious quality which transcends scientific rationalism. His philosophy also approached the model of the person in complementary medicine, as he claimed: 'Healers, whether shamans, humoral physicians, or contemporary western practitioners, rely on the indivisibility of their technical and charismatic power, the technical aspect of their work only having meaning in the relation to the personal and social aspects and vice versa' (2002, p. 84). In line with this, Sulmasy (2002) agreed that spirituality is missing from conventional health care, and proposed the biopsychosocialspiritual model. As an extension of the biopsychosocial model, this author demanded attention to four general domains: religiosity, religious coping and support, spiritual well-being, and spiritual health.

However, including these concepts in a scientific framework will encounter similar problems as the use of term 'holistic' self, because of the inclusion of vague, simple and pseudo-scientific terms (Peters, 1998), such as spirit and soul (Marsella et al., 1985; Shankar and Liao, 2004). Considering the progression of physics in the understanding of the human inner self as embodiment, and the absence of a biophysics understanding of the body as an explanatory framework for the workings of complementary medicine, an extension of the biopsychosocial model to a biophysics-psychosocial model is seen as a better way forward. The biopsychosocial model as it stands, is actually a biochemistry-psychosocial model, which is a sufficient framework for guiding research in western biomedicine. However, as a framework used for the contribution of psychology to the CAM treatment of illness or the identification of its aetiologic and diagnostic correlates (Matarazzo, 1982) from a non-western medicine perspective, a biophysics-psychosocial model will be more adequate.

Summary and future challenges

Health psychology and complementary medicine are based on a different understanding of the world, which has led to different models of the person. Health psychology derives its knowledge from scientific enquiries, which are approved by the psychological academic peer community, and which have evolved over different epistemologies, theoretical perspectives, methodologies and methods during the existence of psychology. Using Crotty's (1998) framework, you could say that the epistemology in psychology started with the domination of subjectivism, in James's pragmatism, Wundt's structuralism and Freud's psychoanalysis as theoretical perspectives. The dominance of positivism as the only way to obtain the truth led to a rejection of their psychologies and to objectivism as the dominant epistemology. Watson's (1913) and Skinner's (1953, 1984) behaviourism became the only acceptable theoretical framework. Through the developments of quantum mechanics in physics, claiming a more probabilistic rather than deterministic model of reality, and developments in sociology and philosophy of science rejecting the positivistic scientific method as the only route to understanding human behaviour, different theoretical frameworks were emerging around the same time. Since the 1960s, the dominance of positivism has lost its ground, and parallel epistemologies such as constructivism and subjectivism were gradually accepted as different but equally valid ways of understanding human reality. Theoretical frameworks such as social constructionism, symbolic interactionism and feminism developed, and different research strands such as experiential, interpretative, discursive, and participatory were elaborated.

Theories of the self followed a similar historical line. A distinction has been made between the individual and social self, with any theories stipulating the inner or unique self being dismissed as non-scientific. Only those models have been taken seriously in academic psychology, in which, for the same reasons as described earlier, general characteristics such as personality traits were 'proven' in the sense of reoccurrence, with a high chance of replication and prediction of the model. This has led to an over-domination of the social cognition and behavioural models, and only a gradual acceptance of any other than the positivism-related 'person models', such as the person as expressed in phenomenology as 'the lived experience', or as in discursive models such as in Harré's (1998, p. 54) expression of selfhood in language, in which the self cannot be more than 'invariants in the flux of action, private and public'; or, the beyond post-modernist 'nomadic self' as described by Fox (1999) for participatory research.

Considering that these epistemologies, theoretical frameworks and methodologies in psychology are not primarily based on the scientific method, they are still part of the scientific enterprise, rather than the arts or humanities. What social science is, and what it is not, has been highlighted and explored in this chapter from the theoretical statements of Feyerabend (1981), Haack (2003), Rosenberg (1980) and Giorgi (1995). The main difference between health psychology and complementary medicine is, as it stands now, that the latter is based on a different epistemology and a different self-concept, and is not accepted by the western scientific community, as yet. The biophysics model of the person is, as has been documented, not grounded in the philosophical ideas of realism and rationalism, on that which we can see and touch, but on idealistic ideas derived from eastern philosophies. The meridians, acupressure points and chakras are still perceived as non-existent by scientists, including health psychologists. More evidence, based on research adhering to the scientific criteria as expressed in this chapter, is necessary.

Nonetheless, new developments are promising. Empirical cell-biological research, especially the work of Shang (2000, 2001) and his colleagues, is gradually providing more support for a different body model and is establishing links with the new physics. Furthermore, the progression of quantum mechanics in the understanding of the coherence of the atomic and sub-atomic field as expressed in the connectivity hypothesis (Laszlo, 2003), offers a new scientific basis for explaining those metaphysical phenomena connected to complementary medicine, which have thus far been covered by a cloud of mysticism. Also, the evolving exploration of the understanding of embodiment rather than the body in the social sciences is hopeful.

Since health psychology and complementary medicine are both focused on people's health and illness, the obstacles in the different models of the person and how to access them should not stand in the way of the two working closer together. As has been shown in this chapter, there have been many psychologists such as James, Wundt, Freud, Jung, Reich, Maslow and Rogers whose model of the person was closely related to that of complementary medicine; it was the accepted epistemology and methodology of that time that disrupted taking these models forward in academic psychology, and to the understandings of health and illness. In addition to their current social cognition models, health psychology could take these models on board and could explore with the currently accepted qualitative research methods, the workings of complementary medicine in an accepted scientific way. Its explanations could go beyond the biopsychosocial model which, as Greaves (2002) has well documented, still falls within the old Newtonian physics paradigm. It could take the new physics of quantum mechanics into account, which has already been documented in the works of Gallo (2002) for the processes of psychopathology and the dealings with mental problems in clinical psychology.

For health psychology, an additional biophysics–psychosocial model could link the workings of the so far absent 'inner self' (which, as shown in this chapter have their basis in the body as embodiment) with the social self, to arrive at a scientific rather than religious or spiritual holistic idea, in which the human being is connected with their deeper inner self to the universe as well as to other people. An inner self, an embodied self which is the basis for the understandings of the working of complementary therapies in the sense that it is supposed to indicate the area where relaxation, meditation, effects of acupuncture and homeopathy, and both self-healing and healing over a distance takes place. An inner self, which in the philosophy of Levinas (1968, 1971, 1979) is the bodily elementary experience of enjoyment preceding the capture in language (think of being massaged), and what MacLachlan (2004) calls 'embodiment' as distinct from the experience of 'the body'.

In line with this, the way forward for health psychology is that, in researching the workings and effects of the various therapies of complementary medicine, not only the chosen research methodology could be reflected upon, but also the dimensions of the experience of the inner and social self of both the researcher and the participants. These, as well as the belief system of the subjects, are important influences in the research process as will be shown in the following chapter in relation to placebo and research literature.

In conclusion, health psychologists have a choice in the use of five broad research methodologies based on different epistemologies. All five will be valuable in furthering the understandings of the workings of complementary therapies for the health and well-being status of people. Depending on the question of research, the most appropriate methodology will be chosen, and different perspectives could be taken into account on the nature of the participants, the researcher and the research process itself. Research in this way resembles the pluralistic method of James and the idea of the researcher as detective in the philosophy of science of Haack. Health psychologists could develop and test this new biophysics–psychosocial model as a working analogy in the area of CAM. As such, it could contribute to the alternative of RCT research frameworks in complex health care, such as whole systems research, by offering an elaborate science-based model of the person which is currently missing.

Beliefs and explanations: experimental and non-experimental psychology

'Doublethink' means the power of holding two contradictory beliefs in one's mind simultaneously, and accepting both of them.
(Excerpt from Goldstein's book in George Orwell's Nineteen-Eighty Four)

Introduction

In this chapter, beliefs and explanations related to health and illness will be explored from the point of view of conventional medicine, complementary and alternative medicine (CAM) and health psychology. The following questions will be addressed: what is the difference between belief and knowledge? How do beliefs or knowledge translate into the practice of health care delivery? Health psychology has collated its knowledge in social cognitive belief models but doubts about the sufficiency in explaining health and illness behaviours have been expressed. Will this also apply to CAM? And if so, will it be possible to identify other components of the models which can be particularly relevant for understanding the workings of CAM?

The experimental method has been valued as *the* method in research leading to knowledge, as setting the gold standard. Nevertheless, other methods such as storytelling have been identified to elicit beliefs in health psychology (Marks et al., 2000). Research findings in CAM have very often been dismissed as anecdotal evidence. Can storytelling, as the narrative method, play a role in this discussion?

Some have questioned the role of psychology in CAM. Yet, looking at colour therapy, music therapy, aromatherapy and massage shows that these are related to the human senses, whose role in human perception began with experimental psychology in the 19th century. Therefore, can psychological knowledge obtained through the experimental method provide explanations for the workings of CAM?

Belief models in health psychology

Belief versus knowledge

In philosophy of science, the difference between belief and knowledge is an ongoing debate. All people have beliefs about what a healthy lifestyle is, or what the causes of illness are, or what the best treatment methods are, but these are not necessarily seen as knowledge. In order to be categorized as knowledge, the most consistent agreement among philosophers is that these beliefs need to be true, reliable (Goldman, 1992), infallible (Kirkham, 1984), and justified (Gettier, 1963). Applied to the social and medical sciences, knowledge is generated through the testing of beliefs as true or false and accepting or rejecting hypotheses by the use of statistics. The more predictable and replicated the hypotheses are, the more we construct the phenomena as knowledge rather than beliefs. So how does this relate to practice?

Clinical guidelines in conventional medicine, not for CAM?

Health psychology as a social science develops, applies and tests models in order to generate knowledge about beliefs, emotions and behaviour related to health and illness. In contemporary western medicine, biomedical knowledge about illness is described in clinical guidelines, and ranked from I–IV (see Table 3.1) depending on the strength of the degree of evidence related to experimental studies, preferably RCTs (van Wersch and Eccles, 1999, 2001). As can been seen from Table 3.1 (Shekelle et al., 1999), a classification of Ia presents the strongest evidence, which leads to the best recommendation for a certain treatment. Non-experimental studies are seen as less scientific (classification III). In the absence of any evidence, assessment via the Delphi Method is used, classified here as category IV. According to this method, 'experts' in the field, in this case specialized clinicians with years of experience, 'agree' to a certain diagnosis or treatment as the best, based on their experience that 'it' worked even though the understanding of how and why it worked has not been tested and is not fully understood.

In that sense, CAM practices can be set in the same light. Beliefs about its workings are not seen as knowledge because of the absence of scientific evidence according to the standards of contemporary medicine. Even though 'evidence' could be brought together via studies according to classification III (case-studies related to CAM are mostly described as anecdotal evidence) and IV (agreement of the experts in the field based on the Delphi Method), development of guidelines related to CAM has thus far not attracted the interest of medical authorities (Paterson, 2007). Suggestions in this direction have been made by authors, such as Franck et al. (2007) who argued that CAM reviews carried out by the British National Institute of Health and Clinical Excellence (NICE) could benefit both patients and the NHS. However, colleagues such as Colquhoun (2007)

Table 3.1 Classification schemes of clinical guidelines

Category of evidence:

Ia – evidence for meta-analysis of randomized controlled trials
Ib – evidence from at least one randomized controlled trial
IIa – evidence from at least one controlled study without randomization
IIb – evidence from at least one other type of quasi-experimental study
III – evidence from non-experimental descriptive studies, such as comparative studies, correlation studies, and case-control studies
IV – evidence from expert committee reports or opinions or clinical experience of respected authorities, or both

---

Strength of recommendation

A – directly based on Category I evidence
B – directly based on Category II evidence or extrapolated recommendation from Category I evidence
C – directly based on Category III evidence or extrapolated recommendation from Category I or II evidence
D – directly based on Category IV evidence or extrapolated recommendation from Category I, II or III evidence

---

Source: adapted from Shekelle et al. (1999).

reasoned against this, with the argument that NICE cannot afford such a re-examination process for practices which have not shown much evidence.

A similar argument can be made for the exclusion of knowledge and beliefs from health psychology in clinical guidelines. The plea for the development and assessment of multi-disciplinary or integrated guidelines, rather than clinical guidelines solely based on biomedicine (van Wersch and Eccles, 1999, 2001) has thus far been ignored. The question is, what knowledge can health psychology contribute to the health and illness domain?

Belief models in health psychology

Individuals have their own beliefs and models about health and illness, referred to as 'common-sense models of illness' (e.g. Leventhal et al., 1980, 2003), which are related to people's own personal experiences (Meyer et al., 1985), and/or social and cultural beliefs (Helman, 2001; Johnson and Helman, 2004). These mental models guide people in their decision-making processes and their acting in health and illness situations (Salovey and Rothman, 2003), and 'may or may not correspond with the medical reality as defined by physicians or outside observers' (Baum et al., 1997, p. 382).

Understanding these lay beliefs and their relation to health behaviours has been one of the main objectives of health psychology. A review of textbooks on health and psychology (e.g. Marks et al., 2000; Forshaw, 2002;

Lyons and Chamberlain, 2006) showed a broad scope of belief models used in research in health and illness. The most reported models are: The Health Belief Model (Rosenstock, 1966; Becker, 1974; Kirscht, 1988; Janz and Becker, 1984); The Theory of Reasoned Action (Ajzen and Fishbein, 1980); The Theory of Planned Behaviour (Ajzen, 1985); Protection Motivation Theory (Rogers, 1983); Transtheoretical model (Prochaska and DiClemente, 1986); Self-regulatory Model for Coping with Illness (Leventhal et al., 1980, 2003) and Health Action Process (Schwarzer, 1992). One of the main criticisms of these models has been the overlap in their components, and the lack of empirical comparison of these models (Salovey and Rothman, 2003). Another criticism is that none of these social–cognitive models provides a comprehensive model of health behaviour (Banyard, 1999).

Bennett (2000) argued in line with Ingham and van Zessen (1997) that the complexity of behaviour contradicts the rationality of social cognition models and that its fullness should be explored rather than trying to artificially simplify it. A means for doing so is the use of qualitative methods. In Chapter 2, we distinguished five research strands as objective positivistic, experiential, interpretative, discursive and participatory, of which the last four are classified as qualitative methods. Storytelling is an important part of these methods in eliciting beliefs (Marks et al., 2000), and in enabling a broader understanding of other important aspects of health and illness such as the integration of individuals and their cultures (Crossley, 1999). This applies to patients as well as health professionals working in the same social and cultural context. The idea that patients' stories are based on naïve beliefs and doctors' stories on medical knowledge (e.g. Godoy-Izquierdo et al., 2007) might not always be as simple and straightforward as it looks.

Storytelling: a valid method?

Loewe et al. (1998) explored the stories of physicians regarding diabetes and showed how not only these narratives differ from patient stories but above all how these reflect the complexity and variability of the expression of doctors' beliefs and knowledge in social interactions. The results elucidated the importance of the social and cultural context of the communication of the chronic illness, and falsify the idea that doctors rigidly apply their medical knowledge based on the clinical guidelines. Bowles (1995) discussed how storytelling among nurses contextualized and humanized their medical knowledge and developed new perspectives, through the recognition and reflection of their roles and motivations. Storytelling, as such, evoked an emotional response, was more pleasurable, reached a deeper level for the person, and facilitated cultural identification through the linguistic and symbolic understanding of the culture.

For CAM therapies, based on the philosophical principle of holism and uniqueness of the person, an exploration of patients and practitioners' stories seems to be a valuable method to elicit both the positive and negative aspects of the healing process. This is especially in addition to RCTs which aim to validate or falsify pre-set hypotheses and ignore these principles from humanities. Heinrich (1992) examined the stories of nurse–student participation in four different CAM practices, in which they shared their beliefs and experiences with each other. This led to different results for each of them, reflecting the uniqueness of the experience, set in an individual context. If Heinrich had used an RCT design looking for certain comparative outcome measures, these valuable unique experiences would not have come to light.

McKay and Bonner (1999) analysed the stories of breast cancer in women's magazines, which they named pathographies after Sigmund Freud, in the sense of 'a study of the life and character of an individual or community as influenced by a disease' (p. 563), and showed that these served three relevant purposes: (i) sharing laywomen's 'medical' advice related to certain symptoms and the various treatments available and used; (ii) asking questions and receiving answers from the medical experts in 'letter columns'; and (iii) expressing personal narrative to share own experiences with the disease. Because of the journalistic nature of the tabloids, the exceptional cases were 'sensationally' presented, very often falsifying existing medical guidelines. Since magazines form an important part of people's lives, these illness stories might be beneficial in the sense of giving coherence and meaning to illness by the readers (McKay and Bonner, 1999) but they might also be risky by misleading women through sharing their own invented stories of illness beliefs and treatment advice which are not based on any rational, or logically rooted illness framework other than own fantasies. Even though McKay and Bonner observed that a lot of answers in the question and answer column ended with 'that the patient should see a medical practitioner' (1999, p. 564), the choice of stories and the discourse of its content were mostly deliberately chosen for its sensation which would ridicule the medical belief system and dangerously open up unjustified or false beliefs. Recently, analysis of similar stories has been taken from message boards on the Internet (Buchanan and Coulson, 2007; van Wersch, 2007).

These, and the tabloid stories, differ from autobiographic illness stories, told and justified by academics such as Frank (1991, 1995) or Ettorre (2005). Both Frank and Ettorre were critical of conventional western medical practices, based on their own experiences which were similar to those of the authors of the tabloid and message board stories, but they both justify the use of stories as the narrative method, and discuss it as a legitimate way to contribute to knowledge and understanding in health and illness. Frank, a sociologist, intellectualized both his experiences with illness related to heart disease and cancer, from analysing his own and other patients' stories, and distinguished three types of narratives reflecting both health and illness beliefs and state of self or identity as: (i) the restitution narrative; (ii) the chaos narrative; and (iii) the quest narrative. In his theoretical framework, the restitution narrative reflects the story told within the belief system of modernist western biomedicine, in which a person's illness is seen as a disturbing part of life. This can be seen as a situation in which fulfilling one's role at work as well as in one's personal and social life is replaced by what Parsons (1978) calls the sick role. The medical profession is there to 'cure' people as fast as possible, and as such there is not much difference between the car mechanic and the physician – they are fixers of the broken vehicles of society. That people are living beings with emotions and beliefs, who might psychologically be able to contribute to this 'fix', is ignored as what we might call 'annoying artefacts'. If the medical profession is not able to 'fix' in the expected way, the tabloid stories of disbelief and distrust might compensate for this dissonance. And that is often when people would turn to CAM practices, but unfortunately, these are not based on this 'quick-fix' belief system.

The chaos narratives in Frank's (1991, 1995) model are utterances of people who have lost the words of their story because their illness experience does not make any sense. Their beliefs and understanding have lost the coherence with reality. As a consequence, their idea of themselves, their social self or social identity is broken apart. In the quest narrative, people have come to terms with their illness, but their beliefs and understanding have changed, and so have their identities. They express a realization that it is the experience of the illness and treatment itself which is making sense, and are even very often grateful that their illness experiences have changed their lives for the better, because of having found a deeper meaning.

The beliefs expressed in these two latter narratives are more in line with the model of the person of complementary medicine. Obstacles such as illness are seen as learning moments inevitably necessary to grow and develop and to become a 'better' person. In that sense the chaos is there to break with the identity before one's illness, as a preparation for establishing a renewed self. The quest narrative reflects this new identity as a responsible person who realized that his/her life path is an answer to life's challenges rather than a determination, or fixed planning of that path (see also Levinas, 1961, 1979). Narratives as such reflect gratitude by the patient for their illness because it made them another person.

Ettorre (2005), a feminist sociologist, published her illness story of thyrotoxicosis, and used autoethnography to contribute to the debate on illness, gender and the body. This illness story could also have been analysed within Frank's (1995) framework of restitution, chaos and quest to show the change and conflict of her belief systems and illness behaviour from conventional western medicine to CAM. The use of her illness narrative contributes to our Class III understanding of CAM, in Ettorre's case, of homeopathy, herbalism and osteopathy, but in a different way than RCTs. It is not the effects of the treatments as such which are 'proven' to be effective or not, it is the whole picture of beliefs, emotions, behaviours, interactions, set in a changing personal and treatment context, which through the method of storytelling has provided us with this knowledge; a knowledge in which the combination of treatment belief (blood tests from conventional medicine combined with the harmless remedies and therapies from CAM), and empathy and trust from the CAM health professionals has been portrayed as opposed to the cold, business-like, guilt-provoking attitude of the physician, who just followed the guidelines. Ettorre's story also elucidated the importance of 'time to heal' rather than the 'quick fix' method of the CAM therapies.

Summary

The advantages of the narrative method for health psychology has been illustrated by Marks et al. (2000). More research, analysing both patients' and practitioners' stories related to illness trajectory and use of CAM, could contribute to the progression of knowledge on the workings of CAM, at least as an exemplar of Category III level research in the guidelines. Frank's (1991, 1995) model of the restitution, chaos and quest narratives forms an interesting theoretical framework from which patients' stories could be analysed to contribute to the knowledge base of health and illness in both conventional and complementary medicine, related to their different models of the person.

Integration of mind–body models

Another criticism of the social-cognition models is the exclusion of the integration of mind and body (Bakal, 1992). Especially for the field of CAM, with the emphasis on the 'inner self', such an omission might lose the essential components of the lay person's understanding of health and illness. Two examples of mind–body integration approaches which might suggest interesting frameworks for future CAM research in health psychology are 'dispositional optimism' and 'somatic awareness'.

Dispositional optimism and positive thinking

Dispositional optimism states that 'positive thinking', defined by generalized positive expectations for the future (Segerstrom, 2005) will guide the healing process in illness and prevent the progression of sickness (Scheier and Carver, 1987). Even though the scientific community views such claims with scepticism, or 'motivated disbelief' (Angell, 1985), Scheier et al. (1989, p. 1024) reported that 'research evidence is beginning to emerge that suggests that this popular folk wisdom may have some basis in fact'. This is supported by Bennett (2000, p. 79) who said that 'the beliefs we have about illness and their associated emotions may, in some cases, prove to be more powerful determinants of the outcome of the disease than the underlying physiological processes'. Indeed, the earlier studies of Greer and Watson (1987) with female breast cancer patients indicated that engaging in positive thinking (a fighting spirit) was associated with an increased likelihood of five-year survival.

Scheier and Carver (1987) invented the term *dispositional optimism* and discussed how this human trait could be related to physical well-being. They elaborated this idea by placing it as a component in their model of behavioural regulation, with the underlying idea that people's actions are affected by their beliefs about the possible outcomes of these (Scheier and Carver, 1988). Subsequently, this theoretical concept has been studied in several health-related projects, such as the health behaviours of older people (Steptoe et al., 2006); HIV-infected men (Cruess et al., 2000; Tomakowsky et al., 2001); and risk of cardiovascular death (Giltay et al., 2006).

The effects of dispositional optimism on the immune system received considerable attention in the literature, however, these appeared to be not as straightforward as originally thought (Scheier and Carver, 1987, 1988). Cruess et al. (2000) found that an optimistic belief system was related to better cellular immunology control of the virus among 40 HIV-positive men. However, when controlled for depression, the regression showed that the lower depression levels of the optimistic men had more explanatory power than optimism as such. Cohen et al. (1999) looked at the acute and persistent stressors and life change events over three months in 39 healthy women and argued that dispositional optimism did act as a buffer between acute stress and the immune response, but with persistent stress the optimists showed an even lower immune response than the pessimists. Szondy (2004) also studied the relationship with stress, and reported from his review that in non-stress situations the immune response was better with optimistic than with pessimistic people. In his view, the sort of stress was the most important variable. He indicated that if the stressor was uncontrollable or if the stressors persisted despite coping efforts, then optimism was related to a lower immune response. In line with this, Segerstrom (2005) argued that the effects of dispositional optimism on health are mixed, especially in the immunological mediated diseases such as HIV or cancer, which might be an explanation of why results of optimism on the immune response are not consistently predicted. Szondy (2004) also hypothesized that optimism correlates negatively with immunity when stressors are complex, persistent and uncontrollable, and positively when stressors are brief, straightforward and controllable.

CAM is often connected with the slogan of positive thinking. Is there a relationship between dispositional optimism and positive thinking? The new trend in CAM and holistic therapies is towards telling people to be positive, which has more the character of an optimistic explanatory style. In a holistic perspective cognitions are intertwined with bodily sensations. But what happens if one thinks positively but one's sensations are not, such as, for example, if one's body is in a state of tense arousal, which according to Thayer (1989, 1996) reflects tension, anxiety and fearfulness? Since there is evidence that cognitions can change this arousal (e.g. Schachter and Singer,

1962), an interesting field for research for health psychology could be to establish under which conditions the repetition of this slogan of 'positive thinking' could have a similar positive arousal effect. Especially since telling oneself to be positive is activated through language and as such is part of the social self, while bodily sensations, such as arousal, belong to the domain of the inner self. Study designs using biofeedback technology might progress the understanding of the connection between the social and inner self through measuring the bodily effects of thinking positively.

Tomakowsky et al. (2001) compared two different forms of optimism with each other and with the immune response in 78 HIV-positive men and found that there was no relation between optimistic explanatory style and dispositional optimism. Even more interesting was that when the men scored high on both of these concepts more subjective health was reported, however, optimistic explanatory style on its own was related to poorer immune status. Exploring various concepts related to positive thinking, as well as the effects of complementary therapies on the different forms of stress or physical conditions will be an interesting way forward for health psychology.

Somatic awareness

Another mind–body approach is *somatic awareness* (Bakal et al., 2006), a theoretical construct indicating the awareness of physical sensations in the body. These sensations are universal and are different from the perceptions which are expressed in words, pictures or images, the latter being the result of socialization in a cultural and social context. Lyons and Chamberlain (2006) discussed studies which show that similar physical sensations have various meanings in health and illness depending on the culture and social group to which one belongs. The absence of medical terminology for certain sensations, especially when these are perceived as pain, have shown to be detrimental for certain groups of people suffering from what are known as medically unexplained symptoms (MUS) (Brown, 2007), such as those of endometriosis (Eastwood, 2006) and myalgic encephalopathy (ME) a decade ago, and others yet to be labelled legitimate illnesses in the future.

That similar sensations can be labelled differently depending on the mood and context of the situation has already been shown in the classic experimental psychology studies of Schachter and Singer (1962), who compared four groups with similar arousal levels and found that perceptions were significantly related to the suggested beliefs in manipulative messages. Since the publication of these findings, the hypothesis that perceptions of bodily sensations can be manipulated has been the topic of further study.

However, that there are different degrees of awareness affecting various degrees of illness, pain or physical conditions has been reported in several publications (McCrae and Lumley, 1998; Bakal, 1999; Broers et al., 2002). Lumley et al. (2000) showed that their 95 participants with silent myocardial ischemia, in which no angina was experienced, used the health services to a significantly lesser degree than patients with symptomatic myocardial ischaemia. In line with this, Carney et al. (1998) reported that patients with silent cardiac ischaemia were more somatically aware, less depressed and less anxious than patients with symptomatic cardiac ischaemia. Van Vliet et al. (1997) revealed similar results with patients diagnosed with insulin-dependent diabetes mellitus. Those with better somatic awareness could sense that their body was in a hypo- or hyper-glucose-dependent state, and they did not need the glucose test to tell them that. For the same reason, they could adjust their diet accordingly.

Because of the dominance of the mind over the body in western thinking, the majority of people seem to have lost the awareness of their bodily sensations. Karlins and Andrews (1972) described this disconnection as a problem for people in the West who have not been brought up listening to their bodily signals. Surrounding oneself with lots of outer noise and keeping busy is another reason why they cut themselves off from their inner world. This disconnection might be the reason why people detect symptoms of illnesses too late, and why they rely on the physicians to make a diagnosis when their body reacts strangely. A stressful life-style which keeps the mind occupied leaves no time for scanning our bodies for proprioceptive sensations. Bakal (1992) distinguished two factors to explain this phenomenon: (i) people are more concerned with their external body than their internal soma because that is what others see and respond to; and (ii) 'unwillingness to self-soothe' (1992, p. 56) related to the western Spartan-based education of ignoring the presence of somatic sensations and 'pushing on' because listening to the signals of one's soma or taking time to relax and pamper oneself is a sign of 'personal weakness' or 'is a sign of laziness'.

In Chapter 2 we showed how these physical proprioceptive sensations as categorized in biopsychology are similar to the experience of the 'inner self' as distinguished in the philosophy of Levinas (1961, 1979). Guiding people to become aware of these sensations or to be in touch with their inner self, is among one of the aims of certain CAM practices such as mediation, relaxation, visualization; practices which in health psychology are known as stress-management techniques (see Chapter 5). A suggestion would be to integrate these body-and-mind variables, such as dispositional optimism and somatic awareness in the social-cognitive health beliefs models to establish a link between body and mind, especially when applied to the area of CAM.

The role of placebo in beliefs and explanations

Another variable in the domain of beliefs and explanations related to health, especially in the area of CAM, is the theoretical construct of 'placebo'. As has been shown in Chapter 2, the main problem of accepting CAM into mainstream conventional medicine is that possible effects are difficult to explain, and are for that reason categorized under the header of 'placebo'. In this section the different meanings and connotations of this concept will be explored in their historical contexts, as well as from the points of view of the social sciences.

Placebo: an example from medical school

Reilly (2001, p. 94) introduced CAM as one of the topics in his lecture to medical students and quoted the reaction of his students as follows:

Oh
isn't
it
just
a
placebo
response

He explained that he had to print this deliberately in this way, 'because it tells us so much':

'Oh' – the emotional tone that surrounds the subject.
'Isn't' – the preconception.
'It' – the idea that it is just one thing.
'Just' – the diminutive, what does it matter anyway?
'Placebo response' – singular.

This illustration brings us right to the heart of the matter of the relation between the role of placebo in complementary medicine and beliefs and explanations. As a medical student, this belief is derived from the context and culture of his or her medical education (Helman, 2001). A medical education, as we have seen in Chapter 2, which is based on a positivist epistemology, with the RCTs as its gold standard. As will be shown in what follows, this is only a small part of the use and understanding of placebo in both clinical and therapy practice and research.

What is placebo?

Placebo became a 'hot topic' in the academic literature after the paper by Beecher (1955). In this publication, he reviewed 15 experimental studies, in which over 1000 patients participated, looking at the effects of an active drug by comparing it in a randomized controlled trial with a placebo drug. He concluded that the improvements in the condition of 35.2% of the patients in the control group – treated with a 'fake medication' – was the result of the powerful placebo effect. Since then, it became a 'truth', cited by the majority of papers looking at placebo, that one-third of the effects in 'fake treatments' in randomized controlled trials is the consequence of the placebo effect.

However, this truth has been strongly criticized by several colleagues. Kienle and Kiene (2001), not only reanalysed the studies Beecher used but also a follow-up of 800 other publications which claimed to have proven the placebo effect in the control arm of their trials, and argued that what these studies had shown was not a placebo effect but other effects as categorized under 10 headings, which they divided into different conceptualizations of placebo (such as where no placebo given at all, or placebo is not a placebo), errors in research methodology (such as both observer and patient bias and ignoring the influence of additional treatments), or oversights (such as disregarding the natural course of a disease) (see Table 3.2 for the full list). They concluded, following the words of Gøtzschke (1994) that the concept of placebo 'cannot be defined in a logically consistent way and leads to contradictions' (2001, p. 15).

Table 3.2 Factors that can cause false impression of placebo effect

1. Natural course of the disease
   - Spontaneous improvement
   - Fluctuation of symptoms
   - Regression to the mean

2. Observer bias
   - Conditional switching of treatment
   - Scaling bias

3. Patient bias
   - Polite answers and experimental subordination
   - Conditional answers
   - Neurotic or psychotic misjudgement

4. Additional treatment

5. Irrelevant response variables

6. No placebo given at all
   - Psychotherapy
   - Psychosomatic phenomena
   - Voodoo medicine

7. The placebo is not a placebo

8. Uncritical reporting of anecdotes

9. Misquotations

10. False assumptions of toxic placebo effects created by
    - Everyday symptoms
    - Misquotation
    - Persistence of symptoms

De Craen et al. (2001) found it hard to understand that Beecher's paper had such an impact since 13 of the 15 papers did not include a non-treatment group and 'could therefore not distinguish between changes caused by the natural course of the disease and those caused by placebo' (2001, p. 180). This was in line with an earlier criticism made by Ernst and Resch (1995) that Beecher confused the observed effect in the placebo group with the placebo effect.

This non-clarity surrounding placebo has several causes. In the history of medical care, the use of placebo followed its literal meaning in Latin 'I shall please', and was used to comfort the suffering of patients by any means possible. With the scientific development of medicine in the western world, based on a positivistic epistemology – in which the bodily functions are understood as a closed circuit from the mind – any practices that could not be objectively proven were dismissed as being based on subjective beliefs. This changed the literal meaning of the word placebo from a subjective practice based on healing the whole person, to a tool in scientific research to discover the 'actual' workings of a drug or treatment. The confusion lies in the 'I' of 'I shall please'.

Who is the I in 'I shall please'?

The question one could ask is: is the 'I' the 'I' of the patient or the 'I' of the practitioner? It looks as though a historical shift has taken place in which the 'I' of the practitioner, who wanted to please the patients (Ernst, 2001), has been replaced by the 'I' of the patient, who pleased the process of healing by responding favourably to a 'fake' treatment. This confusion is reflected in the muddled use of the words placebo and placebo response, a mix-up also highlighted by Kienle and Kiene (2001). In the first meaning of the word 'I', the placebo is the practitioner as healer, and the placebo response is the reaction of the patient. In the second sense, the placebo is a fake drug or treatment used to be compared with the 'real' ones, and the placebo response is an unwanted outcome, portrayed by researchers as a 'taboo' in modern medicine (Stefano et al., 2001); as not fitting into the hard science which has diminished the 'art of medicine' (Peters, 2001); as 'the ghosts that haunt the house of scientific objectivity' (Ernst, 2001, p. 18); as a 'pejorative', threatening the mechanistic paradigm that underpins both medical practice and research (Heron, 2001, p. 191).

These two different ways of understanding both placebo and placebo effect are reflected in the literature, and are not only important in understanding the differences of its use in complementary and western conventional medicine, but also of the criticisms of conventional medicine as undermining the confidence in human practice (Peters, 2001), as 'excluding the discourse of feelings and introspection' (Withers, 2001, p. 116), in which the 'actual consultation is almost lost' (Reilly, 2001, p. 99).

Placebo as healing energy

The placebo as seen in its first meaning is categorized by Kienle and Kiene (1998, 2001) as 'no placebo at all' (see Table 3.2), because psychotherapy and voodoo medicine are based on the practitioners aiming to please the patient, and they work deliberately with psychosomatic phenomena in order for the placebo to be effective and helpful. For several authors this process is unavoidable in clinical contexts. Reilly (2001) named this process 'transformational healing', taking place because of an in-built healing potential within the physician as well as in patients, which is essential in a safe, comfortable, authentic and genuine physician–patient encounter. Withers (2001) explored the placebo effect in therapeutic relationships through the tools of psychoanalysis. He believed that analytical understanding of complementary medicine can help illuminate the operation of the placebo effect as a healing entity and offered explanations from the analytical concepts of psychoanalysis. However, as Peters indicated, one of the problems with conventional medicine is the physicians' over-reliance on technique, which has paralysed this human engagement and 'is arguably a sign of practitioner's boredom, burn-out and depression' (2001, p. xii).

This gloomy picture of conventional medicine does not count for all practitioners. On the contrary, that patients do get better from 'fake' treatment, and in some cases even get the same side effects as from active drugs (nocebo-effect) (Ernst, 2001), is recognized as being the consequence of health care delivery by clinicians who are human beings and not (as yet) robots. That human qualities of a practitioner have led to more placebo healing has been demonstrated in several studies (Bugel et al., 2001; Di Blasi and Kleijnen, 2003). Hawkins (2001) argued that the three components of practitioner behaviour as distinguished by Brody (1997), namely provision of an understandable explanation of the illness, demonstrating care and concern, and holding out an enhanced promise that one can master the symptoms, have a high chance of a positive placebo response from patients. Heron (2001) also constructed the placebo response as an unavoidable phenomenon in the healing context, and saw it as a welcome outcome if it affected patients positively. He illustrated this by making a distinction between the 'observable' and 'experiential' body, the latter being responsible for the placebo response, the first as a too narrow view of the body in conventional medicine. As such Heron says: 'an increasing number of patients, no longer content to skulk passively with their observable bodies and let them be subject purely to external medical control, want to become active agents within their experimental bodies, which are potentially subject to their own control, as the placebo response implies' (2001, p. 192). Bensing and Verhaak (2004) recognized this shift from supply-induced to demand-induced care and from doctor-centred to patient-centred medicine in the provision of medical care. They argued that by applying principles based on patient satisfaction as elucidated by models in health psychology, the 'art of medicine' in the medical encounter could change from powerful placebo to empowering patients. In that sense the 'art' will become 'part' of the practice of contemporary medicine.

Placebo as a fake drug or treatment

The understanding of placebo in the second sense, as a fake drug or treatment in the comparison of the active drug is reflected in other definitions and uses of the words *placebo* and *placebo response* in the literature. Ernst (2001, p. 18) followed a 'consensus definition set at a National Health Institute conference which stated that a placebo effect is "one that includes the many non-specific effects of therapy". He even suggested to replace the word 'placebo effect' with 'non-specific effects' because of the 'considerable difficulties in defining "placebo" ' (2001, p. 18). Among these 'non-specific' effects he reckoned were factors such as physician attention, patient's and physician's expectations of treatment effects, and characteristics of the setting. Kienle and Kiene (2001) did not agree with the definition of the concept of placebo in non-specific terms; for them it is impossible to know all the specific effects which need to be excluded in order to determine the possible non-specific ones. In their view, the best description is taken from Hornung (1994) who defined placebo as an inert preparation that looks like an active medication. Accordingly, the placebo effect is defined by Kienle and Kiene (2001) as the therapeutic effect of a placebo administration.

Beliefs and explanations of placebo

As far as the beliefs and explanations of the placebo effect are concerned, a relation between these two broad different ways of understanding the placebo can be seen as of being part of a 'soft' healing context or a 'hard' scientific paradigm. In research these are reflected in terms of more qualitative or quantitative approaches. The first in the sense of eliciting the meaning of the illness and healing experience, the second in terms of 'proving' that a cure works. Explanations for the effects of placebo are derived from, on the one hand, biopsychological studies (e.g. psychoneuroimmunology (PNI)), and, on the other hand from medical anthropology relating placebo to a micro- and macro-cultural context.

Beliefs and explanations of placebo as healing

The beliefs and explanation of placebo in a healing context are spread out from arguments such as philosophical wisdom and the quantum mechanics-based energy models including Laszlo's (2003) connectivity hypothesis, to the idea of inter-subjectivity in psychotherapy. Reilly (2001) explained placebo from the inter-connectedness of people and the idea that wisdom of healing and self-healing lies within the person. Everybody has a simple in-built understanding based on beliefs:

> These basic understandings are there before they become complicated with words like autonomic nervous system, and psychoneuroimmuno-logy, and placebo and nocebo and the subconscious, and the multi-foiled vocabulary that we then use to begin to get to grips with this simple in-built understanding. The transition into professional life of that knowledge is where a lot of our problems are developing.
>
> (2001, p. 91)

He implied that the placebo response can be a triggering of a true self-healing mechanism, which is connected with the true inner body. A true inner body which Reilly described in a similar way as Levinas portrayed the inner self (see Chapter 2) as 'a blush' which is out of people's conscious control (Reilly, 2001, p. 102); and as 'our breathing and the movements of our hearts' (Reilly, 2001, p. 104). In Reilly's philosophy, what inhibits this healing response is 'deceit', 'self-illusion' and 'woolly thinking'. The healing encounter can only work when both patient and practitioner bring them-selves to a point of complete honesty.

In line with this, Heron (2001) believed in the healing encounter between practitioners and patients, and explained it too with the energy model and the connectivity hypothesis. He described the medical inter-action as the paradigm of participative reality in which the minds participate creatively in the cosmos. As did Reilly, Heron emphasized the inner felt sense of the body (embodiment) – the experiential body – as important in the placebo healing. Bakal et al. (2006) raised the importance of the concept of *somatic awareness*, in which the body is believed to be the unconscious mind. Bodily subjective experiences of the patient, for which no medical diagnosis can be found, are taken seriously in a mind–body connectivity in which the patient recognizes that the source of healing is some inner self-regulated process, which is important to shift the placebo power to the individual. Bakal et al. affirm their beliefs in a biopsychosocial frame-work, however, the case study which they used as an illustration, in which a woman's medically unexplained symptom of heartache were treated by the discovery of the connection of this 'body armour' with early childhood physical abuse of her alcoholic father, would find more explanatory power in the energetic psychology of Reich (1973; see Chapter 2) than Engel's (1977) biopsychosocial model.

Wright and Sayre-Adams (2001) showed how, in their complementary therapy of Therapeutic Touch (TT), the belief of the placebo, in the sense of 'I shall please', is essential in the outcome of the therapy. The definition of placebo as 'any procedure that produces an effect in a patient because of its therapeutic intent and not its specific nature' (2001, p. 171) is in that sense paradoxical because the intent itself is considered to be specific and the aim of TT is to repattern the subject's energy field in order to enhance self-healing. They also explain the working of the healing encounter between practitioner and patient in the energy model in which human beings are all patterns of energy resonating with each other. As in the argument of Heron, TT is also seen as a participatory process in line with Rogers's (1990) 'science of unitary human beings', in which she proposes a particular nursing theory that is allied to modern systems thinking as presented in holism, chaos theory and quantum physics (Bohm, 1973; Zohar, 1990; Dossey, 1997).

Richardson (2001) saw the placebo effect as the therapeutic process arising from an experience that is essentially inter-subjective. Her beliefs are based on phenomenological epistemology and are congruent with Heron's (2001) prerequisites of honesty in the therapeutic relationship for promoting the self-healing capacities of the patient. She believed in a shared healing space, in which being together is seen as more important than the action, as togetherness creates the ability to move through the use of narrative, empathy and openness with the patient. She also talked about inner body feelings in the sense of 'taking the substance of the interaction in my body' (2001, p. 140), and the importance of touch. Furthermore, the significance of personal stories is highlighted. Her explanations are derived from the healing models of Hodges and Scofield (1995) who argue the importance eliciting a placebo response, in particular, in the therapeutic relationship; and Frank's (1984) reported similarities between psychotherapy and placebo in medicine, which are both seen as arousing hope, contributing to emotional arousal, encouraging changed activity and encouraging new ways of seeing oneself and one's problems.

Beliefs and explanations of placebo as fake drug or treatment

The beliefs and explanations of the placebo effect in 'fake' placebo trial experiments are, as mentioned before, different from the healing placebo as highlighted in therapeutic relations. Ernst (2001) discussed how the true placebo effect does exist in randomized controlled trials. But in order to avoid this effect in determining the real action of a drug or treatment, a non-treatment should be included in a three-arm randomized trial. Ernst believed in the placebo as the non-specific effects as discussed before, and argued that researching these in rigorously controlled experiments will make the outcome of the trials more effective. As determinants for studying placebo, ranging from 0 to 100%, he distinguished the nature of the intervention, the therapist, the time factor, the patient, the nature of the complaint and the therapeutic setting. He highlighted that using placebo outside clinical trials has an aftertaste of charlatanism – because it involves deceiving the patient – and it is unethical. He also acknowledged that recently the placebo has been appreciated in its own right, which Harrington (1997) calls the 'third stage of an artefact'. He concluded that if we want to optimize (rather than ignore or control) the placebo effect, we need to understand it better than we do today.

Kienle and Kiene (1998, p. 47) are quite critical about including the therapeutic effect in the understanding of placebo: 'To us, it seems inappropriate to call such therapeutic approaches simply "placebos". Such a label may all too easily mask our own ignorance and lack of understanding when research and attempts at understanding would be more appropriate'. Needless to say for them, placebo is the fake arm in a controlled trial in order to find the 'truth' about a drug or treatment without taking the human factors in account.

Hyland et al. (2006) carried out an open study of self-treatment with self-selected fake Bach flower essences in order to test the role of expectancy hypotheses of placebo in the sense that, if one expects an effect, one will find it. Their quantitative study resulted in an improvement in 58.7% of their sample of 116 participants. The effect of expectancy was highly significant and so was spirituality. The latter was difficult to explain for the authors, however, looking at the items of the spirituality questionnaire it seemed to indicate a positive belief in relying on forces in life other than the drugs themselves.

Explanations of the placebo effect from biopsychological factors

Both Clow (2001) and Fenwick (2001) explained how the workings of placebo effect can be understood from a biopsychological perspective in which the connection between mind and body are illustrated through the workings of the immune system. Clow explored the conditioning of the immune system and showed that brain-hemisphere lateralization is related to cell and humoral mediated immunity, and how the association between brain, emotion and the immune organization is regulated through the autonomic central nervous and neuroendocrine system. These workings are explained and 'proven' through very well designed experimental studies with rodents, rats and human beings. Clow's conclusion was that the immune system can be conditioned in both humoral and cell-mediated branches, and consequently that the immune system is susceptible to the power of belief as suggested by a placebo. She further commented that especially people who are not feeling very well are deprived of their health state, which makes them more susceptible for conditioning (similar to the immune conditioning for the food-and-drink-deprived animals in the experimental studies).

Fenwick (2001) also demonstrated the link between the mind and the body through the immune system, but not through conditioning experiments. He discussed experimental studies which showed the effects of psychological factors such as stress, coping and optimism, on both the cell and humoral cell-mediated immune system, and studies showing the effects of healing on the immune system and illness in general. He concluded that 'meaning is important and that a negative interpretation given to events leads to a reduction in immune system responsiveness and effectiveness'

(2001, p. 223) This again showed the relation between sensation and perceptions with the interference of beliefs, which as Lyons and Chamberlain (2006) have shown, differ between social groups and cultures. Interestingly, Fenwick (2001) used two explanatory models. One is the biopsychological objective epistemology model in which he has reviewed the evidence for the effects of – as he called it – downward causation on the genesis of illness and healing. The other is the energy model in line with the connectivity hypothesis, which he used to explain his review of studies looking at the effects of healing at a distance both by the use of non-contact healing and of prayer:

> Our current physics through the study of quantum mechanical effects suggests that the universe is highly connected and that particles interact with each other at a distance. Thus the idea that mind could also be interactive outside the skull is theoretically possible although at the present time the mechanism by which this could occur is not yet known.
>
> (2001, p. 224)

Stefano et al. (2001) explained the workings of the placebo response too from a biopsychological framework. They followed up Benson et al.'s (1974) earlier claims that the placebo response works neuro-physiologically in the same way as the relaxation response which they have explained in neuro-vascular immunological detail. Their beliefs were that both cognitive and non-cognitive coping influenced the immune phenomena via neuro-immune, vascular-immune and neuro-vascular mechanisms. They believe that the mind, both consciously and unconsciously, depends on the underlying neural substrates to manifest itself. The study showed how the mechanisms and processes work when a person initiates positive mind–body activation. By focusing mentally on certain parts of the body, healing is promoted, the effects of which can be read through physiological measurements of the body.

Explanations for the placebo effect: micro- and macro-social contextual influences

Coming from another discipline, medical anthropology, Helman (2001) argues, as did Lyons and Chamberlain (2006) that placebo is context and culturally dependent, and states that 'placebos that work in one cultural group may not necessarily have the same effect in another'. He developed a model in which micro-contextual influences are different, but related to the macro-contextual. Some of the micro-contextual variables are similar to the ones distinguished by Ernst (2001), and are taken from Claridge (1970) to explain the total drug effect in psychopharmacological experiments. These are additional variables to the active drug ingredient, such as the appearance of the drug (e.g. colour, shape), the prescriber (e.g. attitude, beliefs, self-confidence, air of authority, clothing), the recipient (e.g. psychological state, suggestibility, intelligence, personality), and the setting or physical environment (e.g. home, hospital).

The workings of these additional variables have also been documented in experimental studies. For example, De Craen et al. (2001) showed how different colours of drugs have different placebo effects. Pariente et al. (2005) found that acupuncture did have a demonstrable effect over and above a simple skin prick, which might be explained through the visceroceptive pathway (e.g. Kim, 1964). The Streiberger Needle (SN) was concluded to be an effective placebo as it did not show the same activation in the PET scans as the real acupuncture. They also demonstrated that expectation of, and belief in, treatment have a physiological effect on the brain that appears to mediate a potentially powerful non-specific clinical response to acupuncture. Norheim and Fønnebø (2002) explored the belief system of the prescriber concerning the placebo effect in acupuncture and found that 25% of general practitioners compared to 75% among doctors in other positions believed that the effect of acupuncture was due to placebo; 36% of doctors who used acupuncture in their practice said that placebo explained the treatment effect. Berthelot et al. (2001) studied the beliefs of both recipients and nurses and showed that only 27% of the patients and 58% of the nurses believed that their pain could completely resolve under placebo therapy. Goodenough et al. (1997) researched the effect of placebo cream in reducing needle pain in a RCT with children and did find that belief in the reduction of pain did work. However, they did not have a non-treatment group so the true placebo effect could not be determined.

As the macro-context influences, Helman (2001) pictured the wider, social, cultural and economic milieu which are crucial for the ambience, atmosphere and belief in the efficacy of the healer and their treatments. These influences help create belief in the minds of the patients and their family and friends and accordingly placebo is seen equal to belief. Helman compared these influences in cultures by using the metaphor of the theatre in which there is scenery, costumes, scripts and ritual symbols (body language, music, dance, incense, speech). In that sense understanding the placebo effect is decoding the messages hidden within rituals and the symbols which are associated with it.

The future of placebo

In sum, placebo is a theoretical construct, the meaning of which is not always as clear as one would expect. Its original connotation of 'I shall please' can take on many forms. For future research in CAM it is important to indicate which meaning is attached to the phrase, 'effects are caused by the placebo effect', and whether placebo in the form of healing should be part of the healing encounter or seen as an artefact. In the next section an effort is made to link CAM therapies related to the human senses, the workings of which have been criticized as 'placebo', to experimental studies on human perception in psychology.

Experimental psychology and perception: odour, colour, music and touch in relation to aromatherapy, colour therapy, music therapy and massage

Since Wundt, psychology has been interested in how people perceive the world applying their five senses. Using the experimental method, psychological responses to the elementary sensations of physical stimuli were studied and this approach became known as psychophysics. Since then cognitive and neuro-psychologists have been engaged in research to broaden the understanding of these basic perceptual processes under various different experimental conditions and/or in relation to other variables such as, for example, mood, personality, emotions or pain.

Even though CAM therapies such as aromatherapy, colour therapy, music therapy and massage are based on the psychological perception of these elementary sensations, a link with health psychology has thus far not been made. The question is, should health psychology ignore this body of knowledge from their own discipline, and only concentrate on employing theories, models and concepts from (applied) social psychology, such as motivations, attitudes, beliefs, or social constructions, or should they integrate psychophysics in their research on CAM? In what follows, these questions will be explored.

Smell versus aromatherapy

As early as 1871, a chapter appeared in a psychological textbook on intelligence with the title 'Sensations of Sight, of Smell, of Taste, of Touch, and Their Elements' (Taine, 1871). Since then the effects of scent or odour on human behaviour have been studied in several experimental settings, but as Ilmberger et al. (2001, p. 239) observed, 'scientific research on the effects of essential oils on human behaviour lags behind the promises made by popular aromatherapy'. These thoughts were echoed also by Perry and Perry (2006, p. 257):

> Aromatherapy is currently used worldwide in the management of chronic pain, depression, anxiety, some cognitive disorders, insomnia and stress-related disorders. Although essential oils have been used, reputedly effectively, for centuries as a traditional medicine, there is very little verified science behind this use.

Aromatherapy is defined as a form of alternative medicine that uses volatile liquid plant materials, known as essential oils, and other scented compounds from plants for the purpose of affecting a person's mood or health (e.g. Morrin and Ratneshwar, 2000; Ilmberger et al., 2001). Popular books on aromatherapy claim a variety of effects from the different scents of oils, however, without supporting evidence. Psychophysics has studied the effects of odours on psychological variables, and in several cases these are similar to the scented oils used in aromatherapy.

The majority of experimental studies have been carried out on the effects of perception of odours on anxiety and mood. Lehrner et al. (2000) compared the results of 35 (17 male, 18 female) participants who were in a waiting room for their dental appointment scented with orange essential oils with 37 (14 male, 23 female) subjects in the control group in a waiting room with no scent, and found a significant difference in lower anxiety, positive mood and higher calmness, especially for the women, in the scented room. In 2005, Lehrner and his colleagues replicated the study with 200 (100 women, 100 men) patients and found the same results, this time for both men and women, and not only for the ambient odour of orange, but also for lavender. Burnett et al. (2004) gave 42 women and 31 men an anxiety-provoking task while being exposed to the scents of water, rosemary and lavender. Using the POMS to assess mood and physiological measures of temperature and blood pressure they discovered that when pleasantness of scent was controlled, no differences in physiological measures were the result. However, mood did differ: the rosemary condition showed higher scores on tension-anxiety and confusion-bewilderment relative to the lavender and control conditions, while the lavender and control conditions showed higher mean vigour-activity ratings relative to the rosemary group; furthermore, both rosemary and lavender scents scored lower on the fatigue-inertia sub-scale than the control group. These results were similar to those of Moss et al. (2003) who observed different effects of rosemary and lavender in their experiment in which 144 participants were randomly assigned to three conditions. The subjects in the lavender and control group were less alert than in the rosemary group, and both scented conditions lead to higher contentedness than the control group. In addition, they showed that rosemary had a positive effect on memory. Morrin and Ratneshwar (2000) tested the effects of geranium as the chosen most pleasant scent among rosemary, lavender, geranium, eucalyptus in their experiment of 50 participants, and did not obtain a significant difference in mood states, but did find an improvement in memory. Villemure and Bushnell (2002) showed a significant relation between individually chosen pleasant odours and positive mood changes but only in the absence of pain. If pain was experimentally induced no changes in mood were observed.

The effects of aromas have also been studied in relation to other cognitive tasks such as attention. Ilmberger et al. (2001) tested the effects of peppermint, jasmine and ylang ylang in a speed information-processing task and no significant effect of any of these was observed. However, they did find interesting correlations in the within-group analysis between subjective evaluations of substances and objective performance, which made them conclude that effects of essentials oils or their components on basic forms of attentional behavior are mainly psychological, and not physiological.

Related to health, effects of essential oils have been found on stress, pain and sleep. Komiya et al. (2006) examined the anti-stress action of the essential oils of lavender, rose, and lemon in mice, and concluded that lemon oil had the strongest anti-stress effect in three behavioural tasks. These results suggest that lemon oil possesses anxiolytic, anti-depressant-like effects via the suppression of dopamine (DA) activity in the hippocampus related to enhanced serotonin (5-HT) in the prefrontal cortex and striatum. However, what the effects are on human stress has not been assessed experimentally. As far as pain is concerned, Villemure and Bushnell (2002) reported the opposite of what aromatherapy claims, that pleasant odours alleviate the pain experience. Their results showed a slight worsening of subjects' mood when pleasant odour was present, and no mood change with unscented air during pain induction, an interesting finding with no explanation from the researchers. Gedney et al. (2004) also obtained results along these lines. No lowering of experimental-induced pain was found when comparing quantitative pain scores in air-scented conditions with lavender, rosemary or distilled water (control). Interestingly, when asked on reflection what subjects thought the effects of the ambient scent had been on their pain, the majority thought that their pain had lowered in the lavender condition, and a few even reported this of the rosemary compared to the water condition.

Goel et al. (2005, p. 889) referred to aromatherapy as 'an anecdotal method for modifying sleep and mood'. They carried out a well designed study in which 31 subjects (16 men and 15 women) were monitored for three nights sleeping in the laboratory, half of them receiving scented lavender with a control group receiving distilled water. The results on sleeping pattern and mood were positive: lavender increased the percentage of deep or slow-wave sleep (SWS) in both men and women, and higher vigour was reported the morning after lavender exposure, corroborating the restorative SWS increase. Gender differences were found regarding increased stage 2 (light sleep), decreased rapid-eye movement (REM) sleep and the amount of time to reach wake after first falling asleep (wake after sleep onset latency) in women, and opposite effects in men. Lewith et al. (2005) tested their RCT method in a pilot study with ten volunteers, and their results showed a positive effect of lavender on insomnia.

Comparing these experimental studies of the scents of essential oils with the claimed effects in popular books on aromatherapy such as Worwood's (1995) book with the misleading title, *The Fragrant Mind: Aromatherapy for Personality, Mind, Mood and Emotion*, shows a broad gap between the popular psychological beliefs of aromatherapy and the scientific psychological knowledge of odours on behaviour. For example, the claimed workings of essential oils for concentration such as lemon, orange, rosemary and peppermint have not been supported by the experimental studies just described.

Lavender is supposed to be good for restfulness, which has been revealed in several studies, but so is geranium, which has not been replicated. In popular aromatherapy books broad claims are made of the psychological impact of the scents of essential oils, nonetheless only a few of these have been subjected to experimental psychological research. Many more hypotheses could be drawn from these suggested effects and properly tested in controlled experiments.

This cleavage is very well described in the review article of Martin (1996) on sensations of smell, in which he distinguished 'olfactory psychology' from 'olfactorial remediation'. The first reflects the experimental studies which are reliable because they study 'the effects of exposure to odour on various human psychological processes, such as, mood, cognition, memory, person perception, health, sexual behaviour and ingestive processes' (1996, p. 63) as part of rigorous science, in the sense of 'objective' and 'quantitative' investigations, from which 'to draw meaningful scientific conclusions' (1996, p. 63). ' "Olfactorial remediation" (or aromatherapy), on the other hand, reflects those studies examining the possible therapeutic use of odour to alleviate illness' (1996, p. 63), which might 'add some colour to or provide a vivid illustration' (1996, p. 63), but which results based on 'subjective', 'qualitative' methods are 'speculative' and 'anecdotal'. Probably a combination of both will generate more knowledge about the workings of aromatherapy – which is an interesting challenge for health psychologists.

Vision versus colour therapy

In the electromagnetic spectrum, in which the particles behave as electrons with a certain frequency and wavelength, only waves with a length of between 400 and 700 nanometres can be perceived in the presence of white light as colours by healthy human eyes. Other wavelengths cannot be seen, yet that does not mean to say that these do not exist. In the dark energy surrounding us, there are indirect ways of detecting these waves. For example, the ultraviolet radiation, with waves between 400nm and 10nm can be detected through sunburn on the skin; or the infrared radiation with waves above 700nm to 1500nm as the cooking process in our microwaves. The colours of the visible spectrum are detectable by the approximately 137 million photoreceptors (rods and cones) of the eye, which transform light into electrical impulses which sends information to the visual cortex and gives us information about the colour. Information is also sent to the hypothalamus, where both the pituitary and pineal gland are regulating the autonomic nervous system and the internal functions of the body. As such, colour perception does more than meets the eye.

Still, experimental psychology has mainly concentrated on the visual perception of the brightness and hue of colours. It is as Lindsay and Norman explained (1977, p. 87):

The physical aspects of light and sound are easily studied, defined and measured. A physical wave can be accurately specified by its waveform – the description of its energy or pressure over time – or by its spectrum – the description of how much energy is present at each frequency. The psychological aspects are not easily defined . . . To study psychological impressions, it is necessary to ask people to tell something about their sensations.

However, this has shown to be not very reliable because of the interference of subjects' knowledge of language and social desirability: 'The important thing is to ask the right questions' (1977, p. 79). Psychological experiments as such have been carried out with different colours, different mixtures of light and varying in conditions to study phenomena such as brightness contrast, Mach bands, spatial frequency analysis, contours, depth, critical flicker, after image colour and so on. However, the influences of colour on the central nervous system and the internal systems and regulations, which could link in with suggestions made in CAM, have not been subjected to experimental psychology.

Pak (1998) claimed that the healing power of colour can be used for prevention, treatment and post-treatment recovery but there is no research to support this claim. Demarco and Clarke (2001) distinguished 11 different colour therapies with their so called healing effects on various conditions such as coloured strobe lights for anxiety, depression and post-traumatic stress disorder (PTSD); flickering red lights for migraine; de Marco's colour profile analysis to treat deep-rooted blocked emotions; aura readings with a Kirlian camera to detect physiological and emotional imbalances in the body; and applied kinesiology which is supposed to be able to find a colour needed for a healthy mind and body. Other therapies reported in the literature are Mandel's Esogetic Colour Puncture Therapy (EST) (Cocilovo, 1999; Croke and Dass Bourne, 1999; Demarco and Clark, 2001), in which acupuncture points are treated with coloured light; Bipolar color therapy (Kohler, 1997) based on system information therapy in which a stress ratio is triggered which gives information about a disease, the immunological reaction and the necessary detoxification potentials; and Kosmophon Therapy (Gumbel, 1997) which postulates a related colour for every organ of the body.

Most of the claims of these therapies are based on case studies or anecdotal evidence, which are not very well described. Even the therapy with effects on migraine, insomnia, bronchitis, and uterine fibroids as reported in several research projects such as Mandel's ECT (Croke and Dass Bourne, 1999), have been criticized because of the limitations in research designs and sample size. There is certainly scope for health psychology to study the effects of the various colour therapies for health and well-being in relation to the theoretical understanding of the psychophysics of colour.

Sound versus music therapy

Experimental psychology has carried out studies and developed theories on the perception of sound in order to understand its effects on human behaviour. However, as with vision, research has been limited to certain aspects of psychophysics, such as loudness, pitch, the critical band and auditory space perception. Daveson and Skewes (2002, p. 266) questioned the understanding of rhythm, and criticized music psychologists for their exclusive focus on the quantifiable entities of sound such as pitch, only because these can be easily defined and 'precisely notated'.

As far as listening to music is concerned, experimental psychologists are interested in the question as to which tones can be perceived and why, but not what the effects of music are on health in general, or on the separate organs of the body. Most applied research is carried out on environmental stress such as the effects of noise at work on health (e.g. Sveinsdottir et al., 2007), or noise from traffic, road works or neighbours (Farr, 1967) on public health (Kryter, 1994). Bronzaft (2002) identified this phenomenon as 'noise pollution', indicating that noise is hazardous to good health. However, that sound in the form of music can be beneficial for people's health has received limited attention in psychological research. This is the case even though music therapy, defined as a controlled form of listening to music which has an influence on the physiological, psychological and emotional aspects of the person during treatment of illness or injury (Biley, 1992), has been practised for some time. Again, similar to the studies on colour and aromatherapy, research with good methodology is sparse and a theoretical psychological framework is missing in most of these. This is regrettable because several studies and their findings are interesting but, because of these limitations, difficult to interpret.

For example, studies reported the effects of music therapy on reducing anxiety and distress in paediatric patients receiving non-invasive procedures whereby a musician played guitar and sang children's favourite songs (DeLoach Walworth, 2005); and in MS patients by using the Nordoff Robbins Approach in which both patients and therapists were active in the music-making process (Aldridge et al., 2005). DeLoach Walworth (2005) reported a successful replacement of sedation through the application of music therapy, however, it was not clear how these data were analysed and on which basis this conclusion was drawn. All in all, these studies are vaguely described in the sense that procedures, methods, and results are not very transparent, and for that reason difficult to replicate. Edwards (2005) identified the problems of carrying out Evidence-based Practice (EBP) on music therapy as: (i) the population is too diverse; (ii) the music therapist approach is geared towards patients' responses; and (iii) we are unable to capture the respondents' idiosyncratic voices; pursuing additional well designed experimental studies should be possible and could be carried out by health psychologists.

Other research indicated that listening to relaxing music such as classical, Chinese or New Age music lowers blood pressure but not heart rate or respiratory rate (Wong et al., 2001; Almerud and Petersson, 2003), even in a sample of patients in intensive care, who afterwards reported that they had no memory of the music being played (Almerund and Petersson, 2003). Since certain alternative philosophies, such as the one related to Chinese Wu Xing music, believe in an energy resonance of certain tones of internal organs, there might be scope for the development of a framework by health psychologists, which could be tested in research.

Touch and massage

Touch is a form of human information processing which, unlike smell, vision and sound is not discussed by cognitive experimental psychologists such as Lindsay and Norman (1977). Touch is described by van Dongen (2004) as 'the forgotten sense' in her review of Field's book, *Touch* (2003). In psychology touch has been more the subject of biopsychology than cognitive psychology, because of the interference of the body between the stimulus and the response. However, looking at this from the angle of physics, in which all these stimuli have their basis in energy, the exclusion of the body in the perception of sound, odour and colour is debatable. MacLachlan (2004) argued that these are all part of the embodied experience. Ideas behind music-, light- and aroma-therapy are that the sensations of these energetic particles take place at the level of the body (or the unconscious mind) and not only in the specified organs of the ear, eye and nose as part of the brain.

In the literature claims have been made about the importance of touch for human behaviour, in particular in relation to physical and psychological health and well-being (Heller and Schiff, 1991; Field, 2000, 2003; Brownlee and Dattilo, 2002). As a form of CAM, several touch therapies have been distinguished, which broadly speaking can be divided into two categories: Touch Healing, such as, Reiki and Therapeutic Touch (Kerr et al., 2007), and Therapeutic Massage (Brownlee and Dattilo, 2002) such as aroma-therapy massage, reflexology, sport massage, shiatsu, Swedish (classic) massage (Willison, 2006), Traditional Tai Massage (TTM) (Chatchawan et al., 2005), and the water-massage therapies Watsu and Aix (Faull, 2005). With the first group, there is no physical contact and touch is a form of meta-physical contact in which healing energies come together in line with the paradigm of Laszlo's (2003) connectivity hypothesis. In the second sense, touch is either focused on the acupressure points of the body (e.g. aromatherapy massage, reflexology, shiatsu, TTM), or on the physiology and anatomy of the western model of the body (e.g. sport massage, Swedish massage).

Research has been carried out on these forms of touch, with different outcomes. For example, Frank et al. (2007) compared Therapeutic Touch, a type of energy medicine whereby the therapists moves their hands over the patient's 'energy field', directing the flow of qi or prana to heal the patient (Krieger, 1979) in 42 patients, with sham touch in 40 women undergoing stereotactic core breast biopsy. They did not find any significant differences in easing the discomfort and distress. Clark and Clark (1985) compared the physiological responses (EMG, skin conductance, skin temperature) of 60 college students who were randomly assigned to a Therapeutic Touch versus physical touch group while being exposed to a stressful stimulus, and their results falsified their hypothesis that the Therapeutic Touch group would be more relaxed. In another publication, Clark and Clark (1985) urged us not to be convinced by the weak evidence and concluded that the effects of the treatments of Therapeutic Touch are nothing more than placebo.

Nevertheless, a few studies did find some effects of Therapeutic Touch, mostly a reduction in (state) anxiety (Quinn, 1984; Gagne and Toye, 1994; Spence and Olson, 1997) or an alleviation of pain (Spence and Olson, 1997; Gordon et al., 1998). Yet, as Spence and Olson (1997) concluded from their review of 11 studies, even though there might be some evidence to support the practice of Therapeutic Touch for pain and anxiety, there is a lack of congruity regarding theoretical frameworks, operational definitions and research methods. Unfortunately no empirical studies on Reiki or other forms of Touch Healing were found. On the whole, it is clear that a theoretical framework explaining the working of touch healing with proper designed studies with a sound methodology is necessary.

As far as the second category is concerned, Therapeutic Massage has been researched more extensively. According to Willison (2006), the four massage techniques, effleurage (stroking), petrissage (compression), tapotement (percussion) and vibration and friction, used in a great variety of massage therapies stimulate blood circulation, lower blood pressure, reduce swelling and promote faster healing. Massage is supposed to improve lymphatic fluid circulation, stimulate the immune system and improve cell processes by feeding nutrition and retrieving their waste. However, these effects on the immune system and cell regulation have not been replicated in the study of Goodfellow (2003), who compared the effects of therapeutic back massage on the immune function in the terms of Natural Killer Cell Activity (NKCA) of 42 spouses of patients with cancer. Still, Zeitlin et al. (2000) did find a significant increase in NKCA at the post-massage activity of nine medical healthy females facing an anxiety-provoking academic examination.

A reduction in pain after massage therapy was reported in studies using different massage techniques. Plews-Ogan et al. (2005) compared Mindfulness-based Stress Reduction (MBSR) (see Chapter 5) with Swedish massage in people suffering from chronic muscular pain, fitting the model of Field et al. (2007). They observed that MBSR was more effective, and longer lasting, for mood improvement, while massage was more effective in reducing pain. This was in line with Hasson et al.'s (2004) study, who concluded that massage was more effective than mental relaxation exercises in the pain perception of the 129 people suffering from long-term mus-culoskeletal pain. Interestingly, this difference disappeared at the three-month follow-up, at which stage the pain scores of both group returned to the baseline measurements. Chatchawan et al. (2005), however, compared Traditional Thai Massage with Swedish massage in 180 patients suffering from back pain problems, and found that both massage techniques lowered pain perception significantly after three weeks, and a month after treatment.

Anxiety was also consistently shown to be reduced after therapeutic mas-sage treatment. Cooke et al. (2007) compared aromatherapy massage with a control group in 66 nurse students over a period of 12 weeks, and did discover a significant reduction in anxiety in the massage group. Interestingly, they reported higher anxiety scores in the winter than in the summer. The study of Zeitlin et al. (2000) showed a reduction in anxiety among the nine medical students who received a one-hour full-body massage before an unpleasant bodily examination. Similarly, Ahles et al. (1999) compared a 20-minute shoulder, neck, face and scalp Swedish massage combined with pressure to acupuncture points massage with no massage in their randomized sample of 35 patients undergoing autologous bone marrow transplantation and found a significant reduction in state anxiety at mid-treatment.

Changes in physical measures, such as blood pressure, heart rate and res-piration rate, were measured in several studies (Ahles et al., 1999; Zeitlin et al., 2000; Goodfellow, 2003). Contradictory results were noticed regard-ing blood pressure, indicating the importance of the type of massage. Cambron et al. (2006) reported a significant lowering of systolic (and an increase in diastolic) blood pressure after Swedish massage treatment, but an increase in both systolic and diastolic blood pressure after trigger-point therapy and sport massage in their sample of 150 volunteers. Ahles et al. (1999), on the contrary, observed a significant reduction of diastolic blood pressure after a combined Swedish and acupressure-point massage. Cam-bron et al. (2006) explained this contradiction with the hypothesis that the more painful the massage, the higher the blood pressure (both systolic and diastolic). As far as the other physical measures are concerned, no decrease in heart rate has been found, and only in one study (Zeitlin et al., 2000) a decrease in respiratory rate has been reported.

Other effects of massage described in the literature are the enhancement of mood (Goodfellow, 2003; Boylan, 2005) and the reduction of stress (Zeitlin et al., 2000; Goodfellow et al., 2003; Boylan, 2005) and distress (Ahles et al., 1999). Interestingly, the studies reporting the enhancement of mood were both based on the use of Therapeutic Back Massage. Why this is could be further explored by health psychologists.

Summary

Knowledge has been defined by philosophers as true, reliable, infallible and justified beliefs. The application of the scientific method is the manner by which observations of beliefs and their possible explanations are decided to be true or false. This applies to conventional medicine, CAM and health psychology. The health care system in western countries is still dominated by conventional medicine, and even though developments in the direction of integrated medicine are on their way, it seems that substantial changes are necessary before this mainstream position will be overtaken.

The application of knowledge in conventional medicine is organized in clinical guidelines in which evidence is graded from the sum of RCTs as documented as the strongest in systematic reviews to the weaker non-experimental studies. In this chapter two problems have been observed: knowledge and beliefs from CAM are excluded from these guidelines, but so are those from health psychology. To reflect the knowledge about health and illness more accurately, research outcomes from these disciplines should be included in what could be named as *Integrated Clinical Guidelines*, especially since two of the four categories in the classification scheme of clinical guidelines are not based on experimental research, and the validity of the use of RCTs in CAM are questionable.

As far as health psychology is concerned, knowledge has been presented in psycho-cognitive models. These models have been criticized for their similarity of components and the absence of empirical studies to compare these, for not explaining health beliefs and behaviours in full, and for the exclusion of mind–body models. Regarding the latter, two additional components related to CAM, dispositional optimism and somatic awareness, have been discussed and proposed for a possible inclusion into existing models.

CAM is criticized for the use of case studies to find explanations for its effects. These are often referred to as anecdotal evidence. That storytelling can be a valid method to elicit phenomena important in the understanding of therapies based on the philosophical pillars of 'holism' and uniqueness of the person, has been documented in studies with nurses and as academic autobiographical accounts. Not only for CAM, but also for conventional medicine, the use of the narrative method has offered a broader picture of the application of knowledge in the primary care health care setting by showing that clinical guidelines are not applied as rigidly as the guidelines are suggesting. A theoretical framework regarding the use of stories in research has been presented by Frank (1991, 1995), who distinguished three forms of narratives: restitution, chaos and quest, the first reflecting conventional medicine and the latter two more in line with CAM philosophies.

Because of a lack in the understanding of the functioning of CAM, positive effects are mostly seen as the result of placebo. It has been shown that placebo is a complex concept with principally two different meanings:

placebo as healing and placebo as a fake treatment or drug. Interestingly, several publications used the quantum mechanics-based energy model as the explanation for these placebo beliefs. Appealing explanations for the placebo effect have been offered from the perspective of psychoneuroimmunology.

A link between the psychology of perception of the human senses smell, touch, vision and hearing and the complementary therapies of aroma-therapy, massage, colour therapy and music therapy was made. A gap appeared between the experimental psychological studies and the non-experimental CAM research. Whether the approaches in psychophysics as currently established will be a sufficient theoretical framework for the CAM therapies is debatable. Recent literature on embodiment and eastern phil-osophies of the perception of odour, colour, music and touch are different in the sense that perception does not only take place via the senses of ear, eye, nose and skin, but via the body as a whole, or via certain organs in the body with a similar energy resonance. The physics in this sense is different from psychophysics as theorized and tested in experimental psychology based on Newtonian physics.

In sum, health psychology could contribute to furthering the understand-ing of CAM in various ways: (i) by including body–mind concepts in the belief models. Examples of dispositional optimism and body awareness have been provided as a first step in this direction, but other components could be found and studied; (ii) by using the narrative method or storytelling with users of CAM in order to elicit the beliefs and explanations in a more holistic way than other methods. Frank's theoretical framework could be used to distinguish beliefs and explanations from people in line with the philosophy of conventional medicine, or with complementary medicine; (iii) studies could test the placebo response from different perspectives (healing versus fake drug). Explanations could be tested from the psy-choneuroimmunology frameworks or Laszlo's connectivity hypotheses; and (iv) a theoretical link could be made between the psychology of perception and embodiment regarding music therapy, colour therapy, aromatherapy and massage.

Research and research methods in complementary and alternative medicine

Recent attempts to discredit the emerging evidence base for CAMs may turn out to be a positive sign after all; as Gandhi is reputed to have said 'First they ignore you, then they laugh at you, then they fight you, then you win'.

(MacPherson et al. 2008, p. 360)

The need to research: evidence-based practice

The whole issue of researching CAM is a vast exercise in critical thinking, fraught with the politics of medicine and anti-medicine, which means that summarizing the key issues is bound to lead to simplifying one or other argument or offending this or that stakeholder. However, one thing is clear: we must justify why CAM needs be researched and validated. As Vickers (2000, p. 683) said of the evidence in existence, 'much . . . involves small numbers of patients and is of poor methodological quality'. We took for granted the fact that science had to justify itself, or more recently that medicine should demonstrate its worth in an evidence-based, ethically and sensibly costed fashion. Why do some practitioners of CAM reject this for themselves and is CAM actually different and thus not subject to the principles and regulations with which we bind science? In keeping with this view, the UK Government has made clear (Department of Health, 2001, pp. 5–6) that action against therapists 'who make blatantly unjustifiable claims for their therapy' can be taken, and that they recognize 'the need for strong evidence beyond the placebo effect' for CAMs falling into two categories, one encompassing osteopathy, chiropractic, acupuncture, herbal medicine, homeopathy, and the other, the 'diagnostic' CAMs, as we might call them, including Ayurvedic medicine, Chinese medicine, and other less common ones such as radionics and kinesiology. It is important to note, however, that despite this relatively hard line on potential regulation, the governing powers are not averse *per se*, it seems, to giving CAM the right to exist alongside orthodox practice, where it is proved to be appropriate, stating that this would be in the interests of all parties.

Some would say that we do not need to justify CAM because it is an art rather than a science. Using this argument, it is no different from literature. Reading novels or poetry or viewing works of visual art might have health benefits, indeed it is quite likely because they are forms of relaxation, but they need not be tested for their benefits and rejected if none are found. This is a perfectly legitimate argument but for three things. First, art does not claim health benefits as its principle purpose, and usually not at all. Second, CAM does. Third, people sometimes turn to CAM instead of orthodox medicine. This creates an added dimension, because we have a duty of care to prevent people rejecting something that might work in favour of something that might not (assuming the worst-case scenario). This also leads to a set of legal issues surrounding consumer protection and trades description. You cannot sue an author if you do not like their work but you can prosecute a plumber who fails to provide at-standard plumbing services or an electrician who renders your domestic wiring more dangerous rather than less. Quite simply, CAM is not a set of harmless pursuits. If a chosen therapy is as effective as its supporters would claim, then *de facto* it has the capacity to be dangerous. Only the most ineffectual and futile things are truly harmless. Either CAMs work, in which case regulation and assessment become an imperative, or they do not. If they do not, we need to know this. Either way, complementary and alternative systems and remedies cannot enjoy a special impunity.

It is therefore a matter of ethics, perhaps, that CAM providers be subjected to scientific method, or at least *some* method of enquiry, forced to produce evidence for what they do, and so on. If CAM stands up to our benchmarks of evidence, then there could be no objection to it from any party. If, however, it proves less effective than conventional or orthodox medicine, or even harmful, then there can be but one conclusion, and legislation would possibly follow to regulate the practice of CAM or even obliterate it altogether. It is, therefore, important that we choose our methods of determining evidence carefully, given that the livelihoods of CAM practitioners are at stake, many of whom are innocent, philanthropic, and might be easily able to demonstrate that what they do is helpful and complements other health care services.

We must be fair, however. By that, we mean that we must use objective and appropriate means to assess CAM in all its forms, and also not to give CAM a weaker criterion of success than we attach to science and medicine. For the latter, we use, where possible, Randomized Controlled Trials, and given that most CAM can be subjected to this approach, it seems entirely logical that this is the gold standard for all therapeutic claims. But as Broom et al. (2004) assert, the like of RCTs might not be the best way to approach CAM research. For most CAMs, it is not possible to apply the additional stringent criterion of double-blinding. While it is possible to 'hoodwink' clients with sham versions of therapies (such as in studies of sham acupuncture), the therapist often must know what group a patient falls into, control or intervention. In the case of certain homeopathic remedies, double-blinding would be possible, but impossible for Reiki, therapeutic touch, Rolfing, crystal healing, chromotherapy and many others.

One approach might be to use the four principles of health care in understanding CAMs. These are beneficence, non–maleficence, respect for autonomy, and justice (Beauchamp and Childress, 2001). Of course, we are only too aware of the great debates in terms of defining and applying each of these. However, if we assume a largely simplistic reading of these, then we can instantly accept that CAMs, on the surface, certainly respect autonomy (Sirois and Gick, 2002; Murray and Shepherd, 1993), since essentially they are all about the person, are largely holistic in nature, and rely upon a degree of choice, since they are never foisted upon the person in the way that orthodox health care might be (in the case of accident-related admissions and other cases where consent might be difficult to obtain). Justice, of course, is about fairness or equity, and we have no reason to believe that CAMs are inherently any less just than other forms of health care, except in the fact that they are largely privately purchased and therefore mainly accessible only to those who can afford them (Sirois and Gick, 2002). This model, however, permeates all orthodox health care systems, even those with a national welfare state underpinning them. Rationing, for example, restricts what is available, but those who can afford private health care can top up using their own funds to get what they feel they need. In nations with entirely private systems, personal income becomes the only factor in determining access to health care. Therefore, the lack of fairness in access to CAMs is hardly a reason to condemn them. The much bigger issue arises in relation to beneficence and non-maleficence, or 'do good' and 'do no harm', as they are often converted to. How exactly can we determine that a technique, substance, or other intervention does good, and, by the same token, does no harm? There are simply two ways. The first is to observe, and to reflect. This, of course, is a wholly anecdotal approach. The evidence of our senses is, as we know from countless basic perceptual illusions, simply not, on its own, to be trusted. The outward appearance of things often masks their true nature. 'If it looks like a duck, swims like a duck and quacks like a duck, then it probably is a duck'. The so called 'duck test', in inductive reasoning, is difficult to attribute to a particular person, although it has been in use for decades as a form of semi-serious lay assay. Crude though this may ostensibly appear, it actually paves the way for a systematic approach to categorizing and assessing that which we see before us. The important element of this is that it does not rely on a unitary measure, which actually makes it rather sophisticated. Looking like a duck is not, *per se*, enough, nor is quacking like a duck or swimming like a duck. In probabilistic terms, many things probably quack like a duck. But how many look *and* quack like a duck? Furthermore, how few look, swim *and* quack like a duck? Therefore, to return to our issues of the two crucial principles of health care, an acceptable therapy should do good *and* do no harm. In addition, *appearing* to do good and seeming to do no harm are simply not enough.

We have developed our views of what constitutes evidence partly around such simple, but logical, elements of reasoning such as the duck test. We need more than appearances. In itself, there is nothing about this view that is particularly restrictive, oppressive, or unfair to CAM. All that is being asked is that data exist over and above clients' and therapists' honest but potentially illusory claims that CAMs work. No one wishes to dismiss the patient who says, 'it worked for me', but to accept this alone is tantamount to assuming that tobacco is safe because one can find people who say, 'smoking never did me any harm'. Even if the claim is true, at the level of the individual, we have a responsibility not to allow this to be generalized to a population. This is precisely why we use the scientific method and conduct studies with representative samples in them.

The scientist-practitioner model

The above, rather philosophical discussions of what constitutes evidence is, of course, underpinned by the tradition we have developed over millennia, at least in the West but rather more widely of late, that we call scientific method, empiricism and so on. Further to this, we have equally developed, in orthodox medicine, the concept of the scientist-practitioner. Fundamentally, this is tied up again with the four principles of health care, since this is the true junction of ethics and practice. The scientist-practitioner, in essence, does only what evidence suggests should be done, and where there is no evidence, they seek to gather it, or rather to test hypotheses in a structured manner. In the case of the vast majority of CAMs, there is no reason why this model should be at odds with successful and effective practice. Indeed, even those who politically reject science could indeed use a phrase such as 'artful-practitioner model'. What would an artful practitioner be? We cannot escape the fact that an artful practitioner would be one who gets the job done. They are an 'artisan', perhaps. They are skilled in the therapeutic arts. This sounds very familiar to us, but crucially the scientist-practitioner and the skilled or artful therapist achieve the required outcome. This brings us full circle back to a definition of the required outcome. This must be a change in health state, either physical or mental, in any given patient. Changes in health state themselves come in two forms, the objective and the subjective. It would be wrong to dismiss the subjective, because sometimes it is all we have. In the case of headaches, for example, objective measures are largely pointless. If a patient experiences a headache, then they have a headache. When it subsides, it subsides for real, since reality in the case of headache is all in the experience of it. This is not the case for fractures, tumours, haemorrhages, endocrine disorders, and the like. These are objectively measurable. We can see them. It does not matter what the patient believes or experiences, in a sense. Regardless of a patient's sensation or interpretation of a physical injury or disease, the disease objectively exists. Hypertension is mostly symptomless but is nevertheless important and should not be overlooked. Therefore, the scientist-practitioner, whether they be a surgeon or a homeotherapist, has a responsibility to view objective and subjective conditions and disorders differently, and apply different but appropriate standards of evidence to the two. In the UK the Government has supported a House of Lords recommendation that all CAM therapists should be trained in evidence-based medicine as a matter of course (Department of Health, 2001).

Another crucial aspect to the scientist-practitioner is that they must not select evidence but accept and incorporate all of it into their theories. If they note that 5 out of 10 patients improve as a result of their intervention, they must note also that 5 out of 10 do not. They should also note the extent of the improvement in the first five, and reflect upon the nature of the status of the others (for example, a worsening in their condition). Science should not be blind to failure. In fact, to a true scientist, there is no failure, simply the amassing of evidence in all its forms. Romantic though this may sound, it is central to the maintenance of the scientist-practitioner model, and the pursuit of 'truth'. Truth is yet another concept lying at the heart of science, as is progress. The purpose of orthodox medicine is to progress, and progress is defined partly as the discovery and utilization of truths. Many of the proponents of the more mystical forms of CAM argue that there are many truths, which indeed resonates positively with many people, including physicians, scientists and artists alike. However, it becomes difficult to substantiate this view when it is used as a licence to do absolutely anything in the name of health care, spiritual or otherwise. The average patient is not particularly interested in the philosophical leanings of their therapist, or indeed how many truths there are. They often have a practical problem which they wish to see solved. Again and again, we return to this: when a person has psoriasis and they seek help for it, from whatever source, they wish to find a cure, or an alleviation. They want to see a reduction in affected sites, and/or a reduction in the physical symptoms, and if that cannot be achieved they may wish to receive support in coping with their condition. The existence or not of a number of interpretations of reality, and discussions on the meaning of evidence, do not play on their minds, mostly.

The problem with the scientist-practitioner approach is that there is always a risk that any practitioner could discover, over the course of their work, that what they do is ineffective and inefficient. Arguably, over time, the evidence would speak for itself. The massive investment, in training, time, and all sorts of resources, becomes difficult to justify when faced with the overwhelming conclusion that it was all wasted. This natural, human reaction to such a situation, however, or the fear of it occurring, could prejudice and undermine the very nature of the collection of that evidence, whether consciously or not. We know from Festinger (1957) that in order to reduce cognitive dissonance we reformulate evidence, we become selective, we focus on what supports our hypotheses, and we fail to see the counterarguments. Therefore, relying on individual therapists to be the arbiter of their own success and skill is doomed, however honest, genuine and well intentioned they are. As Carter (2003, p. 138) suggests, 'objective detachment is a considerable departure for most CAM practitioners. Any study design that required a practitioner to work against their philosophical framework would be inappropriate'. Therefore, a true scientist-practitioner is open to assessment by outside bodies, welcomes objective (or at least external) comment, and works with a community rather than alone. This is precisely why, in the orthodox fields, we, as a society, have developed licensing bodies, have opened ourselves up to criticism of both a destructive and constructive nature, have developed legislation to protect citizens from the unqualified, the negligent and the ill-motivated, and so on. Indeed, many CAM practitioners have made significant manoeuvres in the same vein, for the same reasons, and it is important not to homogenize CAM (Carter, 2003). But, it still remains the case that a great many practitioners, and a great many practices, remain outside of these protective mechanisms. The reasons for this are multi-fold, but we live in a cynical age when those who choose to work outside of a system can expect some degree of suspicion, which ultimately does nothing to serve the interests of patients seeking genuine, trustworthy sources of alternative support and treatment. The debates, often malicious, that are generated between orthodox and complementary practitioners are to some degree irrelevant. The important issue is that the public gets what the public wants, and can trust what they get. To many, the scientist-practitioner is one of the ways of achieving that.

Testing therapies and therapists

It is vital that we do not confuse the nature and success of a complementary therapy with the nature and success of its therapists. Van Haselen and Luedtke (2008) make the point that within homeopathy in particular (although this probably is fair to generalize to other CAM practitioners), there are a number of 'gurus' and that rather than evidence-based practice there is 'eminence-based practice'. Much of that eminence may well be deserved but then there is good reason for that to be disseminated so that others can learn from it, and the modern way for that to occur is, arguably, through the publication of peer-reviewed research rather than small-scale training seminars and workshops that unavoidably serve only the few.

Logically, it is possible to have four possible outcomes from the combination of approach and practitioner. This is given in Table 4.1.

Table 4.1 A combination of approach and practitioner

	Skilled Therapist	Unskilled Therapist
Effective Therapy	Positive outcomes	Mixed outcomes
Ineffective Therapy	Mixed outcomes	Poor outcomes

If we are to undertake a proper, fair assessment of CAM, we should do so by investigating the outcomes of all possible theoretical combinations. When we begin, we have a *tabula rasa* situation, which means that we cannot know if a therapy is medically useful, but equally we do not know which therapists are the good and bad ones. This immediately means that we should take a stance which is open to the particular profession selecting its most skilled practitioners to take part in the research, or at least those which have achieved some kind of practising standard, however the profession judges this. It would be unfair and of limited use to select weaker practitioners. Therefore, once we have selected the skilled therapists, we automatically can ignore one half of our legitimate possible combinations, leaving us only with the possibility that the therapy works or does not. After all, one would not wish to take seriously a therapy left in the hands of unskilled, untrained, unvetted, and unqualified practitioners. However, it is not this simple. This only applies where a particular therapy requires a practitioner, as in the case of acupuncture, or indeed almost all Chinese medicine, or chiropractic or Reiki. An entirely different set of standards can be brought to bear in the case of self-care CAMs.

Over-the-counter homeopathic remedies, for example, work on the basis of self-diagnosis and self-treatment, with the practitioner's voice minimized or even completely absent. What is clear, nevertheless, is that any given therapy may or may not be effective. Some proportion of that therapy's effectiveness may be attributable to placebo and related effects, just as the effectiveness of all orthodox medicines is tainted with some element of placebo. Of course, one might expect that the additional placebo benefit of a therapy or CAM would be greatest when a practitioner was required, rather than absent. But, to return to the previous issue of the unskilled practitioner, we should not dismiss researching this out of hand. Imagine, if you will, a situation where an effective therapy did not rely on a practitioner's skill, that is, where the therapist could be poorly trained and lacking knowledge, but with little effect on the outcome. This is possible, one might argue, especially in the case of particularly potent CAMs, should we discover these in the course of time. This, would, naturally, cast significant doubt over the need for a regulated profession in that particular therapeutic approach. In many ways, this is no different from the levels of professional skill that we accept within medicine. We do not think it particularly strange that there is a skill continuum within orthodox healthcare, from highly paid specialist consultants to general nurses, health care assistants, and so on. CAM might develop in a similar fashion, needing only qualified specialists to research and develop particular techniques and interventions, which are then easily passed on and put into practice by the layperson. In a report issued by the UK Government (Department of Health, 2001), the veiled admission, perhaps, is actually that the CAM practitioners could even be seen as the higher authority on CAM, and conventional physicians those who bridge the gap between patient and therapeutic approach. The report contains the following: 'The Government supports the training of conventional healthcare practitioners to standards agreed with the appropriate CAM regulatory body. In some cases there may need to be a gradation of standards which reflect both training and practice at different levels' (2001, p. 8).

From the perspective of good research, it becomes clear that we need to evaluate CAM in a fashion that is not tainted by the success or otherwise of its therapists. Once more, we can easily borrow from the better methodological stances taken by those assessing orthodox medicine. Rather than collect data from a single practitioner, of whatever persuasion, one should aim to minimize individual differences by deriving evidence from a range of practitioners, across practices. Discovering that the vast majority of patients benefit when treated by Therapist X using Technique Y does not tell us whether the success is due to X or Y. If we bring in therapists P, Q and R then potential confounding variables are increasingly less influential.

Therefore, it is logically necessary that we attempt to generalize across therapists when testing a particular CAM approach, whatever it be. However, it would be foolish to ignore the value of researching the successful therapist or practitioner in order to fully understand the nature of their effectiveness and to disseminate good practice more widely. This is where we might need not only to determine that an individual is particularly good at what they do, perhaps through examining patient records and so on to identify trends, but also empirically assessing their work, but then following this up, perhaps, with a more in-depth and enriched, phenomenological investigation, which is where qualitative research comes into its own.

Qualitative versus quantitative research methods

What is the best way to research CAM? In psychology, and more generally across the social and health sciences, we have fostered a dual approach to understanding reality through the twin (albeit often kept separate) children of qualitative and quantitative methods. Quantitative methods have dominated our science for centuries, and still do, and so are often seen as the 'orthodox' methods in contrast with the more nebulous, less rule-bound qualitative ones. If this seems familiar, it is because there is possibly no coincidence that the critical, social constructionist view of research which has been associated with the growth of qualitative methods has been somewhat contemporaneous with the western flourish of interest in CAMs. In fact, one might even postulate that the very people who push for one root for the other. The critical, constructionist view is associated with challenges to medicine, education, and other 'institutions', and is interested in our conceptions and creations of 'otherness' (Levinas, 1979; a concept dating back as early as the works of Hegel). In the last few decades, CAM has come to be one of the 'others', an example of what Camus hints at in the title of his existential work of fiction, *L'Etranger* (1942), which can easily translate as 'outsider', 'stranger', 'foreigner', 'other', 'alien' or even 'irrelevant'. Qualitative methods are 'new' methods, and although they can be used in a politically and socially neutral way, their birth and childhood have not been free from those influences. One might, therefore, make the assumption that qualitative methods could be the most apt methods of inquiry to apply to CAM. If we truly wish to understand what people think and feel about their bodies, and the treatments applied to their bodies, perhaps methods specifically targeted at determining what people think and feel would be ideal. However, given that it is logical to seek the best tools for the job in hand, one might consider the notion expressed earlier that the best way to divide CAM research for the purposes of assessment of it is to consider the outcomes or effects, from the objective or subjective frame.

To repeat our example, headaches are largely a subjective phenomenon, and once serious physical concerns have been ruled out, any intervention that eases the suffering is to be welcomed. We have a choice, then, to measure headaches using some form of crude numerical scale or to explore the experiences of a headache sufferer, perhaps phenomenologically, and to understand the nature of their interaction with a CAM practitioner or their faith in and knowledge of a self-care treatment, purchased in a supermarket or pharmacy. This is clearly best suited to a qualitative approach. Indeed, the very nature of qualitative methods is bound up with views that, in many ways, all things are subjective, and therefore an honestly subjective method is manifestly appropriate for researching an obviously subjective outcome. When the nature of a condition is much more ostensibly physical, then the objective measurements of lesion, trauma, bleeding, and so forth perhaps take on a greater importance. This is not to say that patients' experiences are trivial, or even less important, but that there *is* a way of measuring disease progress without recourse to patient experience. The way forward appears to be clear. When CAM claims are concerned with the alleviation of a subjective experience only, then qualitative methods will probably serve as the ideal research tool. When the CAM is directed at physiological, chemical, or other such objectively measurable disorders, quantitative measures perhaps ought to take precedence. In the words of Broom (2005, p. 73), 'given the fact that very little research has been done on CAM, qualitative methodologies are potentially very useful for exploring the complexities and subjective elements of delivery of care and patient experiences of treatment processes'. However, the problem with qualitative methodologies is that they are still part of the toolbox of the unconventional, as far as many orthodox practitioners are concerned. If it is the case that CAM must get a foot in the door of acceptance, perhaps it is necessary for CAM researchers to borrow the same tools as those used by the conventional health care scientists. Oberbaum et al. (2005, p. 305) put this succinctly: 'Qualitative trials, intriguing as they may be, will not make a mark on the conventional research establishment'. Is the world of science not ready for either CAM or qualitative research? If that is the case, would CAM have to wait for a legitimization of its best research method before progressing, or should it adopt the Randomized Controlled Trial and systematic review, and push on with fighting fire with fire? These are questions that at present we cannot answer.

Systematic reviews

As the number of studies of particular CAMs begins to swell, we start to need some kind of meta-analytic technique to synthesize the growing body of information. Once more, the history of the development of research methods as applied to orthodox medicine has begun to be echoed by the history of the development of complementary and alternative medicine research. A natural by-product of the push for evidence-based medicine is the systematic review, since the evidence collected starts to be unmanageable, and there is quite a task in simplifying and summarizing that for a wider audience to direct them towards the interventions that work and away from those which don't. What systematic reviews can often unequivocally show is that some treatments work time and time again, and others consistently seem to resist attempts at verification and validation.

The number of systematic reviews in the CAM literature is still woefully low, mainly because the number of controlled studies on a single CAM which can be easily included in such a review is also often tiny. Early results from systematic reviews are not especially positive either such as the review of acupuncture analgesia by Madsen et al. (2009), which found only a tiny analgesic effect of acupuncture which could not be clearly attributed to anything other than bias, averaging over 13 trials with 3025 patients. Systematic reviews are, by their very nature, systematic in that they are attempts to filter out studies conducted in problematic ways with poor methods, allowing the best studies to rise and the results of those to be aligned with each other to detect trends. They are also, unfortunately, fraught with problems because of the inherent need to make quality judgements and because of case mix (no two studies are alike, even when attempts are made to replicate previous work). Of course, those quality judgements are not necessarily wholly subjective, as some might argue. Systematic reviews are open to peer review, and the judgement criteria are published along with the findings. It is explicit why certain studies meet the inclusion criteria and others do not. Usually it is on the basis of the methods used.

There is a high degree of inter-rater concordance, because the criteria are so well expressed, leaving little room for debate. However, there are CAM-related systematic reviews making their way into the literature in a way that was almost unheard of 20 years ago, so it is clear, perhaps, that the culture of researching CAM is changing.

The motives of CAM researchers often remain unclear, although in a truly value-free, isolated research system one might argue that these matter little. It is the case from a reading of the literature that many of the CAM studies are conducted and written by either sceptics or adherents, and that likewise the systematic reviews usually come from camps of debunkers or supporters. While this might, on the surface, seem like a poor state of affairs, there is something democratic about this. The protagonists, the antagonists and the ambivalent have a forum for researching and expressing their interpretations of their results, and eventually, the truth will out, as it were. Typically, the argument is made that the CAM supporters are underfunded and relatively powerless to take on the might of the rich traditionalists in orthodox medicine, but this is a flawed argument for two reasons. First, it assumes that all orthodox practitioners, researchers and writers are fundamentally opposed to CAM and have a sworn duty to undermine it. This is simply untrue, as the proportion of physician referrals to CAM practitioners in the western world demonstrates. Second, in the David and Goliath situation David sometimes wins. The truth will out. When Copernicus put forward a heliocentric cosmology, something hinted at much earlier by scholars from the Indian sub-continent and the Arab world, he was derided by the powerful forces at the time, such as the Catholic church, and for following this doctrine Galileo was accused of heresy and was effectively a pariah. These men were essentially early champions of the scientific method, of course. Now, that very method, and those academic ancestors of these pioneering scientists are the very people now and then accused of condemning CAM as unsubstantiated quackery and charlatanism. If CAMs really work, and have a role in health care, then eventually those truths will arise and the veracity of the claims will speak for itself. Of course, not all 'truths' have made their way into orthodoxy, and we shall never know about those which were successfully suppressed perhaps thousands of years ago. CAMs however, despite opposition, will not go away, and so they have a status way beyond the proclamations of an individual eccentric who is easily silenced and lost in history.

It is likely in the future, then, that systematic reviews of CAM literature will be a 'socially accepted' way for CAM to demonstrate its usefulness where indeed it is possible to do that.

Single-case studies

Single-case studies are often misunderstood, and yet provide an important method, potentially, for the study of CAM. For many, single-case studies become fused in their understanding with the notion of case studies, which are entirely qualitative, largely subjective, and represent a writing-up of the history and details of treatment of an individual patient. Single-case studies, on the contrary, are experimental tests of an intervention which can be highly complicated, but nevertheless are rule-governed and perfect examples of the use of the scientific method applied to individuals in a medico-therapeutic context.

The single-case design was championed by Sidman (1960) who argued that if something was real, and was clinically significant, it was likely to be demonstrable in small samples, often as small as one. His argument at the other end of the scale, as it were, was that if (as is often the case) some effects can only be demonstrated through the application of statistical testing in large-scale population studies, one might wonder if they are worth remarking on at all. Tiny effects can be statistically significant, primarily because they are consistent across large samples, but clinically meaningless. An improvement in a health outcome of a tenth of a percentage point on a scale could be barely detectable and measurable, but as long it *is* measurable and keeps on occurring then that effect could prove statistically significant. In real terms, that improvement has a negligible impact on the health status of any individual. Imagine a treatment which produces a drop of a half millimetre of mercury in systolic blood pressure. The change is real, and measurable. Whether half a millimetre makes any difference to the mortality or quality of life of anyone is called into question, however. But, as Sidman claimed, truly important, *clinically* significant effects are demonstrable with much smaller samples. In psychology, we are highly familiar with the primacy and recency effects in memory. We tend to remember the first and the last few items in a list we have just heard or read. We can demonstrate this effect in one just one individual; there is no need to repeatedly demonstrate it across thousands. The effect is robust, replicable, and for those very reasons, we assume it is as 'real' as it gets.

Single-case designs allow us to test out hypotheses about the effectiveness of particular interventions on individuals. They are particularly useful because often we need to tailor our interventions to meet the needs of one person, and so generalizing to the wider population is only a secondary, tertiary or even quaternary issue. Currently, clinical psychologists are probably the main group who utilize single-case designs within health care settings. It is also possible to fuse a collection of single-case designs to create a single-case-series design, showing patterns of effects of an intervention in multiple patients.

The most basic single-case design is that referred to as A-B. In this case, there is a period of baseline measurement of some problem variable (a health outcome), followed by measurement of that variable during an intervention (the B phase). Naturally, this is not perfect, since spontaneous recovery could mean that the intervention was not responsible for any change in variable state. Therefore, the most fundamental single-case design in common use is the A-B-A, which corresponds to baseline, intervention, then a period when the intervention is withdrawn. If there is an improvement in health status during the intervention phase, then it disappears when the intervention is withdrawn (the second A phase), we can assume that the intervention is likely to have caused the effect. However, this raises two further problems. Some interventions are one-offs, and once they are applied the patient changes forever. They cannot unlearn the intervention, and so they remain changed, even when the intervention is taken away again. Counselling and psychotherapy are examples of more conventional interventions which can show this pattern of effects. Moreover, there are ethical issues in ending a trial with a phase where the intervention is removed, and so for those reasons we often would aim to use an A-B-A-B design instead.

Single-case designs can be much more complicated. It is possible to introduce multiple interventions, and it is also possible to chart the progress of an intervention when it is applied in staged doses, for example where a drug or homeopathic treatment is commenced with a mild application and then is stepped up to an effective level.

However one uses single-case designs, it is clear that they provide the CAM practitioner with a simple way to log the progress of patients in a clear fashion that does not require sophisticated statistical knowledge, and which can be converted to a graphical representation suitable for showing to patients themselves. It is often little more complicated than 'before-and-after' photographs. It is, nevertheless, a scientific approach to evidence-based practice, and carried out properly the single-case design is well suited to purpose. It is much superior in many ways to the rather more anecdotal case reports that are subject to considerably more bias and interpretation, even when written without prejudice or agenda.

The issue of triangulation

When we wish to truly investigate something, inside and out, our best bet is a multi-method approach (Mason et al., 2002; Broom et al., 2004). In fact, CAMs lend themselves very neatly to such tests of their usefulness. The very nature of CAMs is that they tend to be filling a niche somewhere between the psychological and the physical worlds for patients who largely share CAM philosophies (Astin, 1998). Being holistic, as so many CAMs are, they aim to 'put right' not only the physical conditions pertaining to an individual but to also make them feel better, or in some cases, help to adapt them to their situation, help them to feel more at peace with the world and themselves, and so on. While it is relatively easy to measure a change in physical state, psychological development can be much more difficult to pin down using somewhat crude questionnaire measures and scales. For some patients, some of the time, a particular CAM approach might be more useful in dealing with the physical rather than the psychological, but sometimes the reverse is true, and sometimes CAMs might be useful in both ways or neither. In order to make sure that we miss nothing, the recommended approach is, arguably, one where we aim to triangulate sources of information in a coherent way to tell a consistent story. Without taking all factors and angles into account, we may fail to notice a great benefit that a treatment has but, more alarmingly, we could be blind to a danger. If a CAM approach had significant psychological benefits it would seem worth pursuing, but if we were to measure physical progress of a disease or illness and find that there had been a *worsening* during CAM treatment, then this is not something we should ignore. Thus, we should take all steps to research CAM (as indeed is expected in orthodox medicine), so that we are fully aware of the facts before concluding what should and should not be done in any given situation.

Resistance to research: can and will CAM be investigated?

It might be the case that a reframing of the questions concerning researching CAMs is needed. One could argue that the way that CAM research has been used as a weapon against its adherents created animosity that need never have arisen. What do we mean by this? There has been something of an accusatory tone to the notion of researching CAM. The assumption has been, in some circles, that CAMs are inherently nothing more than snake oil, and research is the way in which the charlatans and purveyors can be 'found out' and flattened, paving the way for yet more orthodox medicine. Vickers (2000, p. 685) explains that considerable anger has coloured the debates between the two 'sides' and that 'practitioners of conventional medicine have used legal sanctions to harass and even jail practitioners of complementary medicine'. A commentary by Haynes in the *British Medical Journal* is entitled, 'A Warning to Complementary Medicine Practitioners: Get Empirical or Else' (1999). Understandably, this has caused some recalcitrance in CAM environments, and perhaps some backing-away from research, just as people would back away from a knife pointed at them. In fact, in the case of some CAM practitioners, there is possibly a very real fear because they know that their particular brand of intervention is in reality devoid of substance.

Not all CAM practitioners are genuine; to some it is a way to make money, nothing more. But for those who truly believe in what they do, and feel that they see the evidence daily in their work, a new approach is needed. Research is about fine-tuning, about progress, and certainly not about throwing the baby out with the bathwater. Traditionally, CAM practitioners are not well versed in research, and so additional resistance can be found simply out of ignorance, or out of a concern that becoming a scientist-practitioner will necessitate training and learning which the working practitioner feels is a drain on resources. As we have seen, however, some basic research techniques, such as single-case designs, are not beyond the ken of the average practitioner. Research is good for CAM, research will help CAM become part of the modern panoply of health care techniques, and research will refine CAM, sorting the wheat from the chaff and demystifying some rather ancient and ill-understood phenomena. If CAM is mature and healthy, it will survive being researched. If it is weak and failing, research may be its saviour.

It is worth quoting Mason et al. (2002, p. 832) at length here:

> Complementary medicine should be evaluated as rigorously as conventional medicine to protect the public from charlatans and unsafe practices, but many practitioners of complementary medicine are reticent about evaluation of their practice. Sceptics maintain that this is because of fear that investigations will find treatments ineffective and threaten livelihoods. In defence, many practitioners argue that research methods dissect their practice in a reductionist manner and fail to take into account complementary medicine's holistic nature leading to invalid evaluation.

There is something of a rosy glow on the horizon for CAM, provided that it can take up the challenge of becoming a mature and wholesome complement to orthodox medicine, although doing so will require something of a sea change in attitudes to research, since the traditional power base associated with research is extremely powerful and shows no sign of weakening and withering. Winnick (2005) has characterized the historical evolution of attitudes to CAM as progressing through three distinct phases. The first was *condemnation*, which roughly corresponded in her study with a decade spanning the 1960s and 1970s. (One could, incidentally, argue that for many this phase is not over.) In this phase the medical profession mainly attacked, insulted and ridiculed CAM. CAMs, of course, persevered, and the second stage, *reassessment*, occurred. At this time, from the mid-1970s to the early 1990s, medicine was beginning to question itself, and this led to something of a softening of attitudes towards CAM, since the orthodox practitioners reflected on their own shortcomings in a way that they had never before. Holism was a growing philosophy in orthodox medicine, and the notion that the patient was important and had a role to play was gaining credence. Finally, the current era is labelled *integration*, by Winnick, and she argues that CAM is becoming a force to be reckoned with, and in some circles worked with. The future, according to Winnick, will be *cooptation*. This represents a challenge for CAM much greater than the ridicule and contempt of old. What could happen is that those CAMs which have been shown to work will be eaten up by the medical profession, and become part of standard, orthodox practice, subjected to the same biomedical model theorizing as established treatments, and CAM practitioners will, at worst, be outlawed and forced to take up medical training or lose their livelihoods. The medical profession could, potentially, become the new CAM practitioners. There is precedent for this. Sociologist Oakley (1984) describes the situation that occurred concerning the profession of midwifery when childbirth became increasingly medicalized, as the medical profession absorbed what was a normal, human act into their repertoire. If we have learned from history, this extreme scenario can be avoided. At best, on the other hand, what will happen is that there will be a new-found respect for CAM among physicians, and complementary and orthodox approaches will co-exist harmoniously, with referrals back and forth, and room for both as part of a well-functioning, mature health care system.

Summary and conclusion

We have seen how CAM cannot be seen as immune to research, for two reasons. Research helps us to progress, and research puts what we do into context and allows us to reject the bad and accept the good. Some systematic reviews of CAM techniques and interventions have begun to arise, and there is a growth in qualitative research, which is possibly best directed at those CAM interventions aimed at subjective experiences such as pain. Single-case designs can be seen to be a suitable experimental design which span the gap between hard-line empirical research and anecdotal evidence, upon which too many CAM practitioners still, it seems, rely.

Critics of CAM point to the lack of research to substantiate it. The reaction to this, it seems, is to reject research, rather than stand up to the critics by meeting them on their own terms. Lyles (2005) argues that this is a 'self-perpetuating cycle', whereby those critics reject CAM because of its paucity of peer-reviewed research, and use the 'otherness' and unconventionality of CAM to deny CAM researchers access to research funds which would solve the problem, preferring instead to continue funding orthodox work.

It is true that many studies into CAM are likely to yield negative results, but this is no different from research into orthodox treatments. There is nothing to fear in this respect. As van Haselen and Luedtke (2008, p. 60) write, 'the advancement of knowledge can only be achieved through trial and error, by verifying or falsifying postulations. From this perspective, "negative" results are essential and steps in the advancement of knowledge, and negative results can therefore be "positive" in the broader sense that a lot can be learnt'.

One of the most important characteristics of research is not, as some might fear, that it stifles practice and can be at best an irrelevance and at worst a hindrance to the development of a complementary approach. Indeed, it is a key technique or supporting aspects of CAM which have value, and for filtering out the good and the less so. Furthermore, research is the way in which we refine what we do, how we learn to do things better, how we decide what to leave behind and what to take with us on our journey. It is not the enemy of any approach, CAM or otherwise. It can be a neutral tool, but so easily becomes imbued with the politics of those that use it.

CHAPTER
5

Stress, appraisal, coping, moderators and stress management

To live is to suffer. To survive is to cope. To succeed is to adapt effectively and creatively.

(Wong & Wong, 2006, p. 267)

Introduction

Stress-related illnesses have increasingly been shown to be a burden on society and as such have become the target of several complementary and mindfulness interventions (Garland, 2007). Health psychology has stress management as one of its concerns, and interestingly, apart from the cognitive techniques, several of these are derived from eastern practices, such as relaxation and visualization. Other 'eastern' approaches imported to alleviate stressful lifestyles are complementary practices such as yoga, tai chi and meditation. But what are the consequences of this importation? Are the understandings of stress and stress management practices similar in western and 'eastern' belief systems? Or, if they are different, what does that mean for health psychologists working from a western stress model?

Stress is an over-used word, with so many different meanings that scholars such as Evans et al. (2000) indicate that it is almost impossible to define. Not only is it frequently used in newspapers, magazines and other more popular literature, it also pops up, academically, as a concept in books, academic publications, conference presentations, health websites and illness leaflets, with the assumption that there is a common understanding of its meaning.

That people's experience of stress can be different in similar contexts, and is not necessarily related to stressful life events, has already been demonstrated by the many criticisms of the first and most used psychological measurements of stress developed in America by Holmes and Rahé (1967). Their SRRS (Social Readjustment Rating Scale) life events scale, which ranked the most stressful events to the least, has been under scrutiny from the moment it was made accessible (e.g. Scully et al., 2000). Apart from its culturally biased, white, middle-class application, other criticisms were directed to the assumed life events itself. For example, death of spouse or moving house as one of the most strenuous life events, could be a relief of stress if one cared for a terminally ill spouse, or when the move was from a damp house, in a grey, colourless, noisy area to a house in beautiful colourful surroundings.

So what is stress, which factors influence it, how does it impact on health and illness, and how can it be managed? For decennia, psychologists have been engaged in elucidating this concept and the many different ways in which it affected people's lives. For health psychology, the knowledge of the influence of stress on health and illness has advanced through the progression of stress-related immunology studies, such as proposed in psychoneuroimmunology (PNI). In what way this knowledge can progress further through insights from 'eastern' philosophies will be the focus of this chapter.

Stress, appraisal, coping and health and illness: psychological theories versus non-western perspectives

Generally, stress reflects an imbalance of a desirable homeostatic state, which diverts from a situation in which human beings find themselves physiologically and psychologically in harmony, or 'at ease with oneself', 'at peace', 'relaxed', 'happy' or 'comfortable' (e.g. Lyke, 2009). The stress experience has been described as positive ('eu-stress'; Selye, 1950; Garhammer, 2002) when people are on a 'high' because of exciting good news, or negative (e.g. Bale, 2006) when life is not what one expect it to be, but seems to go hand in hand with a continuous effort to maintain a sort of balance (e.g. van Vegchel et al., 2005). Whether this urge for 'harmony' is a more a physiologically or psychologically driven phenomenon is an interesting question to ask. In lay terms, 'being stressed' means 'being uncomfortable', indicating an undesirable state, which one would like to change. This might be a survival mechanism knowing that prolonged stress can have detrimental effects on people's health, as demonstrated by psychoneuroimmunologists such as Evans et al. (2000).

This basic understanding of stress is similar in psychological theories applied to conventional health systems as in the philosophical underpinnings of non-conventional health approaches. However, differences have been recognized, especially as to how the meaning of stress is embedded within its culture. For example, Palsane and Lam (1996) highlighted a distinction between a western negative connotation of stress detrimental to one's health and an eastern positive perspective, in which stress is part of life's necessary challenges. Along these lines, the papers of Wong and Wong (2006) and

Laungani (1995a) discussed how different religious and humanistic beliefs impact on cultural values, dominating the ways in which people view and deal with the stressors. Cultural variations, according to Laungani (1995a, 1995b) can be identified along the four dimensions of individualism-collectivism, cognitive versus emotionalism, free will versus determinism and materialism versus spiritualism. This categorization resembles Hofstede's (2001) dimensions of cultural difference, which he and others identified and validated in 64 countries, opposing developed and western from less developed and eastern countries, in which he placed the USA as the most individualistic (concern for oneself) and China and India as more collective (concern for community) societies. However, these dimensions have been criticized for their over-generalizations (Much, 1995; McSweeney, 2002; Chiavacci, 2005; Cheug and Kwan, 2009), and should be taken as simplifications of cultural differences when referred to in this chapter. When talking about western cultures, the emphasis is on the degree to which people in these cultures adhere to the understanding of stress and coping as an individual experience which can be dealt with either cognitively or emotionally and which is based on free will and materialism. When using the term 'eastern' in this chapter, reference is mainly made to people adhering to Buddhist, Confucian, Hindu and Taoist belief systems, whether residing in their own or in a host culture.

Taking into account that prominent 'thinkers' (e.g. James and Skinner), who have led western psychology over the last century, are from the USA, it might be no surprise that western theories and models on stress, coping and illness are based on a more individualistic philosophy.

Background: stress and coping in the western world

Stress research began with Cannon (1914, 1939) who described stress as a disturbance of the homeostatic state of humans and animals caused by an internal (e.g. hunger, thirst) or external (e.g. appearance of a bear) disruptive stimulus. He believed all reactions to this stress to be similar in the sense that one either fights for a solution to deal with the stressor, or one flees away from it ('fight-flight response'). This original model has been at the basis of psychological theories and research models which through testing and intellectualizing have been elaborated since. Selye (1936, 1950), who mainly worked with animals such as mice, developed the General Adaptation Syndrome (GAS), to demonstrate the three-staged stress response which can be observed when efforts to deal with the stressor effectively fail: (1) alarm, (2) resistance and (3) exhaustion; the latter eventually resulting in death when stress continues. Both Cannon and Selye based their models of stress on animal studies.

The first psychologists to apply these to human beings were Lazarus and Folkman (1984), with their cognitive theory on stress and coping often referred to as 'The Transactional Model of Stress and Coping'. In this model, they distinguished the cognitive and behavioural capabilities of humans over and above the reflexive ways of animals dealing with taxing circumstances, by separating the balancing efforts into new concepts such as primary and secondary appraisal. Primary appraisal concerns what is at stake by 'scanning' how harmful, challenging or a threat a stressor is to a person. Secondary appraisal has been formulated as the process of scanning the possible solutions as to how best to deal with this stressor. These have come to be known as coping strategies, reflecting the continuously changing rather than static efforts of people 'to manage the demands which are exceeding their resources' (Lazarus and Folkman, 1984). In their follow-up work (e.g. Folkman et al., 1986), they categorized these into problem and emotional-focused forms of coping and indicated that these are the result of both appraisals which differ per person and per situation. However, the way people dealt with their stressors was assessed with their stress questionnaire with pre-set items phrased in their words.

Even though follow-up research did validate these coping strategies, more and different categories have been found since, depending on the context of the studies, such as coping with a cancer diagnosis (e.g. Tarakeshwar et al., 2006), coping with endoscopy (Eberhardt et al., 2006) coping with MS (e.g. Pakenham, 2006); or coping with AIDS risk behaviour (Hobfoll and Schroder, 2001). British health psychologists interested in stress, such as Ferguson and Cox (1997) proposed different categorizations. For example, they distinguished the coping process in coping style and coping function, and saw coping style as the individual's ways of dealing with a particular stressor, assessed by asking people to write these down in their own words. Coping function was based on these individual reflections and assessed by a Likert scale-answer format to establish the degree to which the style (for example, crying, shouting, talking to one's husband) served one of the following functions: approach, avoidance, reappraisal or emotional relief. Not only is this a less rigid form of enquiring about coping, it also showed that one can deal with a certain stressor through employing a variety of coping styles concurrently, which also serve a mixture of coping functions, some of which can be approaching and emotional relief at the same time (Flynn et al., 2004). Wong and Wong (2006) referred to this as 'eastern' dualistic rather than western dichotomic thinking, the latter in the sense of processes being 'either' 'or', but not simultaneously present. In 'eastern' dichotomous thinking paradoxical phenomena can occur simultaneously. For example, as Wong and Wong (2006) refer to, one can be both optimistic and pessimistic at the same time (Wong and McDonald, 2002) or embrace both internal and external control (Wong and Sproule, 1984). However, one can wonder if it is a dual dimension or a multiple dimension, as Chun et al. (2006) argued that people have often multiple competing goals in a situation in which one is simultaneously self and other focused. In other words, people have multiple ways of appraising and coping with stress at the same time.

Background: stress and coping in the 'eastern' world

Stressful life events and daily hassles in certain eastern traditions may not be constructed as irritating individual frustrations and struggles with the 'planned' or expected course of life. On the contrary, these obstacles are seen as necessary ingredients for the healthy development of a person. The reason for this is that dealing with stressful events is embedded in eastern philosophy of life, based on old philosophical, religious or spiritual teachings.

For example, scholars have shown how in Chinese culture, stress, coping and illness cannot be understood from western belief systems, because of the embedment of the principles of Confucianism and Taoism in all aspects of people's behaviours and beliefs (Dahlsgaard et al., 2005; Chen, 2006; Jing-Huaibin, 2007). In Table 5.1, the nine domains of Confucian thoughts have been laid out, and as one can see in domain 2, stress and coping imply that adversity of stressful events could help people grow by developing good traits.

Taoism, also practised in China, differs from Confucianism in that it uses nature as the healing power (Dahlsgaard et al., 2005; Chen, 2006). Tao, in the sense of being selfless, spontaneous and authentic (Chen, 2006), implies that doing nothing is the best way of coping when under stress, because all things will take care of themselves. Since one's life path has already been decided by nature, life will take its own course and will not be under the power or will of the human mind (Legge, 1888). In that sense, passive acceptance of obstruction in life's course is highly valued (Wong and Ujimoto, 1998; Tweed and Conway 2006).

Table 5.1 Nine domains of Confucian thought

---

1. *Meaning of life*: humans possess an essence which is different from the conception of God in Christianity, as believed in western societies.
2. *Stress and coping*: Confucianism emphasizes that adversity the of stressful events could help people grow by developing good traits.
3. *Immortality of the human soul*: In western belief systems people die when their bodies die; in Confucianism the essence of people never die because it lies in the soul and the soul embodies temporarily in a human existence on earth to learn and develop and to continue after death.
4. *Not harming oneself* when in pain or when losing a loved one.
5. *Self-regulation*: humans should become full persons by adopting self-regulation techniques such as introspection, self-examination and meditation and so on.
6. *Interpersonal skills*: these should be more from me (as essence, or inner self; see Chapter 2), to you (social self) than the western concept of empathy which stresses "from you to you".
7. *Social skills*: one should consider the interests of all people before one comes to a decision.
8. *Personal development*: the ideal virtuous person is 'benevolent', 'ritual' and 'intelligent'.
9. *Self-learning approach as counselling technique.*

Source: adapted from Jing-Huaibin (2007).

Again, such a spiritual coping style is difficult to understand in the western world where planning and goal achievement are the norm and where doing nothing is seen as laziness, and where the possible consequences of poverty and social exclusion are seen as one's own fault for lack of choice, decision or action. However, in Lazslo's connectivity hypothesis (see Chapter 2) 'doing nothing' would mean a relaxed response of contemplation, connecting to the inner rather than the social self in which a solution of how to handle the situation might come to mind without conscious effort. In what way this response can be understood in the western categories of primary and secondary appraisal processes is an interesting question to ask. Contemplation as seen from certain eastern philosophies has the form of energy-based mind–body–universe integration for which it seems that answers will be found in tranquillity. Tranquillity in the form of relaxation and meditation has also been recognized as a coping strategy or stress-management technique in the western world including health psychology.

Buddhism, on the other hand, as another philosophical-spiritual embedment of countries such as India, finds its basis in particular on the dimension materialism-spiritualism. According to Buddhism, stress in the western world is constructed as the result of external pressures, while the primary source of stress and suffering lies within the individual through the psychological mechanisms of need rather than longing (e.g. Levinas, 1961), demand rather than asking, keeping busy rather than silence, grasping rather than waiting, and craving for more and repugnance (Dahlsgaard et al., 2005; Chen, 2006). Buddhism sees everyday life as full of pain and suffering caused by people's ignorance, greed and hatred. A stressful event can only be dealt with properly by believing in the process of enlightenment or total wisdom (see also Chapter 2), through aiming for Nirvana. The teachings show that this can be reached by following the eight-fold path of disciplines, which incorporates rules such as not to speak, act or make a living by hurting others or oneself, and to practise mindfulness every day.

Mindfulness as a technique forms the basis of mindfulness meditation. This is one of the western stress-management techniques, which is lifted from this eastern religion to be planted in western life. The difference is that these Buddhist teachings are a way of coping with stress by offering a pathway to be free from the daily hassles and life events (Mirza Tahir, 1998). In that sense, its aims are not stress reduction but stress transformation through mental discipline and enlightenment (Chen, 2006), which does not mean that people do not experience pain and suffering through stressful events but that these mentally strengthen them by dealing with it all through inner strength (Dahlsgaard et al., 2005).

As can be seen from these Confucian, Taoist or Buddhist teachings, people's dealings with stress, coping and illness are permeated by the basic principles of mind–body–spirit integration, in which the beliefs about the meaning of life and death are an answer to all questions of suffering. Believing that one's path in life has already been established makes acceptance of stressful circumstances easier to deal with than the idea that one is not only responsible for creating one's own life path, but moreover that failure to deal successfully with stressors, including becoming ill, is seen as one's own fault.

Furthermore, rather than a personal failure, in certain eastern cultures sickness is constructed as a healing process for the person as a whole. For example, Sarojjakool described in his book entitled, *When Sickness Heals: The Place of Religious Beliefs in Health Care* (2006), how sickness is constructed as a disturbance of yin and yang in a Taoist worldview, and how this leads to a spiritual journey of healing for patients rather than a healing of the body alone. Chui et al. (2005) as well as Lee (1998) discuss how chi, the invisible energy responsible for all living, is perceived as out of balance in the yin yang process when a person is ill, and how these beliefs and practices are embedded in Traditional Chinese Medicine (TCM) and how important it is for health care practitioners to work with Chinese people. In order to enhance an understanding of different cultural beliefs and practices, Chamberlain (1998) described yin and yang as the six phases of chi in relation to health and disease, not as a schematic system but as description of human experience, in order for health professionals to understand when to intervene for the benefit of a patient. This leads us to the question how these two main distinctions in cultural heritage relate to our understanding of stress.

Western stress models interpreted in certain eastern philosophies

Since the introduction of the stress model by Lazarus and Folkman (1984), academics working in western epistemologies have verified or elaborated this basic model of stress to deepen the understanding of the influences of intra- and interpersonal variables (e.g. Stroebe et al., 2007). These are reflected in differences in primary and secondary appraisal, and stress moderators. Current understandings of stress are still along similar lines as those its founders described, and can be captured in a framework as presented in Figure 5.1, in which the relationships between these variables are illustrated. Stress appraisals and stress moderators have been shown to be of influence on the effects of stressful events and the perceived stress experience and on health and illness.

Regarding the stress experience, if coping strategies and moderators are inadequate, and loss, threat and harm are still experienced, then this will have an effect on the immune system, threatening one's well-being with illness as a result. The relationship between stress and illness mediated through the immune system has been shown for several diseases, such as HIV and cancer.

In what follows the components of the stress–illness model will be examined in more detail on the basis of findings in the literature. The variables classified in this model are a selection only. So moderators social support, personality and immunology will be discussed, and not other

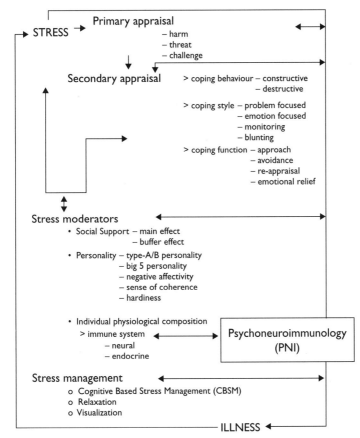

Figure 5.1 Stress and illness model.

moderators such as resources (time or money). Immunology, classified as the last moderator, will be examined in a separate section of this chapter, because of its having become a discipline in its own right, and its greater emphasis on biological rather than psychological terminology. Stress management will be explored in a separate section as well because of introducing eastern practices such as meditation, tai chi and yoga alongside the western techniques as distinguished in this model.

Primary appraisal

As far as primary appraisal is concerned, the majority of studies followed Lazarus and Folkman's (1984) scanning of a stressor as harmful, threatening or challenging, and this process has been described as the most important in relation to health and illness when facing changes in health status (e.g. Oliver and Brough, 2002; Ahmad, 2005; Curtis et al., 2004; King, 2005). In line with this, Schweizer and Dobrich (2003) researched the relationship between self-reported health, appraisal, coping and stress in 8158 teachers and their structural equation modelling revealed that 23% of self-reported health was predicted by these variables, with style of appraisal receiving the highest path coefficient while the coping strategies seemed to be negligible. However, what the actual appraisal of the participants was has not been made clear in these studies and they are for that reason difficult to interpret.

Pakenham and his colleagues, on the other hand, were very specific and defined different categories for primary appraisal than Lazarus and Folkman (1984, 1986). In his studies with patients suffering from Huntington's Disease (Pakenham et al., 2004), depression (Pakenham et al., 2007), and multiple sclerosis (Pakenham, 2006), Pakenham distinguished control, threat and self efficacy as the primary appraisal rather than harm, threat and challenge. The replacement of challenge for self-efficacy would be more in line with eastern philosophy, because self-efficacy not only implies that one has the confidence to face the stressor, which is implicit in challenge, but above all it holds the belief that one can deal with it. Interestingly, this idea was also revealed by Karademas and Kalantzi-Azizi (2004), who found that self-efficacy served as a key variable in the appraisal process, as well as being a mediator between inner cognitive structures and stress outcome.

The opposite applies to control, as also shown by O'Connor and Shimizu (2002) who argued that the relationship between personal control, stress and coping has a 'western bias' because it only reflects an individualistic western value, different from eastern collectivist values. This is, on the basis of his comparative study of British and Japanese samples, in which this relationship with control was only supported for the British, but not for the Japanese participants.

In other words, 'eastern' ways of primary stress appraisal are different from the western categories of threat, harm and control. Only challenge from Lazarus and Folkman's categorization, and self-efficacy from Pakenhams' et al.'s studies, seem to be applicable. As demonstrated earlier, in certain eastern philosophies, stressors are not constructed as harmful or threatening or not controllable, but as a necessary challenge for growth. Believing in the truth of their religious traditions will exclude the appraisal of a stressor as such, because one 'needs' to be harmed and threatened to experience fulfilment of the development as a person, and the process of believing is already a measure of control, because 'stressful events' will happen for a reason, so rather than avoiding these, one 'welcomes' the unexpected.

Secondary appraisal or coping

As far as secondary appraisal or coping is concerned, people use various behaviours to deal with their stressors, some of which are more constructive such as going for a walk, listening to music, reading, or praying while others are more destructive such as smoking or excessive eating or alcohol abuse.

Folkman et al. (1986) categorized these in their functional meaning, and named their coping scales confronting, distancing, self-control, seeking social support, accepting responsibility, escape-avoidance, planful problem solving and positive reappraisal, which they further classified as cognitive and emotional coping styles. In contrast to these western functions of coping, Jing-Huaibin's (2007) Confucian Coping Questionnaire (CES-D) revealed the following factors which he labelled optimism in adversity, viewpoints to faith, responsibility as human beings, and the role of adversity in individual growth. As one would expect from the cultural divide high-lighted by Hofstede (2001) and Laungani (1995a), these factors reflect more a collective, determined and spiritual meaning to dealing with stress than the individualistic coping categories as distinguished by Folkman et al. (1986).

Laungani (1995a) argued that in eastern cultures where Taoism and Zen are the predominant philosophies, stress and coping operate more on an emotional rather than cognitive dimension, because they view life as essen-tially predetermined, rather than based on a possibility for choice related to the western philosophy of free will. Values of life are expressed in spiritual terms such as fulfilment, wisdom and peace and not in materialistic needs such as a bigger house, a better job and more money (Palsane and Lam, 1996).

Interestingly, the coping function frequently reported in the West as maladaptive is avoidance or denial, and this coping function is absent from 'eastern' coping measurements, such as in Jing-Huaibin's (2007) coping scale. Pakenham (2005), for example, studied the coping antecedents in relation to positive outcomes and distress in 502 patients suffering from Multiple Sclerosis (MS), and found that personal health control, emotional release, physical assistance, and acceptance as coping style were related to positive outcomes, but the most important variable related to distress was avoiding the problems related to the illness. Awasthi and Mishra (2007) examined the role of coping strategies in 100 diabetic women and also reported that approach coping reduced the severity of the perceived illness consequences while avoidance increased these consequences, showing that escapism made the experience more stressful.

Rather than categorizing the mastery of stressors in emotional and cogni-tive coping styles or cognitive appraisal, other researchers have distinguished the more context-specific strategies of monitoring and blunting, or a combination of both, as a person's reaction to the appraisal of a stressor as threat. Shiloh and Orgler-Shoob (2006) examined monitoring, which has been defined as a cognitive coping style in which people tend to seek information about threats, and unexpectedly found more information seeking in emotion rather than problem-focused coping.

Blunting has been defined as avoiding or distracting oneself from threat-relevant information (Miller, 1987) such as through daydreaming or sleeping. Van Zuuren and Dooper (1999) found that blunters were less likely to engage in health-protection activities. However, it would be interesting to see what the role of religion, spirituality or one's philosophy of life would be in the so called 'blunters'. Especially from certain eastern philosophies of life, threats are seen as unavoidable on one's path, so why prepare for it or take protective actions?

Religion and spirituality are belief systems which provide faith to people believing in their principles. Their important role has already been documented for certain eastern ways of dealing with stress. However, even though religion is not embedded in western philosophy of life in a similar fashion, it still has many followers and an important role to play in the experience of stress and illness. The question is where to place these belief systems in western stress models?

Role of religion and spirituality in stress, appraisal, coping and illness

Several studies have shown the importance of religion in offering challenge as a primary appraisal of stress. For example, Park (2006) explored the relationship between religiousness, meaning and adjustment in 83 elderly people and their results revealed that religion was important in giving meaning to stressors appraised as challenges, but not that this was enough to adjust to stressful life events in later life. Maltby and Day (2003) studied the relationship between religious orientation, religious coping and appraisals of stress in two UK studies with a total of 826 participants and showed how the use of challenge appraisals was the most important predictor for religious coping and well-being. Another important finding was that cognitive appraisal of the stressor for people with a religious orientation was seen as important for their personal development and growth. These findings are in line with the influence of certain eastern philosophies in dealing with stress.

Religion and spirituality as a coping function have shown to be a positive influence on adaptive coping and positive mood. In their study with 37 mothers of children diagnosed with cancer, Elkin et al. (2007) reported that the 30% of women scoring high on the depression scale scored low on religious beliefs. On the other hand, mothers who showed positive coping outcomes also scored high on religious beliefs and the 38 survivors of prostate cancer in Bowie et al.'s (2004) study who coped well with their illness showed beneficial effects of faith and religious beliefs. Similar results were found in Keefe et al.'s (2003) study with participants suffering from rheumatoid arthritis and in Dunn and Horgas's (2000) research with the elderly.

Looking specifically at the coping strategies of non-western populations, Parks (2007), who studied the narratives of the coping strategies of African-Americans in response to stress, crisis and trauma found that four elements (spirituality, ritual, the power of words and dreams) were the most important. Of the 14 African-American mothers of serious ill children in Wilson and Miles's (2001) study, only two had difficulty relating to a God or spirit, the others indicating feeling supported through their value systems. Similarly, in Ghana, women diagnosed which HIV/AIDS who coped well with their diagnosis did so through their faith, spirituality, fatalism and hope (Perry et al., 2007). Iwasaki and Bartlett (2006) showed how Australian-Aboriginal people suffering from diabetes cope with the stress related to this through what they call, 'culturally meaningful leisure', by which they mean practising native arts, aboriginal dancing, music, spiritual reading, or going to the reserves.

This collective link with the healing practices of aboriginal people was also expressed by McCormick and Wong (2006) in which rituals, medicine men, and drumming were all part of community dealing with the individual whose feelings of unwellness were expressed in terms of connectivity with surrounding energy, similar to Laszlo's theory of connectivity (see Chapter 2). Being unwell for the aboriginal people meant being out of balance physically, mentally, emotionally and spiritually, or as the whole self, which can be restored by contacting the connected energy of the universe through the collective healing practices of their community (Epes-Brown, 1989). Aboriginal therapies such as Vision Quest and Seat Lodge are based on these cultural values and are not dissimilar to energy-balancing practises such as tai chi, qi gong in China and Japan, and yoga in India.

Interestingly, one would think that religion and/or spirituality are the main differences in western and 'eastern' ways of coping. In Lazarus and Folkman's (1984) model, religious and spiritual coping methods have in recent studies been incorporated alongside problem and emotion-focused coping (Pargament et al., 2000; Folkman and Moskowitz, 2004; Klaassen et al., 2006). However, most of these studies have been carried out in the USA with largely Christian (Protestant) people, or Confucian or Buddhist belief systems of people living in western cultures. Klaassen et al. (2006) argued that religion and spirituality are not just coping behaviours in a model such as Lazarus and Folkman's, but that they infuse all variables. In this sense, religiousness or spirituality are a process rather than a product (as a variable) which cannot be simply reduced to coping behaviours such as going to church or praying.

Stress moderators

Social support

Social support has been distinguished as functioning as a buffer in the stress and coping process (e.g. Zimmerman et al., 2000), or as a main effect (e.g. House, 1981; McMahon and Jason, 2000; Park et al., 2008). The latter more in the sense that people will utilize their social network as a way of coping with their stressor, such as using one's friends, family or social network as a shoulder to cry on (emotional support) or to talk to (cognitive support). As far as social support as a buffer is concerned, it implies that people have access to a social network which they are aware of, and which is accessible when needed. In both 'eastern' and western cultures such a 'silent form' of social support has been shown to be an important moderator in the stress and illness process.

Steptoe and Hamer (2007) investigated epidemiological surveys, naturalistic everyday life-monitoring studies and laboratory psychophysiological stress testing in western cultures and found evidence that social support buffered acute physiological stress activation and addictive behavioural responses, while social isolation and loneliness were related to impaired psychobiological function. Cropley and Steptoe (2005), on the other hand, only found support for the buffering function of social support for recent but not for chronic stress. Wu (2006) studied the social support buffer model related to work stress in Taiwan, and interestingly explicitly referred to the East–West divide: 'We apply stress-social support theory (a western model) to examine daily life and work stressors in an eastern cultural environment (Taiwan)' (2006, p. 145). This author did find support for the role of social support as a buffer for work stress.

However, gender differences have also been revealed as reported by Holahan and Moos (1985) in their research with 267 families which they split in high and low stress groups. According to these authors there was a higher relationship with social support for the women in the stress-resistant group with a better health record, but for the men self-confidence was more important. Hughes (2007) examined the effects of social support on cardiovascular stress responses in 92 men and women, and showed that these were beneficial for women but not for men.

Other current research has acknowledged the importance of social support not as a separate variable mediating the stress–illness process but as an inherent construct of the stress experience. For example, Kayser et al. (2007) examined the cancer experience as a 'we' disease, in which the process of coping with the diagnosis and treatment of breast cancer was explored in 10 couples from a relational perspective. Two types of relational coping emerged in their qualitative research, mutual responsiveness and disengaged avoidance, highlighting the importance of awareness, authenticity and mutuality, concepts more related to certain eastern than western philosophies.

Personality factors

Personality styles which, in particular, have been found to be related to the stress experience in relation to health and illness from a western philosophy of life are Type A versus Type B (e.g. Suls and Sanders, 1988), the Big 5 personality traits (e.g. Grant and Langan-Fox, 2007), negative affectivity (e.g. Oliver and Brough, 2002), Sense of Coherence (e.g. Yueping et al., 2004) and hardiness (e.g. Maddi, 1999, 2002). Hofstede (2001) describes how personality in the sense of an idea of a self separate from others is absent in those 'eastern' cultures which he found to be high scorers on the 'collective' rather than 'individualistic' dimensions, and refers to Hsu's (1971) study concluding that 'the Chinese tradition has no equivalent for the western concept of personality: a separate entity distinct from society and culture' (2001, p. 210), and Riesman et al.'s (1953) finding that 'that the tradition-directed person . . . hardly thinks of himself as an individual' (2001, p. 210).

However, in western psychology, the Type A personality was originally distinguished by Friedman and Rosenman (1974) as a type of person who was always stressed, a person who was constantly pressed for time, irritable and hostile, and who had been found to be highly susceptible to coronary heart disease (e.g. Borg and Shapiro, 1996; Kirkcaldy et al., 1999). This personality type was studied extensively in the 1970s, 1980s and 1990s, but because of substantial criticism of its construct validity and lack of explanatory power, its focus has diminished over time. For example, Suls and Sanders (1988) reviewed the research on Type A behaviour in relation to physical disorders and concluded that Type A on its own is not a general risk factor for illnesses, and that higher correlations have been found between Type A and having accidents or dying from accidents or violence.

Type B, as the counterpart of Type A, could be criticized for the same reasons because of its static, out-of-context, isolated appearance; however, interestingly it does reflect attributes similar to certain eastern ways of living. Thomas (1986) distinguished characteristics related to type B as living life at a more peaceful pace than Type A, experiencing less stress as a frustration of daily life, less pressure when there are too many things to do, more likely to enjoy life and less worried about the meaning of life. Research found that coronary heart disease was hardly related to these Type B traits (Rhodewalt et al., 1984; Nowack, 1986; Thomas, 1986).

Regardless of the criticisms of the validity of personality theories per se (e.g. Mischel, 1968), the Big 5 personality profile (openness, conscientiousness, extraversion, agreeableness and neuroticism) seems to have an explanatory power such as to justify its use (e.g. McCrae and Costa, 1990; Costa et al., 2001) even across cultures such as USA and China (Trull and Geary, 1997), and several West European countries such as Belgium and Hungary (De Fruyt et al., 2004).

Exploring the items of the five personality constructs implied that openness, in the sense of being receptive to ideas and imagination, and agreeableness as feeling and caring for other people, most closely reflect certain eastern belief systems of dealing with stress. On the other hand, neuroticism as being moody, irritable and stressed, extraversion as talking a lot and seeking attention and conscientiousness as being prepared, liking order and following a schedule seemed to reflect a western, goal-achieving way of life.

This has been supported in the literature as well. For example, a direct and indirect effect of neuroticism has been found to be related to the coping style of avoidance in a sample of 265 11–14 year-old young adolescents (Kardum and Krapić, 2001). Grant and Langan-Fox (2007) looked at the role of the Big 5 personality traits in the occupational stressor–strain relation in 211 managers and found that neuroticism and physical strain were mediated by perceived role conflict and substance misuse. The relationship between neuroticism and psychological strain however was shown to be mediated by perceived stress. As one would expect from certain eastern philosophies, openness and agreeableness were unrelated to strain.

Deary and Frier (1995) examined the Big 5 personality styles and the stress of the worry of hypoglaemia in 141 diabetic patients. Of these, only neuroticism correlated significantly with emotion-oriented worry behaviour and coping and illness severity. They tested their hypotheses using Lazarus and Folkman's (1984) transactional model of stress and found another 'personality trait' to be the most important mediator for maladaptive coping, namely negative affectivity. This style, in the sense of being moody and expressing a negative atmosphere, represented attributions opposing certain eastern belief systems. Other studies also highlighted the important mediating effect of negative affectivity, but what is meant by this?

Negative affectivity has been defined as reflecting individual differences in negative emotions and self-concept (Watson et al., 1988). Both Oliver and Brough (2002) and Hoyle (1995) indicated that negative affectivity plays a complex and substantive role in the stress process. Some argue that negative affectivity is a dispositional variable, as described in the research of Kahn et al. (2003) with 100 elderly people. Kressin et al. (2000) as well as Denollet (1991) saw negative affectivity as a personality trait in the sense of a pervasive disposition to experience any subjective distress from an aversive mood state in which one is angry, disgusted, guilty and fearful, which according to Watson et al. (1988) will appear across time and regardless of the situation. In concert with social inhibition, negative affectivity is now construed as D-Type personality, reflecting low social support and poor well-being with chronic tensions, pessimism and depressive symptoms (Kahn, 2008), all attributes of an individualistic personality style which seems to oppose communal eastern value systems.

Another reported mediating variable in the stress and illness literature is Antonovsky's Sense of Coherence (SoC) concept, which strictly speaking, is not a personality trait but a state of the person in which values, norms, feelings, cognitions and behaviours are experienced in a coherent rather than disoriented way; this he named the state of salutogenesis (Antonovsky, 1979, 1987, 1993). Antonovsky (1979) defines SoC as the extent to which one has a pervasive, enduring though dynamic, feeling of confidence that one's environment is predictable and that things will work out as well as can reasonably be expected. Although this relates to the western psychological concepts of self-efficacy and control, the three factors important for sense of coherence which he named comprehensibility, manageability and meaningfulness, relate more to a coherent understanding of life which infiltrates the whole stress, coping and well-being process similarly to 'eastern' ways.

Because of the embedment of an empathic, relaxed and responsive eastern philosophy of life in all aspects of being, 'stress-management' techniques such as relaxation, visualization, and mindfulness meditation are not necessary set-aside practices from daily life. In the West, these are seen as a type of exercise one practices as a form of leisure along the same lines as sport, going to the movies or going out for a meal or drink; as counterbalancing a busy, stressful, goal-achieving life. Eastern forms of stress management, as such, are consequently not coherent with other aspects of one's life in the western world. The question is whether this matters, and if it does, what research from the SoC model can contribute to the understanding of these differences in 'eastern' and western lifestyles.

Research so far has given some informative findings. For example, Yueping et al. (2004) found with their self-developed Sense of Coherence Scale that their subjects in Shanghai with a high SoC reported the lowest stress, which made them conclude that SoC is an important variable to maintain health and prevent illness. Strong SoC is assumed to promote and protect health in stressful situations such as serious illness. Also in the East, Bishop (1993) studied 186 people in Singapore and showed that daily hassles were a significant predictor of both number and severity of illness. If there was a high SoC then there was no relationship between stress and illness but with low SoC there were higher numbers and severity of illness.

In the West, value systems close to eastern philosophies are often measured as spirituality (e.g. Strang and Strang, 2001; Delgado, 2007) with interesting gender differences favouring higher SoC in relation to stress in females than males (e.g. Gustavsson-Lilius et al., 2007; Nielsen and Hansson, 2007). The reason for these differences have not been discussed by the authors but raises interesting questions for future research for health psychologists, especially related to differences in value systems and behaviours associated with complementary medicine, for which gender differences have also been reported (see Chapter 1).

Nonetheless, Geyer (1997) is quite critical of the concept of SoC because there is not much evidence of the stability of this concept. He sees SoC more as an attitude of people who are well educated, in rather privileged social positions with opportunities for decision making. Especially because of the high negative correlation between SoC, anxiety and depression, he questioned whether the instruments are not measuring the same concepts. However, this can be said of several different concepts used in the social sciences, hence the attraction of SoC as the inclusion of the importance of coherency of value systems such as philosophy, religion or spirituality, in relation to people's appraisals of stress and their effects on well-being.

The personality concept which probably best mirrors the eastern person's view is Kobasa's (1979) hardiness construct, which suggests that people who have a personality style which shows commitment, control and challenge are less likely to get stressed and are in better health. However, what is the difference with the 'eastern' model?

Maddi (1999, 2002) researched hardiness extensively and found consistently in cross-cultural studies that the higher the hardiness level as measured with the Personal Views Survey, the more constructive the coping behaviour and the lower the reported illness symptoms. Maddi also found that more transformational coping was inspired by hardiness level, and that avoidant coping which he called, 'regressive coping' was unrelated to the contexts of events and hardiness. In his recent publication of 2006, Maddi named hardiness as the courage to grow from stresses, because people with high scores consistently showed that they were able to turn around stressful circumstances from potential disasters into opportunities for growth. Support for enhanced resistance in 'hardy' people to stress-induced illness has been revealed in several studies (e.g. Allred and Smith, 1989; Beasley et al., 2003) with gender differences favouring males over females (Klag and Bradley, 2004; Dolbier et al., 2007).

Also in these studies, negative affectivity seem to have been an important mediating variable. If people were moody and expressed negative emotions then a high score on hardiness did not necessarily lead to fewer illness symptoms under stress. This in an interesting finding, especially since this combination of a committed person who perceives stressors as challenges and who feels in control but who at the same time is negative and moody, is opposing the 'eastern' representations of the person dealing with stressors. The same can be said about studies combining Type A personality and hardiness, especially since people showing Type A characteristics also seem to be irritable and bad tempered but in combination with experiencing constant time and workload pressure (Schmied and Lawler, 1986; Nowack, 1991).

Interesting questions can be raised from these findings, especially, since Type A personality type people appear to be very committed to their work situation, as hardiness also implies. However, the opposite is true. Is this because of the hard-working ethos as the result of a Protestant religion, or is it an avoidance strategy to not feel the moral demands of the inner self (Levinas, 1972), a lack of self-efficacy, or part of the capitalistic drive for more money and status? All of these are different from certain 'eastern' value systems.

Psychoneuroimmunology

Due to Cartesian dualism, health and illness have primarily been constructed from a bodily perspective, hence the domination of the medical model in studying illness aetiology and progression. Since Hans Selye showed a connection between stress and illness and even death with his GAS model, more questions have been raised about possible connections between mind and body. However, observational studies examining this link were dismissed by peer academics as anecdotal and non-scientific. As Kiecolt-Glaser et al. (1987) have shown, psychosomatic research had been conducted since the 1930s but it was not until the 1970s that a new approach named psychoneuroimmunology (PNI) obtained more ground in the scientific community. When Ader's book was published in 1981 with the title *Psychoneuroimmunology*, the efforts to establish links between mind and body through the mapping of behaviour and neuroendocrine and immunological processes in relation to health and illness were finally given a name. Ader (2000, p. 167) even refers to PNI as a paradigm shift:

> These and subsequent studies have led to the general acknowledgment that the nervous and immune systems are components of an integrated system of adaptive processes, and that immunoregulatory processes can no longer be studied as the independent activity of an autonomous immune system. This paradigm shift in the study of immunoregulatory processes and the elaboration of the mechanisms underlying behaviorally induced alterations of immune function promise a better understanding and a new appreciation of the multi-determined etiology of pathophysiological states.

Even though other names, such as psychoneuroendocrinology, or PENI, have been suggested, PNI is the most common name used in the many books and publications which subsequently followed. Cohen and Herbert (1996) were the first to relate PNI to health psychology and, since 2007, PNI has been one of the required fields of study embedded in the set curriculum for the professional training of health psychologists in the UK (BPS, 2007). Also in the UK, psychologists such as Evans et al. (2000), who defined psychoneuroimmunology as an inter-disciplinary science that examines the neural and neuroendocrine links between immunology and psychology, have carried out valuable work relating the immune reaction to stress.

The basic model of PNI is that the cognitive and emotional components of people's behaviour are at a biological level understood through the workings of the brain via two pathways: neural and endocrine. The first is through sympathetic nerve stimulation of the Autonomous Nervous System (ANS) to the lymphoid organs and glands, where T lymphocytes receive stimulation from the neurotransmitter noradrenaline and peptides through their β-adrenergic receptors. The second endocrine pathway is understood through the processes in which the brain communicates with target cells through the stimulation of the production of hormones.

Regarding stress and illness, the most influential endocrine-immunological system is the immonoregulatory role of the hypothalamic-pituitary-adrenal (HPA)-axis, especially the processes in which the adrenal cortex responds to stimulation of ACTH (adrenocorticotrophic hormone) by producing glucocorticoids such as cortisol, which is often referred to as the stress hormone, and DHEA (dehydroepiandrosterone) (e.g. Haddy and Clover, 2001). These two hormones are the most important in keeping the balance of the two T-helper-cell populations, Th1 and Th2, and are described by Evans et al. (2000) as the most important indicators in the recognition of acute versus chronic stress, a distinction essential in the body's sustainability against illness.

In the case of Th1 dominance as in acute stress, the body's neuro-endocrine response strengthens the immune system by more trafficking of lymphocytes, less trafficking of circulating lymphocytes, more efficient lymphocytes, more circulating NK cells, enhanced cytotoxiticy and enhanced secretion of (non-specific) sIgA, while for Th2 domination the reverse is the case (see Evans et al., 2000). A Th2 supremacy as the result of chronic stress shows a weakening of the immune response, making the person more susceptible to disease progression, such as promotion of bacterial and viral infection, acceleration of tumour development and increased auto-immune response (e.g. Sun et al., 2007).

Miller et al. (2002) developed a pathway to show how chronic stress altered the course of inflammatory disease on the basis of their research with 50 parents of children with cancer versus parents with healthy children, by establishing the effect of cortisol on the pro-inflammatory cytokine interleukin 6. Song (2001) also studied the interactions with interleukin 6 but in relation to anxiety. From Miller et al.'s study it is not clear which aspect of the stress response was responsible for the change in interleukin 6, but considering the fear associated with the uncertainty of losing a child with cancer, it might well be that anxiety was a major contributor to the effects.

However, as has been documented by several scholars, this process is not as simple and straightforward as one wants to believe. For example, Plotnikoff et al. (2007) highlighted the difficulties of the Th1 and Th2 categorization, in particular from the point of view of the contradictory results regarding studies using cortisol as their main immune measurement. They argue that more clarity will only be obtained by a repeated measures design in which cortisol measures are taken 20–30 minutes after waking up and at several points during the day depending on the intervention. A daily course of cortisol secretion is also described by Evans et al. (2000), and according to Clow et al. (2003) is most accurate when measured in relation to IgA. Cortisol measured on its own is not very reliable because of its temporary variation under acute stress, with rapid recovery after the release of the stress stimulus, such as for example exam stress (Gilbert et al., 1996).

Overall, the PNI processes in relation to stress and illness are more complicated than initially thought. Evans et al. (2000, p. 40) say: 'Many psychologists, biologists and certainly immunologists are deeply suspicious of the term "stress" (as coined by Selye) since it is so difficult to define and there is so much cognitive overlay resulting in marked individual differences in response to any particular situation and stimulus'. Also, Malarkey and Mills (2007) highlighted, in their mini-review of research published in *Brain, Behaviour and Immunity* during the last 20 years, the complexity of the interaction between the endocrine hormonal system and the cytokine immune system in acute and chronic stress, and their relation with various illnesses.

Nonetheless, that psychological factors do have an effect on the endocrine and immune system in such a way that vulnerability of the person to attract illnesses is enhanced, is well established (e.g. Tosevski and Milovancevic, 2006). The variation of the process depends not only on the individual differences of the human beings studied but also on the various psychological and physical variables selected in the research design, the choice of population under study, the selected outcome measures, the time scale of measurement, and the methods of analyses.

For example, in the review articles of both Glaser and Kiecolt-Glaser (2005) and Toveski and Milovancevic (2006), the relation between stressful life events on the sudden onset or worsening of a variety of illnesses has been discussed in connection with certain behaviours and the complex interaction between the Central Nervous System and the endocrine and immune system. Thornton et al. (2007) and Kiecolt-Glaser et al. (1998) on the other hand, emphasized the importance of stress appraisals such as threat or challenge on the effects of the immune system and health outcomes. Wadee et al. (2001) studied the immune response of 10 postgraduate students on the subjective appraisal of the stressfulness of their exams in relation to having an anxious personality (high-score trait anxiety) and found that anxious students who appraised their exams as a threat displayed more efficient phagocyte function but decreased proliferation of their lymphocyte function at the time of stress. In the ecological model of Segerstrom (2007, 2008) (described in more detail later) this might be explained by the body benefitting for the stress in the short term (doing well at the exam), but spending less energy on protection in the long term.

Other academics concentrated more on the way people cope with their stressors (e.g. Erikson et al., 1999) or in what way personality factors influenced the immune response. For example, the influence of religion (Cohen and Herbert, 1996; Herberman, 2002), humour and laughter (Lefcourt and Thomas, 1998) and the degree to which people experience a sense of coherence (Post-White, 1998) all had a positive effect on immune measures. On the other hand studies looking at personality factors such as Type A, hostility and pessimism (Lee, Meehan, Robinson & Smith, 1995) have shown a relation between these and a worsening of the immune function.

Koenig et al. (2001) developed a model regarding the relationship between religion and medicine, and not only emphasized similar roles of social support but also how religion's promotion of healthy behaviours prevents alcohol and drug abuse, and certain sexual diseases which might contribute to better immune response and good physical health in religious people. However, the role of psychological factors has not been incorporated into this model.

Segerstrom (2007, 2008) proposed to look at the relationship between stress, appraisal, coping, personality, immunity and health from a broader ecological perspective, in which the immune system is regarded as an energetically costly system whose functioning depends on the energy necessary for a person's performance as a whole. Her argument was that in some cases immune suppression under stressful circumstances can be more beneficial to the well-being of a person, for example, finishing a task rather than becoming ill and experiencing extra stress because of not having finished it. Explanations derived from this model might clarify why some people tend to get ill in their spare time such as weekends or holidays.

Regarding variation in methods of analyses, Sephton (2007) highlighted the discrepancy in methods interpreting NK cytotoxicity data, used as an outcome measure in studies looking at immune resistance to viral and other serious diseases. Her new model illustrated this in her PhD on breast cancer, but is in need of further testing which might be of interest to health psychologists.

Research has been carried out to show the link between stress, PNI and health and illness for several conditions. Apart from psychological disorders such as depression (e.g. Irwin, 1991; Malarkey and Mills, 2007) and post-traumatic stress disorder (e.g. Wong, 2002; Wong and Yehuda, 2002), the majority of studies have looked at physical disorders such as HIV/AIDS (e.g. Robinson et al., 2000; Irinson et al., 2002; McCain et al., 2008) and cancer (Cella and Holland, 1988; Bovbjerg and Valdimarsdottir, 2001; Finn, 2001). In particular, the role of NK cells in HIV and cancer aetiology and progression has been well established, as well as the effects of chronic stress on the function of these killer cells.

Herberman (2002) explained the important role of these cells because of their function as 'immunosurveillance' in which NK cells start operating without having to recognize a specific antigen. These are stimulated by cytokines and their enhanced capacity to find and destroy cells which express unrecognizable molecules, such as is the case with malignant and deformed cells. In his chapter he showed how this is related to cancer progression. McCain et al. (2005) also refer to the Immune Surveillance Theory as the system in which NK cells destroy tumour cells and protect against tumour growth. However, they too recognized that the processes are more complex than the theory states, for example, that especially in cancer patients the NK cells have an even greater cytotoxic capacity when activated by certain cytokines (e.g. IFN-γ, IL-2 and IL-12), which are then named the Lymphokine Activated Killer (LAK) cells.

That the neuro-immune profile will vary with the diversity of health outcomes, quality of life or physical health, is very well documented in the publications of McCain et al. (2005, 2008), who developed research frameworks with different neuro-immune (and psycho-social) variables and diverse ways of measuring immune response for their study on HIV and cancer. For example, for HIV their selected neuro-endocrine mediators were cortisol (salivary) and DHEA, while for breast cancer they selected cortisol (urinary) and Leu-Enkaphalin Beta-Endorphin. The selected immunology indicators were similar for NK cell cytotoxicity, Type 1 (IFN γ, TNFα) and Type 2 (IL-4, -6 & -10) cells, cytokine production and lymphocyte proliferation, but differed in that CD4+, CD8+ and CD57+ were measured for HIV but not for breast cancer, and Type 1 cytokine production for IL-1β and -12 for breast cancer but not for HIV. Other health outcomes related to PNI, as especially documented by the PNI group in Chicago, are those related to aging and negative emotions. Kiecolt-Glaser et al. (2002) reviewed literature that showed how the production of pro-inflammatory cytokines influenced the onset and course of conditions associated with ageing such as cardiovascular disease, osteoporosis, arthritis, Type 2 diabetes, certain cancers, Alzheimer's disease, and frailty and functional decline. In their own studies they revealed how important the influence of negative emotions was to prolonged infection and delayed wound healing, mediated by close personal relations.

In sum, more research is necessary, especially in relation to the mediating role of complementary therapies and their effects on the immune system in the stress–illness process in which health psychologists could play an important role. Some of this research has already been performed in relation to stress management as will be discussed in the next section.

Stress management in health psychology versus meditation, tai chi and yoga

In older American health psychology textbooks, one would find a chapter on stress management techniques (e.g. Harvey, 1988; Taylor, 1991; Sheridan and Radmacher, 1992), but not in British-authored ones (e.g. Ogden, 1996; Bennett and Murphy, 1997). One of the reasons might be that health psychologists in the USA were more involved in health care practice, in the sense of direct client work, than in the UK. In these books several practices for health psychology have been introduced, varying from relaxation and visualization programmes such as progressive muscle relaxation (Jacobson, 1938, 1978), and guided imagery (Kirsch et al., 1977), to more cognitive programmes such as Rational Emotive Therapy (RET) (Ellis, 1957) and Stress Inoculation Therapy (Meichenbaum and Cameron, 1983). Biofeedback (Lawrence, 1976) was introduced as another method in which biological processes were monitored which were normally beyond conscious control (Bonso et al., 2005). In relation to stress, biological responses were measured by electronic instruments, and auditory or visual feedback of heartbeat or alpha brain waves were immediate assessable to the participants. In that way the effects of breathing techniques or other forms of stress management could be seen and heard, and the desired 'relaxed' states obtained.

Looking at contemporary publications on stress-management programmes, in particular related to stress in sufferers from chronic diseases such as HIV+/AIDS and cancer, one would expect an important role for the involvement of health psychology.

Scott-Sheldon et al. (2008) studied the effects of stress management with

HIV-positive people. They conducted a meta-analysis of 35 studies which were based on RCTs and found that 46 different interventions were used with a total of 3077 patients. Among these were western as well as 'eastern' stress-management programmes such as Cognitive Behavioural Stress Management (CBSM), Cognitive Behavioural Group Program, tai chi and yogic breathing. They concluded that overall they could see a trend that stress-management techniques were effective in reducing anxiety, depression, distress and fatigue and did improve quality of life. However, they did not find any verification for an improved immune response measured with CD4+ counts, viral loads or hormonal outcomes, but did acknowledge that the immune measures taken were varied and mostly only obtained one week after the intervention. Because the type of stress-management technique was not taken into account, it is not clear whether there was a difference between the more accepted techniques in psychology, such as relaxation or biofeedback, and the more alternative practices.

Eastern forms of stress management

Mindfulness meditation

Mindfulness meditation as a concept stands for people's sense of being in the here and now with an awareness and attentive focus of one's thoughts, to whatever one is thinking and whatever one is doing (Kostanski and Hassed, 2008) in a non-judgemental way (Kabat-Zinn, 2003). Mindfulness meditation, which has its origins in Buddhism, was introduced to the western world by scholars such as Kabat-Zinn et al. (1985). It has been shown to be a good practice for stress reduction (e.g. Carmody and Ruth, 2008), improving quality of life (e.g. Fernros et al., 2008), and for lowering anxiety and depression (e.g. Toneatto and Nguyen, 2007). However, it is not always clear from these studies what form of mindfulness meditation has been practised, how it has been taught and whether it is integrated in one's lifestyle as a whole, as the original teachings imply. Even the contents of specifically developed mindfulness programmes such as the Mindfulness-Based Stress Reduction (MBSR) programme by Kabat-Zinn (1994) are not always as straightforward as we might think.

Williams (2006) carried out research on MBSR in a worksite wellness programme. He asserted that MBSR is consistent with social cognitive theory used for behavioural change. In the MBSR programme participants were given the opportunity to develop skills to increase the behavioural capacity for self-control as well as self-efficacy. Williams argued that MBSR is based on a theoretical framework addressing cognitive and somatic dimensions of stress and that, unlike health promotion and Cognitive Behavioural Therapy (CBT), mindfulness training focuses on cultivating inner resources rather than on what is wrong with the person. In other words, it is focused on cultivating the calmness of the mind rather than a larger perspective on the difficulties of life. By decreasing emotional reactivity and enhancing cognitive appraisal, a positive response to stress was the result. Mindfulness reduced resistance to change and fostered conditions conducive to the elimination of dysfunctional behavioural patterns. This study questioned the difference with other cognitive stress-reduction programmes, such as Cognitive Behavioural Stress Management (CBSM), which will be discussed later in this section.

Garland (2007) did not think that mindfulness could be constructed as *a type* of stress management in western models. He showed, on the basis of his review of stress and mindfulness studies, that mindfulness should be seen as a second-order cybernetics, a trans-disciplinary conceptional framework which highlights the constant interplay between the individual and their context. He constructed the meaning of mindfulness in a novel causal model of stress, meta-cognition and coping, in which mindfulness was hypothesized to reinforce coping processes by widening positive reappraisal, justifying catastrophizing and stimulating self-transcendence.

Tai chi

Tai chi is a form of exercise, practised standing up, while performing a ritual of slow described movements of the body (Taylor-Piliae et al., 2006). Originally portrayed in Confucianism and Taoist philosophy as a martial art, nowadays it is better known as a method to channel yin and yang energy in one's body in order to feel in harmony and at peace with oneself and one's surroundings (Lan et al., 2002). It is a daily undertaking integrated in Chinese way of life to feel well and it is, visible by watching Chinese people practising it in quiet natural places such as parks, gardens, rivers or by the sea (Li et al., 2001).

Western cultures have imported tai chi for stress management and health-promotion reasons, and even though tai chi exercise classes are to be found in the majority of big cities, research showing its effects are still in its infancy (Sun et al., 1996). Regarding the influence of tai chi on health, positive relations have been found on cardiovascular functioning (e.g. Sun et al., 1996; Taylor-Piliae et al., 2006), sleeping patterns (Irwin et al., 2008), depressive symptoms (e.g. Sjösten et al., 2008) and fall prevention with the elderly (Li et al., 2008).

As far as the effects of tai chi as a stress-management technique are concerned, comparative research has been carried out. McCain et al. (2008) designed an RCT to measure the effects of conventional versus alternative forms of stress management in 252 people with HIV and found that the interventions were effective in all three groups (cognitive-behavioural relaxation training; focused tai chi training and spiritual growth groups) in the sense that lymphocyte proliferative function was enhanced. Even though the cortisol measures adhered to a valid protocol in which wake-up cortisol was assessed in addition to the pre- and post-intervention measurements, no significant change in cortisol was found in the stress-management groups. The authors' explanation was that the participants were not particularly distressed at the start of the intervention, probably because they had already accepted their diagnosis. Strangely, the authors did not look at the belief systems of the participants. The only psychosocial difference was that the first two groups used a less emotion-focused coping style than the latter group, a finding which the authors could not explain. Interestingly though, 60% of their sample were involved in some form of non-traditional therapy but this variable was not controlled for. So what went wrong?

Without understanding the value system of the participants, in particular their beliefs regarding life and death and the after-life, and possible connections to the chi, or life or cosmos energy in light of Lazslo's connectivity hypothesis, comparisons of these stress-management practices will not reveal relevant answers. The comparison, performed as an RCT, only measured a short-term effect on the coping functions and immune system for all three techniques, but long-term effects with additional cultural and value measures might have given different results. Especially if the focused tai chi training had been taught within its original cultural teachings, it would have been more than just an exercise class. The same applies to the spiritual growth group, if more information had been given as to what this actually involved. In other words, without a qualitative element of exploring value systems of health, illness and related or non-related religious, spiritual, philosophical or humanistic orientation in the short term as well as long term, the real meaning of these different stress-management techniques might not come to light.

Yoga

Yoga is a form of exercise derived from Hindu philosophy, embedded in Indian culture. Yoga (meaning 'union' in Sanskrit) is the overall name of several different yoga disciplines, however, the one practised the most in the West is hatha yoga (Saper, 2004). As with tai chi, yoga also involves a series of 'calm' stretching exercises whose aim to unite the body and mind with the universal energy, the main difference being the inclusion of breathing exercises ('pranayamas') to circulate 'prana' (the whole life-energy of the universe) through the body as the connecting medium (Birkel, 2000; Raub, 2002; Gura, 2007). The goal of yoga may range from improving health to achieving 'Moksha', which is similar to the Buddhist's aim to achieve enlightenment, in the sense of a liberation of life's suffering and reaching unity with Brahman, the permeation of all experiences (Raub, 2002; Gura, 2007).

Raub (2002) in his literature review assessing the psycho-physiological effects of yoga showed that these were found for cardiovascular and pulmonary function, osteoarthritis of the hand, carpal tunnel syndrome, and management of chronic illnesses such as multiple sclerosis. Other more 'anecdotal' studies seem to indicate a positive relation with lower back pain (Schaeffer, 2000a; Galantino, 2004) and headaches (Schaeffer, 2000b).

Regarding stress management, not much research has been published in peer-reviewed journals as yet. Gura (2007) described how yoga at work could lead to the release of tension and a decrease job stress yet no studies have been carried out to validate these statements. Milligan (2006) described the development and implementation of a Yoga for Stress Management Program (YSMP) as a counselling approach for college students. However, yet again no evaluation has been documented. More recent research into the effects of yoga on stress has interestingly been conducted by PhD students, indicating a current research interest. Coleman (2008) examined yoga as a treatment for secondary traumatic stress in mental health professionals, and Fallon (2008) as an intervention for stress reduction and enhanced well-being in African-American athletes, while Smith (2008) studied the effects on stress among college students in a post-Katrina population. This pioneering work asks for continuation of studies using robust methodologies, which might be a good opportunity for health psychologists.

Western forms of stress management

Cognitive Based Stress Management (CBSM)

The stress-management method most consistently researched and published in the literature is Cognitive Based Stress Management methods (CBSM), the effects of which have been studied in several populations such as breast cancer patients (Cruess et al., 2000), caregivers of dementia patients (Lancer, 2007) and sufferers from HIV/AIDS (Antoni et al., 1991; Schneiderman et al., 1992). However, even though some guidance on a CBSM training package seems to exist (Antoni et al., 1991) different programme contents with different time scales are reported in the various publications.

In Schneiderman's (1999) studies, in which men who were HIV positive were compared to a control group in the CBSM intervention, awareness of stress and negative thoughts were taught and ways were offered as to how to restructure these cognitions and coping skills. These authors found a buffering effect of the skills training on anxiety and depressed affect. As far as the immune response was concerned they discovered that for those men who reported greater stress at diagnosis and more HIV specific denial coping and lower intervention adherence, lower CD4 cell counts and poorer lymphoproliferative responses to PHA were found at a year follow-up, and a faster progression of the disease two years later. Overall, they concluded that interventions using CBSM are useful for decreasing distress, buffering the stressful effect of the diagnosis and improving immune functioning.

Berger and O'Brien (1998) also looked at the effects of a five-weekly practice of CBSM, which was composed of information provision over stress and immunity, autogenic relaxation and breathing exercises in an

RCT of 53 undergraduate students. They found significant stress reduction in the psychological reports of the students in the intervention group, but not in the amounts of salivary immunoglobin A (sIgA). Their conclusion was that the intervention reduced stress but was not improving the immune system. Possible explanations might be that the stress experience was not severe enough at baseline, that cortisol was not measured in relation to sIgA, or that the intervention was too short or not enjoyable.

Gaab et al. (2006) carried out an RCT to examine the psychoneuroendocrine effects of CBSM. They tested the effect of a four-weekly session on 28 economy students. Salivary cortisol (cortisol-awakening response and short circadian cortisol profile) was repeatedly measured at baseline and on the day of the exam. Also cognitive appraisal was assessed on the day of the exam. The CBSM students scored lower anxiety and less somatic symptoms throughout the period before exam. On exam day, control attenuated cortisol levels in their cortisol awakening stress response. No difference in circadian cortisol levels were found. Differences in cortisol response and cognitive appraisal were reported in the control but not in the experimental group. Reasons presented for this dissociation were also in line with current psychoendocrine models as a result of dysregulated HPA axis, probably as a consequence of long-lasting stress. In this study IgA measures were not taken. According to Clow et al. (2003) it is the results of the interaction of IgA and circadian cortisol profile which gives the most accurate picture of the immune response regarding stress and stress-management interventions.

Relaxation and visualization

The most frequent form of stress management used by 63% of the 100 cancer patients in Sparber et al.'s (2000) study were relaxation and imagery, which all patients believed helped them to achieve an improved quality of life, a more effective way of coping with stress, a decreased discomfort from illness and treatment, and a better sense of control. Similar results were found in Petry's (2000) review with surgical patients. Distress and relief of distress through relaxation, hypnosis, suggestion and imagery were chosen as a choice of therapy because of their role as a coping style and as a form of locus of control. Suarez and Reese (2000) too found that users of meditation and visualization classes showed significantly more adaptive coping behaviours and higher levels of control in their sample of 73 males suffering from HIV and AIDS.

Nunes et al. (2007) studied the effects of Relaxation and Visualization Therapy (RVT) on psychological distress, cortisol levels and immunological parameters (lymphocytes for T-cell proliferation and sensitivity to glucocorticoids) in an RCT comparing 20 breast cancer patients who were receiving radiotherapy with 14 non-patients in a control group, and found effects on the psychological measures of stress, anxiety and depression but not on the immunological parameters. One of the explanations for this, also highlighted by the authors themselves, is that RVTs over a period of three weeks is, maybe, too short. Other results, according to the authors, might also have been found with more severe psychological morbidity at baseline.

Gruzelier et al. (2001) examined the outcomes of the effects of immune-related imagery and relaxation imagery (and named this self-hypnosis) on immune function, mood and health during medical examinations in 31 medical students. Three weekly group plus homework sessions with an audiotape were assessed comparing instructions of improved immune function with relaxation training, and both groups receiving instructions to increase energy, alertness, concentration and happiness. Immune assays involved CH3, CD4, CD8, CD19 lymphocytes, CD56, NK cells and blood cortisol. Better results were obtained for immune-related imagery rather than relaxation imagery in buffering decline in total lymphocytes and sub-sets. Independent of the instructions, self-hypnosis buffered the decline in CD8 cytotoxic T-cells, an effect associated with hypnotic susceptibility. Dissociations between negative mood and raised cortisol following hypnosis were also reported. Interestingly, it seemed that the cognitive aspect of this relaxation/visualization stress-management programme, in the sense of instruction on immune function, was the most influential.

Burns (1997) compared the use of humour versus relaxation training on the improvement of immunocompetence, in terms of changes in Secretory Immunoglobin A (sIgA), by collecting samples before and after the experiment which were bio-assessed for sIgA concentrations in 160 men divided over three groups (humour, relaxation and humour plus relaxation) 'because of its crucial importance as one of the initial defences against foreign organisms invading the body' (1997, p. 5319) and it is easy access through saliva as a non-invasive technique. They found significant effects for all three, with humour producing higher elevations of sIgA than humour and relaxation, which were higher than relaxation on its own.

Other forms of stress management

Bova et al. (2008) reported the results of their Positive Life Skills Workshop project which they conducted over six years with 187 HIV infected women in the age group of 23–62 years. Women worked weekly in small groups for 10 consecutive weeks on changing their cognitive appraisal of the stressors linked with their illness by exploring the power of art, science and alternative medicine in reframing the meaning of HIV in their lives. Even though the authors claim that the workshops were effective in increasing anti-retroviral drug adherence and improving mental well-being and reducing stress, it is difficult to understand what the dynamics were in the groups and what elements of the skills were the most effective in influencing this change.

Kennedy et al. (2005) examined the effects of a Coping Effectiveness Training (CET) based on Lazarus and Folkman's theory in people with spinal cord injury and did find positive effects in the sense that appraisal and coping skills were enhanced. However, they concluded that this training could be maximized by reducing the time between the onset of the spinal cord injury and the start of the intervention.

In sum, stress-management techniques have been offered and researched in many different forms, with various time scales and a range of diverse outcome measures. Studies comparing western and 'eastern' forms have found similar outcomes. For example, Baum et al. (1995) reviewed studies on stress-management techniques, such as CBSM, biofeedback, relaxation, guided imagery, and hypnosis on immune function and concluded that the application of all these techniques offered constructive coping styles and had promising results on chronic diseases and quality of life. Irinson et al. (2002) also reviewed stress-management methods such as CBSM, relaxation, exercise and massage, and argued that these had a buffering or positive effect on the quality of life of HIV and AIDS suffers at various stages of their disease, with positive effects on their endocrine and immune system.

The main differences between certain eastern and western forms of stress management are to be found in the way in which these methods and skills are embedded within one's daily life. In certain eastern cultures meditation and doing one's tai chi or yoga exercises are not part of a separate class which is only practised at certain hours of the week for a set length of time. On the contrary, these are entangled within one's philosophy, value system and as such part are of one's daily life. Whether the gap in values and life philosophies is an obstacle in the effects of stress-management techniques in the longer term is hard to say. Most studies examining these effects are short lived. Using patient groups exploring these effects in longitudinal studies would deepen the understanding of the differences between the practices from the East and West. Health psychologists could play a role in this.

Summary and moving forward

The majority of the complementary practices have their origin in 'eastern civilizations'. Chun et al. (2006) argue that culture is missing in most stress models. Some models do incorporate the variable 'culture' (e.g. Moos, 2002) but the other variables in the model are still based on western operationalizations of stress, coping and illness. Culture in the understanding of the shared meaning of norms, beliefs and values could be grounded in these models and infiltrated throughout their constructs, but cannot be expressed by a single variable in the model named 'culture'.

The western models of stress, coping and illness have been criticized for being too compartmental and losing sight of the overall picture. The context is mostly not taken into account and since the majority of psychological models are developed and tested in western cultures, these seem not applicable in non-western cultures or for people with self-acquired or socialized non-western belief systems residing in the western world. Simply including spirituality, religion or alternative healing practices as separate variables into these models, as a way of coping or as an independent factor, does not seem to work. The norms, values and practices attached to these are too fundamentally embedded in the way people experience life, stress, coping, and illness that it will miss the most important aspects.

There is a need for elucidating belief systems regarding values related to stress and coping, such as about life and death, sickness and health, living for oneself or others, and work and leisure. Also, 'contemplation in tranquillity' as an appraisal and coping strategy of stress in certain eastern cultures, could be explored further in order to enhance our understanding of stress transformation rather than stress reduction as a new way of dealing with stress in western cultures. The belief systems mostly incorporated in stress research are religion or spirituality, but then as separate variables related to coping or social support, and not as a meta-cognition in a trans-disciplinary conceptional framework as proposed by Garland (2007), which reinforces coping processes in a way similar to 'eastern' practices of positive reappraisal, justifying catastrophe and stimulating self-transcendence. Analogous with this, Jing (2007) coping scale also looked at the effects of contemplation of stressors in relation to eastern belief systems such as optimism in adversity, viewpoints to faith, or responsibility as human beings. Interestingly, scientific rather than humanistic or religious beliefs have not been found in any of the stress studies discussed in this chapter. Exploration of these newer scientific understandings of connectivity between people and the universe such as based on quantum mechanics and the connectivity hypothesis of Laszlo on the stress and illness process would be another interesting step forward.

It seems that both Antonovsky's (1993) Sense of Coherence concept and Kobasa's (1979) hardiness personality style reflect the 'eastern' ways of dealing with stress the best. However, that studies showed different results for males and females in that Sense of Coherence seems to be important in the stress and illness process for women but not for men, and vice versa for hardiness, is not easy to understand, and it would be interesting to explore this further in relation to complementary therapies.

That a positive outlook on life, in the sense of optimism, low negative affectivity, and use of humour was consistently associated with less reported illness and or a better immune profile when under stress, should also not be ignored for future studies. Wong and Wong (2006) and Schwartzer and Knoll (2003) suggested that proactive coping should get more attention in the sense of building up personal resources such as competencies, skills, self-efficacy and optimistic beliefs. There could be an important role for health psychologists in developing these skills programmes and to apply and evaluate these, in addition to the stress-management initiatives reported in this chapter.

Psychoneuroimmunology is a fascinating new area for health psychology, and including immune measures in research on stress and illness could progress our knowledge and understanding in this field. Including stress management as a practical element in health psychology in action is another way forward. Not only will the acquirement of stress-management techniques applied in psychology for decennia, advance the opportunities for professional training in health psychology, but studying imported 'eastern' practices such as mindfulness, yoga and tai chi will also offer a new area of research in need for further exploration in the stress and illness process. In particular, qualitative research exploring value systems and the meaning of appraisals and coping mechanisms could be a significant addition to the current understandings of the stress–illness process as described in this chapter.

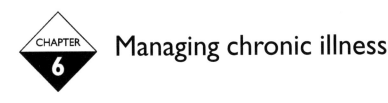 Managing chronic illness

Chronic disease means living with illness in a world of health.
(Radley, 1994, p. 139)

Introduction

Improvements in public health and medicine in developed countries have increased longevity but also created new challenges in managing the concomitant rise of chronic illnesses such as cancer, heart disease, stroke, HIV/AIDS and diabetes. Data from household surveys in England in 2001 and 2002 show that 60% of the adult population have chronic health problems (Wilson et al., 2005). Other estimates are somewhat lower, depending on how chronic illness is defined; most definitions are based on timescale (e.g. exceeding three or, most commonly, six months), rather than symptom management (not curable) or disability. The World Health Organization (2003) predict that chronic disease will be the main cause of disability by 2020.

This has significant implications for the provision of health care and the relationship between allopathic and complementary medicine. Chronic illness presents particular challenges to the biomedical model; the needs of those with chronic illness are complex and difficult to treat within an interventionist model. The pluralistic model of health seeking frequently adopted by those with chronic conditions is one consequence of this tension between patient needs and health care provision. However, it is widely recognized by both allopathic and complementary medicine that complex interventions[1] are more effective than simpler ones and that the engagement of the patient is crucial in long-term management of chronic complaints. This suggests that the area of chronic illness provides the most potential for dialogue between allopathic and complementary health care.

The impact of chronic illness and psychological approaches to adjustment

People with long-term conditions are significantly more likely to visit their GP and use inpatient health services (Wilson et al., 2005). Moreover, health care utilization increases alongside the number of problems reported, particularly among older people (Wilson et al., 2005). Use of CAM is also much higher among people suffering from chronic illnesses, particularly those with difficult-to-treat complaints (Vincent and Furnham, 1996; Kelner and Wellman, 1997; Eisenberg et al., 1998). Additionally CAM is frequently used to aid the management of side effects of conventional treatments for conditions such as HIV/AIDS (Pawluch et al., 2000) and cancer (Lewith, 1996).

The impact of chronic illness on the individual, their family and the health care system is complex and multi-faceted, and changes over the course of the illness. Although variable, most chronic illnesses require adjustments in lifestyle, restrictions in daily activities and some level of pain and disability, in addition to adjustment to a chronic-disease label and loss of 'health'. Treatment usually entails long-term medication since chronic conditions, by definition, cannot be cured. Research with a variety of chronic conditions indicates that patients are concerned about the effects of taking long-term medication (Donovan and Blake, 1992; Britten, 1994; Horne et al., 1999) and often adjust their medication to fit in with their own beliefs about their condition or to assume control over their health (Conrad, 1985). Not surprisingly then, chronic illness can have serious psychological consequences with higher rates of anxiety and depression among the chronically ill compared with the 'normal' population, particularly when pain and disability are experienced (Prince et al., 1998; Vilhjalmsson, 1998) and when more time is spent living with illness (Schnittker, 2005). Moreover, patients may experience depressive symptoms at sub-clinical levels; such negative affect has serious ramifications for adjustment and self-management of a chronic condition and yet may remain undetected (Sharpe and Curran, 2006).

Chronic illness encompasses a heterogeneous cluster of conditions, which vary considerably in their seriousness, disease course (e.g. progressive vs. stable), degree of incapacitation, level of life threat, and invasiveness of treatment regimen. Thus the impact on the individual's daily life will vary enormously. Similarly, as seen in Chapter 5 (stress, coping and stress self-management) individuals vary in both the internal and external resources which facilitate adjustment to long-term illness. While the majority of patients are able to adapt positively to chronic conditions, a minority demonstrate adjustment difficulties (Stanton and Revenson, 2005). Failure to adjust to illness may not only result in psychological difficulties but also negatively impact on ability to manage the condition, which can result in medical complications. Poor psychosocial adjustment to a chronic condition is also associated with higher use of health care services (Browne et al., 1994; Watt et al., 1997).

Individual variation in the physical and psychological consequences of long-term illness can only partially be explained by differences in disease severity. Numerous other psychosocial factors influence how well an individual adjusts to their condition, for example, social support, perceptions of control and coping styles (see Chapter 5). The decision to use CAM is one such coping response which is likely to interact with these psychosocial variables, as discussed in Chapter 1. Although evidence for the efficacy of CAM for chronic complaints is mixed, there is substantial evidence that CAM makes people 'feel better' and helps adjustment to illness (Luff and Thomas, 2000; Thorne et al., 2002; Paterson, 2004; Verhoef et al., 2005). Much of the psychological literature has focused on the factors associated with adjustment in order to facilitate positive adaptation to chronic illness, improve quality of life, and reduce the incidence of physical and psychological impairment.

Within health psychology, particular attention has been placed on people's perceptions of their illness, since health professionals can modify beliefs in order to maximize positive adjustment or to improve the circumstances of those with adjustment difficulties. Additionally, this may be one mechanism through which complementary therapies may be effective in changing people's beliefs about their illness. Two particular psychological models relevant to chronic illness will be explored here: attribution theory and the self-regulatory model of adjustment. However, the role of illness narratives, as discussed in Chapter 3, is also particularly salient to the understanding of meaning in long-term illness and demonstrates the importance of broadening the approach of health psychology. Stam (2000) cautions against an uncritical stance towards constructs such as 'adjustment' and argues that we must negotiate their meaning together with those affected in order to develop interventions that reflect patients' needs and which facilitate empowerment.

Causal attributions

In order to make sense of chronic illness, people seek to understand why they have developed a particular complaint. According to attribution theory, by identifying causal explanations for events such as illness, we make our world more predictable, stable and controllable (Weiner, 1982). In the health context, the link between causal attributions and adjustment is of particular interest. It has been suggested that patients with causal explanations have better outcomes although the relationship between specific causal attributions and adjustment is somewhat equivocal (Turnquist et al., 1988). In a meta-analysis, Roesch and Weiner (2001) found that the direct effect of attributions on adjustment is actually relatively small, but that they also demonstrate an indirect relationship with outcomes via coping. Evidence suggests that controllability is a key feature underlying the relationship between attributions and outcomes.

The belief that one is able to control the course of one's illness has been associated with cognitive adaptation and psychological well-being, providing that this is not undermined by the physical realities of the disease (Taylor et al., 1984; Thompson et al., 1998). In contrast, blaming others is consistently associated with maladaptive outcomes (Taylor et al., 1984; Affleck et al., 1987). However, there are mixed findings regarding the relationship between self-blame and adjustment, with some studies finding a positive relationship (Tennen et al., 1984), others a negative relationship (Schiaffino et al., 1998; Glinder and Compas, 1999). This is likely to reflect the distinction between behavioural (modifiable) and characterological (non-modifiable) blame (Tennen et al., 1986), or more precisely, whether taking responsibility for the cause of one's condition enables control over the future course of the illness. This is well illustrated in a qualitative study in which MI patients were interviewed shortly after their myocardial infarction (French et al., 2005). It was found that participants attempted to avoid blame for their MI while seeking control over the future course of their illness; for example, the popular attribution of stress was seen as unavoidable prior to the MI but something that could be controlled in the future. Additionally, attributions focused on reasons for the acute trigger of MI rather than chronic causal factors, which contrasts with the approach adopted by health professionals.

Indeed, evidence suggests that there are considerable discrepancies between the attributions of patients and health professionals. For example, in interviews with patients with Type I diabetes and health professionals, Cohen et al. (1994) found that health professionals focused on the biomedical factors associated with diabetes, whereas patients focused on more personal causal factors occurring around the time of diagnosis. Health professionals were unaware of patients' attributions. As discussed in Chapter 1, belief congruency is often cited as a key factor underlying decisions to use CAM. Several studies have shown that patients with chronic illness feel disbelieved by health professionals as well as having their own theories of their illness ridiculed (Thorne et al., 2000; Whitehead, 2006). Additionally, patients frequently report that explanations provided by conventional medicine are inadequate, and they are attracted to the in-depth and holistic attention to psychosocial causes and solutions provided by CAM.

Self-regulation model

Leventhal and colleagues (Leventhal et al., 1980, 1984; Leventhal and Diefenbach, 1991) have explored a wider range of illness cognitions or 'common sense beliefs' about specific illness episodes. The self-regulation model suggests that the content of an illness representation shapes the individual's choice of coping strategy and appraisal of its outcome. Evidence suggests that when people are diagnosed with a chronic illness, they initially employ an acute model of illness consistent with previous illness experiences, but this shifts to a chronic model over time (Meyer et al., 1985; Leventhal, 1986). The model proposes at least two 'partially independent processing systems' which operate when people respond to health threats: cognitive and emotional regulatory systems. The former represents the 'psychologically objective' representation of the health threat and the development of a coping plan to deal with the perceived threat. Emotional regulation represents the 'psychologically subjective' processing system, which involves the emotional response to the threat and the coping plan devised to manage this emotional reaction and the cognitions specific to it. The existence of two distinct regulatory systems is consistent with the coping literature which distinguishes between problem-focused and emotion-focused strategies (Folkman and Lazarus, 1980).

Research with a variety of chronic illnesses has demonstrated significant relationships between illness perceptions, coping and health outcomes (for a review, see Hagger and Orbell, 2003). Whereas beliefs in a strong illness identity and severe consequences are associated with avoidance and emotion-focused coping strategies, beliefs about cure/control are consistently associated with the more adaptive active problem-focused coping strategies (Moss-Morris et al., 1996; Heijmans, 1998, 1999; Sharloo et al., 1998). Similarly, perceptions of a strong identity, severe consequences and chronic timeline are consistently associated with negative health outcomes in both cross-sectional and prospective studies (Moss-Morris et al., 1996; Heijmans, 1998, 1999; Sharloo et al., 1998; Cartwright et al., 2009). Interventions based on the self-regulation model, particularly in patients with myocardial infarction, have been successful in changing patients' views of their illness and facilitating recovery (Petrie et al., 2002).

This raises some interesting questions regarding potential processes operating in CAM consultations. The decision to use CAM may be one of a range of coping strategies utilized by an individual with chronic illness to deal with either (or both) the cognitive (e.g. explanation) or emotional (e.g. reassurance) dimensions of their illness. Several factors common to most complementary therapies, such as the longer patient-centred consultation, attention to patient history and holistic explanation, suggest that patients' illness representations are more likely to be addressed within the complementary medicine framework. Research in this area is still limited; prospective studies are needed to examine changes in perceptions over time and to assess whether CAM acts as an 'intervention' to change people's maladaptive beliefs about their illness and promote a more positive view of one's illness and coping resources.

Psychological interventions have tended to focus on three main areas in treating chronic illness (Petrie and Revenson, 2005). First, multi-modal interventions to aid adjustment and management of illness by providing training in areas such as pain management, stress management, coping skills, and communication skills. Second, interventions such as biofeedback which aim to treat the physiological effects of disease by reducing or controlling symptoms. Third, the provision of adjunctive care and techniques to cope with unpleasant medical treatments, particularly in the case of cancer (Anderson, 2002). The extent to which CAM may incorporate such techniques will be considered in this chapter.

The challenges of managing chronic illness

Chronically ill persons frequently experience a crumbling away of their former self images without simultaneous development of equally valued new ones.

(Charmaz, 1983, p. 168)

Chronic illness has physical, social, and emotional consequences for the individual, making it difficult to provide a comprehensive care package which addresses all these needs. Moreover, chronic illness is incompatible with the traditional biomedical focus on disease, cure and medical control: 'When an illness is chronic, the medical system has inherently failed in its socially ascribed promise to cure disease' (Thorne et al., 2000, p. 303). The response to chronic illness has been criticized for being 'narrow and paternalistic', dominated by the scientific model and the discourse of individualism (Wellard, 1998; Prilleltensky and Prilleltensky, 2003). The focus on 'normalization' and independence means that those with illness are compared with the 'normal' healthy population, while treatment focuses on a return to 'normal' functioning and physical independence. Wellard argues that this approach 'fails to acknowledge a reality beyond the physical body of chronically ill people for whom cure is not attainable' (1998, p. 50).

Current strategies for managing chronic illness emphasize the importance of individualized collaborative care which is patient centred and serves to engage patients and their families (Von Korff et al., 2002). While such 'holistic' care is integral to most complementary health care, Campbell and McGauley (2005) argue that doctors may be ill-prepared to engage in the psycho-emotional experiences of patients, while differences between multi-disciplinary team members have the potential to disrupt continuity of care (van Wersch, Bonnema et al., 1997; van Wersch, de Boer et al., 1997). Similarly, Thorne et al. (2000) highlight the contradictions in traditional assumptions about health care relationships caused by chronic illness, with the focus on patient (vs. professional) expertise, long-term outcomes, and the inherent incompatibility of notions of compliance and self-reliance.

Such tensions are also evident in evaluations of the Expert Patient Programme (EPP), a critical part of the support package for self-care of chronic complaints, as favoured by current health policy. The programme, based on self-efficacy theory, consists of six weekly sessions run by an 'expert patient'. The discourse of empowerment is central to such programmes, which aim to facilitate patients' self-management of their condition. The EPP could therefore be seen as a bridge between traditional biomedical approaches and complementary medicine. Several criticisms have, however, been levelled at the EPP, both in terms of its effectiveness and its realization of the goals of patient empowerment. Evaluations have shown only modest psychological improvements, with the suggestion that a generic course fails to address patient variability and condition-specific needs (Kennedy et al., 2007). There is also considerable debate over the extent to which programmes founded on the biomedical paradigm are able to empower the patient (Wilson, 2001; Davidson, 2005). In a qualitative study, Wilson et al. (2007) identified 'a paradox of patient empowerment and medical dominance'; on the one hand the course structure reinforced the medical paradigm, but on the other, it supported the subjective experience of living with long-term illness. Indeed, this appears to reflect a wider tension between the new discourse of 'agentic patient' and existing biomedical discourses (Salmon and Hall, 2003). Moreover programmes such as the EPP must be considered within the wider context of the illness experience. For example, Wilson et al. (2007) found that patients felt more confident in communicating with health professionals following EPP but that their expertise was devalued by doctors.

This has several implications for both conventional and complementary health care. Clearly, more people with long-term illness are actively electing to use CAM outside of their standard treatment package, suggesting that this is meeting an unmet health need. Is this incompatibility with biomedical assumptions a reason why people are turning to CAM for a more individualized and contextual approach? There is evidence that CAM has wider 'whole-person' and transformational effects that extend beyond the limited scope of illness (Paterson and Britten, 2003; Verhoef et al., 2005). Additionally, many areas of chronic health care are including complementary therapies as an integral part of treatment in recognition of the limitations of the biomedical approach (e.g. in pain clinics and cancer care). It also raises questions for health psychologists regarding how we measure outcomes and whether we are truly representing the voices of the patients themselves or continuing to apply biomedical assumptions regarding the importance of 'objective' indices of health outcomes.

One of the key psychological consequences of chronic illness is a 'loss of self' or a threat to people's sense of identity as one is forced to modify the self-concept to incorporate the label of illness (Charmaz, 1983; Frank, 1991, 1995; Whitehead, 2006). This can lead to social isolation and separation, with further consequences for the self, as reflected in Frank's (1991, 1995) chaos narrative (see Chapter 3). Chronic illness might therefore be viewed as a 'psychosocial construction' which entails biographical disruption and role changes (Bury, 1982; Williams, 1984; Thorne, 1999); a reinterpretation of circumstances and understanding of causal events is necessary in order to regain a coherent sense of self. 'Narrativising the chronic illness within the framework of one's own life history makes it possible to give meaning to events that have disrupted and changed the course of one's life' (Whitehead, 2006, p. 1024), which Frank (1991, 1995) named the Quest narrative. Within the framework of Leventhal's self-regulation model, it is argued that the development of illness representations is driven by the need to regulate the self and maintain equilibrium. Successful adjustment therefore requires an adjustment of the self-representation to accommodate the illness representation (Brownlee et al., 2000).

In a phenomenological study, Aujoulat et al. (2008) found that empowerment in chronic illness was a *process* of transformation which reflected both a 'holding-on' to pre-illness self-representations, and a 'letting-go' or acceptance that not everything is controllable. The former enabled a differentiation of self from illness, whereas the latter process was associated with a sense of coherence and meaning in life. It is hardly surprising, given the personal nature of such narratives, that lay and clinical perspectives are frequently at odds with each other, causing communication difficulties and lay–professional conflict (Kleinman, 1980; Whitehead, 2006). It has been suggested that health professionals can facilitate the process of empowerment through the use of patient narratives to integrate medical explanations within a more meaningful biographical context (Kleinman, 1988; Aujoulat et al., 2008). The extent to which such narratives are employed in CAM consultations deserves further exploration.

Of course, the 'burden of illness' is not restricted only to the individual, but rather impacts on the family as whole (Bury, 1982; Thorne, 1999). This may affect family dynamics as well as necessitating lifestyle changes. For example, spouses may have to adopt roles previously assumed by the 'sick person' as well as dealing with difficulties faced by those in the sick role. While this may negatively impact on relationships, there is also evidence that serious, particularly life-threatening illness can have a positive impact on relationships and overall life view, for example through a re-evaluation of what is important in life (Sodergren et al., 2002; Danoff-Burg and Revenson, 2005). Additionally, Sodergren et al. (2002) suggest that positivity can be facilitated by rehabilitation. Several qualitative studies suggest that using CAM may be part of this re-evaluation process leading to changes not only in perceptions of illness but also to changes in personal and social identity (Cassidy, 1998; Paterson and Britten, 2003; Cartwright and Torr, 2005; Verhoef et al., 2005).

Coping with complex treatment regimens is one of the key difficulties faced by people with long-term conditions. Adherence rates are notoriously low for chronic illnesses; it is estimated that 50–70% of patients do not take their medication as prescribed (Wertheimer and Santella, 2003), with potentially serious consequences for health and an increased risk of complications (Simpson et al., 2006). While perceptions of treatment effectiveness and necessity are significant predictors of medication adherence (Hampson,

1997; Horne, 1999), the absence of such beliefs are important precursors to seeking CAM. Decisions to seek CAM treatments may in part reflect people's concerns about the toxic nature of medication, but are frequently also a means to help patients to cope with the iatrogenic effects of conventional care.

It can be seen that chronic illness presents various challenges for conventional medicine, both conceptually and practically, in terms of the complexity of the health care needs of those with long-term illness. Greater attention to patient empowerment and involvement in health care suggests a compatibility between conventional and complementary approaches, although there is clearly some way to go. The health care needs of those with chronic complaints are not currently being met within the orthodox system, hence the increasing numbers turning to CAM, often at personal cost. It is necessary, therefore to consider (a) the extent to which CAM is meeting those needs and expectations, and (b) the issues surrounding the integration of conventional and complementary medicine.

Optimal care: the role of complementary medicine

Research considered earlier suggests that psychosocial adjustment to and attitudes towards illness are more important determinants of outcomes (health care utilization, functioning and well-being) than illness severity. Successful interventions that address issues of adjustment and empowerment as well as the physical consequences of chronic illness are therefore most likely to have the broadest impact. It has been suggested that CAM is a complex intervention which addresses the health care needs of patients that are not met by conventional care (Paterson, 2004). Clearly, there are differing perspectives as regards successful treatment outcomes and the evidence required to demonstrate effectiveness. While the biomedical perspective primarily focuses on treatment efficacy demonstrated through Randomized Controlled Trials, patients are more concerned with the personal impact of treatment on symptoms, quality of life and well-being (Thorne et al., 2002; Kelner and Wellman, 2003). Since it is beyond the scope of this chapter to review the efficacy of complementary therapies for the treatment of specific disorders, the aim is to explore key areas in which CAM is seen to aid adjustment to long-term or chronic illness, particularly drawing on research that explores the patient's perspective.

One of the most important outcomes for both patients and health professionals alike, is the reduction of symptoms or improvement of the primary condition. A qualitative study with older people using CAM for chronic complaints found that symptom/pain relief and improvements in mobility were the primary outcomes valued by patients, despite the fact that such improvements were generally short term (Cartwright, 2007). Temporary relief from pain and other symptoms enables people to regain some sense of normalcy and to participate in everyday activities. This engagement has been shown to relate to better adjustment and a more coherent sense of self (Bryant et al., 2001; Borglin et al., 2005). The majority of people using CAM for chronic conditions use it in tandem with conventional medicine, and it therefore represents an additional means of effectively managing one's condition particularly in the context of limited conventional treatment options (Thorne et al., 2002).

Another key facet of adjustment is learning to cope with the consequences of long-term illness, both in terms of regulation of the self-concept and more pragmatically with respect to treatment regimes and lifestyle changes. Qualitative research looking at the experiences of using CAM suggests that the treatment process may enhance an individual's coping resources, enabling them to either reinterpret potentially stressful circumstances or deal with difficulties in a more adaptive manner, factors that can strongly impact on well-being (Cassidy, 1998; Cartwright and Torr, 2005; Verhoef et al., 2005). As described in Chapter 5, Lazarus and Folkman (1984) stated that coping behaviour is made up of primary and secondary appraisal, in which the individual evaluates the threat and considers the availability of coping resources. Treatment can facilitate adaptation on both levels, through reappraisal (e.g. viewing one's illness in a more positive light) and expansion of coping resources (e.g. support, advice and increased energy). Mind/body therapies in particular may improve emotional well-being by facilitating positive emotions such as optimism and encouraging a sense of purpose (Verhoef et al., 2005). Such factors have been associated with psychological resilience and adaptive coping. While there is a considerable body of research into the positive health effects of resilience (e.g. Fredrickson, 2005), this has not been explored in relation to treatment effects, but suggests another interesting avenue for future research.

One particular strategy of self-management given much attention within health psychology is having a sense of control either over one's illness or the treatment process. Studies within CAM suggest that users report learning to listen to their own body and take responsibility for their own health, strategies also promoted within conventional medicine (Luff and Thomas, 2000; Pawluch et al., 2000; Gould and MacPherson, 2001; Thorne et al., 2002). In Thorne et al.'s (2002) study, this was associated with an increased sense of power and reduction in reliance on health care providers. Indeed, several studies indicate that patients feel empowered through the use of CAM, which is frequently contrasted with the paternalistic experiences of conventional medicine (Conway and Hockey, 1998; Andrews, 2002; Cartwright, 2007). Additionally, the active decision to use CAM may be empowering in and of itself, irrespective of the actual treatment. However, there remains much to learn about the impact of treatment that empowers the patient and the extent to which it facilitates behaviour change through patient engagement and increased self-efficacy. These are issues that are of great interest to both complementary and conventional practitioners and require longitudinal studies to explore the relationships between patients' beliefs, treatment experiences and outcomes.

Given the challenges of managing chronic illness, and the limitations of conventional care in treating the multiple demands faced by sufferers, CAM may be one measure taken by both patients and health care providers to maximize health and quality of life. Many patients are also concerned about the consequences of conventional treatment, ranging from worries about the effects of long-term medication, to the physical and psychological effects of aggressive treatments such as chemotherapy. Certainly, patients would prefer to take as little medication as possible (Pound et al., 2005) and frequently turn to CAM as a means to reduce medication (Sharma, 1992; Cassidy, 1998; Richardson, 2004). It has therefore been suggested that integrated medicine is the way forward in the treatment of chronic conditions in order to effectively bring together the strengths of both conventional and complementary medicine (Vickers, 2000; Rees, 2001; White, 2003). The Consortium of Academic Health Centers for Integrative Medicine has defined integrative medicine as 'the practice of medicine that reaffirms the importance of the relationship between practitioner and patient, focuses on the whole person, is informed by evidence, and makes use of all appropriate therapeutic approaches, healthcare professionals and disciplines to achieve optimal health and healing' (2004). In an editorial in the *British Medical Journal*, Rees argues that integrated medicine 'is about restoring core values which have been eroded by social and economic forces' (2001, p. 120). Integration is more prevalent in areas of health care which support multidisciplinary care, such as pain clinics and oncology, where conventional treatments alone are limited in scope.

Cancer care

The role of CAM as a treatment for cancer patients is particularly relevant since the shock of diagnosis, life-threatening nature of cancer, and unpleasant side-effects of treatment inevitably impact on physical and psychological health and well-being. Fatigue, nausea, pain, anxiety, depression, and sleep disturbance are all common symptoms experienced by cancer patients (Fallowfield, 1990; Ashbury et al., 1998). CAM use among cancer patients is therefore particularly prevalent, almost invariably in conjunction with or subsequent to conventional treatment. A systematic review across 13 countries indicated that over 30% of adult cancer patients use CAM, although there were large differences across studies (range 7%–64%) (Ernst and Cassileth, 1998). The motivations underlying recourse to CAM generally reflect the wish to maximize quality of life and regain some control over their lives (Truant and Bottorff, 1999; Boon et al., 2000), rather than a sense of dissatisfaction with conventional treatments (Balneaves et al., 1999).

Integrated cancer care that incorporates complementary therapies is increasingly common in the UK and elsewhere. A survey in England and Wales found that 70% of oncology centres provided access to some form of CAM (White, 1998). This appears to reflect the greater congruency in approach between conventional and complementary medicine within cancer care and the recognition that patient-centred outcomes, such as quality of life and well-being are of paramount importance. Additionally the palliative care movement in the latter part of the 20th century paved the way for a more integrative approach that recognizes the broader needs of those suffering from cancer. Pioneered by Dame Cecily Saunders, it sought to improve the quality of care for people with cancer, promoting holistic care that addressed the physical, psycho-emotional and spiritual needs of those with advanced, progressive illness. This concept of 'total care' is congruent with the current discourse of 'supportive care', which seeks to empower people with cancer and enable them to live as well as possible with the disease. This was a fundamental premise of the NHS cancer plan in 2000 and complementary therapies were designated as one of 11 components of this supportive care model (Tavares, 2003). National guidelines on best practice have also been developed by the National Council for Hospice and Specialist Care Services and the Prince of Wales Foundation for Integrated Health (Tavares, 2003). These guidelines acknowledge the limitations of allopathic medicine in addressing the wide-ranging consequences of cancer, while recognizing the widespread use of CAM by people with cancer.

Given this combination of factors, attitudes towards CAM are more favourable among oncologists compared with specialists in other areas (Bourgeault, 1996; Lewith et al., 2001), although there remain concerns that patients will reject conventional treatments in favour of untested cancer cures. Despite the emphasis on evidence-based medicine, it is acknowledged that 'we still only have a partial understanding of how effective complementary medicine may be in the management of cancer' (Lewith, 1996, p. 245). This is echoed in several reviews of common therapies used to treat cancer, most commonly acupuncture, dietary supplements, herbal medicine and supportive therapies such as relaxation (Lewith, 1996; Ernst, 2000; Ernst and Stevinson, 2004). Interestingly, the NICE manual for guidance on cancer services acknowledges that while 'evidence is not as rigorous as might be desired . . . the fact that these therapies are already in wide and effective use in the NHS and voluntary sector may be taken as a significant indication of their value' (NICE, 2004, p. 151).

There is, however, substantial evidence for the effectiveness of acupuncture and hypnotherapy for pain relief and reduction of nausea, and relaxation techniques for reducing pain, anxiety and stress (Lewith, 1996; Ernst, 2000; Weiger et al., 2002). Indeed, consensus statements have been issued by the National Institutes of Health in the USA supporting the use of acupuncture for pain and nausea, and hypnosis for pain relief (Vickers, 2000). Aromatherapy is frequently provided as part of the palliative care package, and massage is reputedly one of the most commonly used complementary therapies used within the NHS (Trevelyan, 1996). Despite its popularity within conventional medicine, systematic evidence is limited although descriptive studies suggest that it can alleviate symptoms, increase relaxation, and improve sleep (Fellowes et al., 2004). Inevitably however, there is some question whether the 'feel good' effect of such treatments is enough evidence to provide complementary treatments as routine practice.

The majority of CAM treatments are used as part of the supportive care package for patients rather than as 'cancer cures'. Studies suggest that patients typically seek CAM in order to maximize quality of life, manage pain and other symptoms, and improve emotional well-being (Corner and Harewood, 2004; Scott et al., 2005). However, surveys suggest that a small percentage of patients have unrealistic expectations that CAM will cure their cancer (Richardson et al., 2000; Lewith et al., 2002), with potentially negative consequences for subsequent well-being. We know rather less about those who eschew allopathic treatments in favour of CAM since the majority of studies are based on clinical samples. Other attractive elements of CAM include the opportunity to exert some control over their illness and treatment, and also to negotiate a more active position in their health care (Bishop and Yardley, 2004). The empowerment of patients may be particularly important in cancer care where patients can feel dehumanized by invasive allopathic treatments. A reduction in distress may therefore reflect several pathways, including a reduction of symptoms, enhanced coping skills, perceptions of control and hope, suggesting that CAM meets important psychological needs in patients with cancer.

Overall, research shows that complementary therapies can serve a beneficial function for cancer patients, particularly in terms of controlling pain and nausea, reducing distress, and improving well-being. However, people with cancer are also a vulnerable group facing a life-threatening condition. It is therefore important that patients are encouraged to have realistic expectations about treatment and understand the potential benefits and safety risks of various therapies, particularly when both CAM and conventional treatments are used in conjunction with each other. Such support is essential to enable informed decision making regarding possible treatment options. Indeed, this is a strong argument for integrated cancer care, enabling regulation of practitioners and communication between allopathic and CAM practitioners. More broadly, integrated care enables 'a far more patient-centred and holistic treatment protocol in which the patient rather than the illness or the medical practitioner becomes the central focus of treatment' (Lewith, 1996, p. 245). Evidence from psychoneuroimmunology suggests that holistic psychosocial interventions not only improve quality of life, but also have the potential to prolong survival in cancer (Spiegel et al., 1989). Clearly such findings warrant further systematic investigation.

Implications for research and practice

"Western medicine is often viewed as having a mechanistic-reductionist approach, where it may be logical to try to extract component effects. In contrast, complementary therapies generally take a holistic and functional view, where the diagnostic process, the therapy, the therapist and patient all interact to achieve the desired outcome" (Hilsden and Verhoef, 1999, p. 104). Here lies a fundamental difference in the perspectives of allopathic and complementary medicine. In the former, the focus on evidence-based medicine gives greatest credibility to efficacy studies assessing the specific effects of treatments within a controlled but artificial setting. For patients and many CAM practitioners, the focus is rather on total treatment and synergistic effects and assessment of wider benefits on a range of psychosocial outcomes. Difficulties in the evaluation of treatment effects are certainly not unique to CAM, but rather apply to all 'complex interventions which are made up of various interconnecting parts' (Campbell et al., 2000, p. 694).

Chronic illness is a particularly interesting case, since the focus of treatment is primarily on the management of illness, alleviation of symptoms (especially pain) and reduction of disability, rather than cure. This requires a holistic package of care which passes control over to the patient to facilitate effective management of their condition. From a research perspective, it suggests the importance of a variety of research methods to address each world-view, including qualitative research to gain an 'insider's perspective' in order to understand patients' subjective experiences of treatment. While researchers and clinicians have traditionally focused on 'hard' objective outcome measures, there has been a shift towards patient-centred measures, such as quality of life and well-being in recent years, although they remain underused in clinical trials (Higginson and Carr, 2001).

The current focus within conventional chronic care on the 'expert patient' and patient-led care is congruent with a 'bottom-up' approach which encourages those experiencing and managing long-term illness to identify salient outcomes. Thorne (1999, p. 399) argues that

> the knowledge forms we legitimise within the health sciences have made it difficult to rationalize meaning as relevant and important . . . if we can isolate and interpret the meanings that are commonly shared, we can better understand and help other people as they strive to find meaning in their own illness experiences.

Additionally, the meaning of illness is inexorably shaped by the wider socio-cultural environment. It has been suggested that outcome measures need to be more inclusive to account for the patient experience, since they 'may inadequately reflect the whole experience of the patient' (Gould and MacPherson, 2001, p. 262). For example, in a qualitative study comparing several patient-centred measures, Paterson and Britten (2003) found that they were limited in their capacity to record the diversity of experience reported by participants. In addition to ceiling effects, the measures failed to assess changes in energy/tiredness (a key outcome for patients) and changes in self/social identity. Mixed-methods designs are interesting in revealing difficulties in assessing change using purely quantitative methods; for example an RCT of a mind/body intervention for people with HIV/AIDS showed an increase in stressors following the intervention and minimal improvement in quality of life, but an embedded qualitative dimension revealed a personal growth process towards well-being, although this was not always a comfortable process (Brazier et al., 2006).

Health psychologists therefore play a crucial role in developing methods that capture meaningful outcomes for people with chronic illness and which are in line with participatory approaches to treatment and research. Such methods are relevant to the evaluation of both allopathic and complementary medicine. Additionally, recent interest in the positive effects of illness, together with the popularity of positive psychology suggest the importance of measuring well-being and transformative change. The importance of long-term follow-up must also be considered in research designs for long-term illness where successful adaptation may be a gradual process; a recent RCT of acupuncture for lower back pain showed a greater positive effect at 24- versus 12-month evaluation (Thomas et al., 2006).

From an integration perspective, evidence of the cost effectiveness of treatment is also of primary concern and yet remains relatively undocumented. An evaluation comparing the costs of a short course of acupuncture with improvements in QALYs (quality-adjusted life years) suggested that acupuncture is a cost-effective treatment for lower back pain (Ratcliffe, et al., 2006). Additionally, costs may be reduced indirectly through reductions in care seeking and medication usage. Of particular interest to health psychologists is the role of CAM in instigating lifestyle changes that are frequently central to treatment regimens for chronic conditions such as diabetes and coronary heart disease. Descriptive evidence suggests that users of CAM are more likely to adopt healthier lifestyle practices (Gould and MacPherson, 2001), although this may simply be a function of those who seek out CAM being more orientated towards preventative health behaviour. There is certainly a need to systematically examine the evidence for positive lifestyle changes arising from specific treatments, in addition to the processes underlying such improvements, essentially the cornerstone of health psychology.

Summary

Research indicates that people with chronic disease take a pragmatic approach to their health care, using both conventional and complementary treatments to meet their needs. Patients appear able to reconcile differences in worldviews and approaches to illness between the two approaches, since each provides support for different aspects of the condition. Many patients are willing to pay considerable sums for complementary health care in the hope that it will ameliorate their condition and help them to manage their illness within the context of their everyday lives. Patient demand for CAM to be more readily available is therefore high, but the extent to which CAM is integrated with conventional treatments for chronic diseases is variable. The inclusion of CAM as part of the health care package is not always evidence led, but is most prevalent for conditions such as cancer where it is recognized that psychosocial treatments are central to the provision of a good quality care programme.

Whether CAM forms part of an integrated package or is accessed privately, it clearly plays an important role for a significant number of people with chronic illness. This reflects the complexity of living with a chronic condition, in addition to the demands of long-term and often invasive conventional treatments. Evidence suggests that CAM: (a) is able to offer an alternative to conventional treatments for certain conditions/symptoms and iatrogenic effects of treatment such as pain relief and nausea control; (b) is effective in providing supportive care by improving quality of life and reducing emotional distress; (c) is able to maximize non-specific elements of care such as empathy and encourage active engagement of patients; and (d) has the potential to change people's beliefs about their illness with concomitant implications for health outcomes and behaviour. While the provision of CAM in an integrated package with conventional medicine inevitably requires recognition of the biomedical, evidence-led approach, it is important that health psychologists also propagate a more meaning-centred approach to understand the patients' perspective of the experience of chronic illness and its treatment.

Note

1. Complex interventions are 'built up from a number of components, which may act both independently and interdependently' (Campbell et al., 2007, p. 455)

 Conclusion

Health psychology is blossoming and, arguably, is ready to take on new challenges, one of which can be the full investigation of CAM from a perspective of the informed, open-minded, independent assessor. But perhaps health psychology needs to change further to meet that gauntlet. As a subject in its infancy it is still, to some extent, buried in proving itself, to gain the approval of the traditional sciences and medicine. This, however, is to overlook the fact that this tradition has itself changed over the last few decades. There is a new physics, and a newer medicine, and psychology, if it can work with these groups of theorists and professionals, can become something of real value to the patient, the physician, and to society generally.

Complementary and alternative medicine offers an exciting new area in health and illness, and is certainly in need of further empirical investigations, carried out with the use of quantitative and qualitative scientific research methods. Throughout this book, health psychology in particular has been challenged to take on this role, because of its grounding in empiricism, and its range of sub-disciplines such as psychophysics, biopsychology, social psychology, the psychology of individual differences and research methods, as well as its proponents' training in the application of this knowledge specifically to the field of health and illness. This is not to say that other researchers, such as nurses, physicians, health scientists, other psychologists and social scientists, and CAM practitioners could not add valuable contributions to this fascinating new sub-discipline as well. It is just that, unlike other available texts on CAM, this book has concentrated on the 'pros and cons' of the heritage of psychology and health psychology so far, in particular in relation to the difficulties and possibilities of integrating CAM practices into the western scientific tradition, with the acknowledgement that the eastern traditions are based on a different epistemology, models of the person and ideas of health and illness.

This is a tradition, which can also be recognized in current conventional western medical care, where the provision of health care follows a scientific-practitioner model guided by clinical guidelines with randomized controlled trials as the preferred methodology helping to achieve the 'gold standard'. On the other hand, western societies have values of freedom and choice, which for people's health and well-being is reflected in their fervent and frequent use of CAM, notwithstanding its legislation, despite the financial outlay associated with it, and regardless of the disapproval from standard western medical authorities. Especially for those suffering from chronic illness, their choice for well-being and quality of life through integrated care packages has shown to be more important than scientific proof, regulation or legislation. One of the arguments of this book is that even though RCTs are important, other empirical research methods, which can also further our understanding of CAM, should not be dismissed; since two of the four categories of proof in the clinical guidelines supporting conventional practice are based on non-experimental studies as well, no reason can be seen for its the dismissal of CAM or indeed any non-RCT empirical evidence. Accordingly, in this volume, special thought has been given to the use of single case studies, the use of systematic reviews, and the value of the analyses of stories of CAM as presented in the media, diaries or autobiographical accounts. Generating more evidence, based on these qualitative methods, will enhance the development of guidelines, preferably in a multi-disciplinary fashion, forming future 'integrated' clinical guidelines.

Complementary and alternative approaches are typically underpinned by different models of the body, based on meridians, chakras and acupressure points rather than muscles and neurons which also hinders integration into western belief systems. Working from a biopsychosocial model does not suffice when attempting to explain CAM practices, as this model is still rooted in the old Newtonian paradigm in physics. It has been proposed that we consider the new physics of quantum mechanics and that we work from a biophysics-psychosocial rather than the bio(chemistry)-psychosocial model. New developments in biophysics are promising, as further empirical evidence is appearing to show that quantum processes, including electromagnetic forces, can explain communication and information processes in the body. This, for example, could be through light transmission (biophotons) in DNA, which can trigger some biochemical reactions in and between cells (Popp, 1998). Other evidence, which has demonstrated potential links between 'meridans' and 'chakras' and physiological processes, has come from Shang's (2000, 2001) morphogenetic singularity theory or Kim's (1964) Kyungrak System. An exciting new theory, applied specifically to health and illness based on the controlling quantum electrodynamic field (human body field), is Fraser and Massey's Nutri-Energetic Systems (NES). Evaluating these evolving theories in relation to health and illness with a critical and investigative mind is a new challenge to the health psychologist and to health professionals more widely. It is important to note just how far physics has come in redefining itself. The quantum world is very far removed from the Newtonian one, and has in many ways embraced uncertainty, chaos, and possibilities and probabilities rather than certainties and hard facts.

Just as CAM holds to a holistic model of the person, a biophysics-psychosocial model has been proposed for health psychology. This is in line with Laszlo's connectivity hypothesis, which, also based on quantum mechanics, proposes a model of energetic connection within and between people and the cosmos. From this hypothesis CAM practices such as Radionics, Reiki and Therapeutic Touch could be examined. It has been identified that the model of the person in psychology progressed in its developments as a social science, and as such became more concerned with a 'social self' separated from an 'inner self'. The 'inner self' is akin to the 'wordless' sensations (proprioceptions, Harré, 1998), uncluttered by the language of the 'social self'. For example, in the case of the bodily elementary experience of enjoyment (Levinas, 1961, 1979) a massage feels different from the words used to describe it, which to some extent constrain things. This tension is what MacLachlan (2004) refers to in the label 'embodiment' as distinct from the experience of 'the body'. A biophysics-psychosocial model could link these sensations with the psychosocial self, to reflect a connection between the deeper inner self of people with others and the universe, from a scientific rather than religious or spiritual holistic reference point. An embodied connected self, which has been identified as the basis of bodily awareness, and where stress-management practices, such as, relaxation, meditation, yoga, and tai chi take place, could make for a rich area of investigation.

As an example of the application of psychological theory to some CAM practices, comparisons have been made between the psychology of perception of the human senses (olfaction, sensation, gustation, vision and audition) and the complementary therapies of aromatherapy, massage, colour therapy and music therapy. A gap has been identified between experimental psychological research and non-experimental CAM studies. Whether the approaches in psychophysics as currently established will be a sufficient theoretical framework for the CAM therapies is debatable. Recent literatures on embodiment and eastern philosophies of the perception of odour, colour, music and touch are different in the sense that they claim that perception does not only take place via the traditional sense organs, but via the body as a whole, or via certain organs in the body with a similar energy resonance. Sheldrake (1988) explains this with his theory of morphogenetic fields and morphic resonance, claiming that people communicate with themselves, others and the cosmos through these fields, which act as antennas outside the body. In this vision, our minds are supposed to communicate with these fields as a telephone number with its receiver. The physics in this sense is different from psychophysics as theorized and tested in experimental psychology based on Newtonian physics, hence the proposal for future research investigating the comparison with the biophysics-psychosocial model. However, as we have noted, modern physics is working in a new paradigm, which has taken on board newer ideas about energies and connections.

The quantum world is a strange world, and much less tinged with self-confidence than the Newtonian one. There was a time when x-rays, gravity and radio waves were fanciful ideas, little more than useful numbers in equations, but then we found ways to detect them and use them to our benefit. We are only too aware that today's unseen force is potentially tomorrow's harnessed power. Dark matter represents a major challenge for the modern physicist, as something 'out there' (and inside too, in fact almost everywhere) which we know woefully little about. Some of the energies that CAM therapists claim are the basis of their work could, theoretically, exist, and we simply have to find them. Some of the vibrational energies spoken of by CAM practitioners could, potentially, find a home in string theory. Equally, of course, they might not, but it will be wrong to base anything on supposition or prejudice; we must research, fairly, dispassion-ately, and with precision. Psychology must catch up with physics, in a way, in accepting that some things do not always make sense on the surface, and in fact can seem rather mystical, and together we can work in a truly inter-disciplinary fashion, with physicians too, and with the CAM practitioners, for the good of all, and most of all for patients.

Another application which has been examined in detail is the process of stress and illness, one of the main areas of health psychology. Through assessing the literature it has been shown how the appraisal of, and coping with, stress in relation to health and illness is mediated by social support, personality characteristics, the immune system and the application of stress-management techniques. Special attention has been given to the relatively young discipline of psychoneuroimmunology (PNI), as a fascinating new area for health psychologists to include in their research on stress and illness, by mapping behaviour and neuroendocrine and immunological processes to health and illness. Linking PNI to the electromagnetic processes as identi-fied by biophysics might advance the understanding of these relations even more. Set in a cross-cultural divide, differences in cultural values between certain eastern and western belief systems have helped to identify relevant future directions for stress research. One of these is the importance of elicit-ing values about life and death, sickness and health, living for oneself or others, and work and leisure from the participants in stress research, rather than establishing religious orientation or spirituality as a separate variable in a rigid statistically modelled analysis. This is especially salient, since it has been demonstrated that in certain eastern traditions these values are embed-ded within the stress and coping process as a whole, as different from a more segregated process in the West. Another worthwhile direction is the practice and research of stress-management techniques, which have been shown to overlap in content but differ in conduct. Future studies could look into whether separate stress-management classes set aside from a busy and stressful lifestyle in western life differ from stress-management techniques embedded in one's daily life as a whole, as is more common in the east.

One cannot push for a paradigm shift any more than one can push for language change; things happen when they are ready to happen. Neologisms are naturally occurring; no one can make a word appear in a dictionary because they want it to. The issue is one of timing. One could argue that psychology is ready to change again, as it has many times in its short existence, but it is not easy to make that shift occur. As a forward-looking branch, health psychology is well placed to grasp the nettle and move on to the new science. If we can take the physicists, the doctors, and the CAM practitioners with us on our journey, then all the better. Good science is about exploring possibilities, and not about doing the same old things in the same old way because it is convenient and politically expedient. Too often, we claim that we are keen to explore the darkness, but only when we know where the light switch is. The best scientists are willing to explore the room when they don't even know if there is any light to be found at all. From the cracked cocoon we glimpse the emergent butterfly of health psychology, and CAMs are a rich feeding ground, provided we are willing to taste new things. So frequently we are bound up with appearances; we are concerned how it will look if we mix with the 'wrong crowd'. To research CAM is not to wholeheartedly accept it, nor is it to unequivocally reject it. There *is* a middle ground. It is possible to be open minded without being gullible. It is possible to be rigorous without being blinded by one's own science. One can explore possibilities without assuming that they are always probable. We must be willing to make our own paths through untrodden territory, because interesting things are found in unusual places.

 Glossary

Acupuncture
A bodily treatment originating from Traditional Chinese Medicine, wherein very fine and small needles are inserted in certain points on the body in order to help the body's own healing response. The points are called acupuncture points, which are 'invisible dots' on the skin running consecutively along the meridians. They have all been named, and have special functions. Stimulation is believed to clear the meridians and to improve the flow of energy (qi or ki).

Allopathic medicine
A term first coined in 1842 by the founder of homeopathy, Samuel Hahnemann, to refer to conventional medicine (as opposed to homeopathy).

Aromatherapy
A form of CAM in which essential oils are used, based on plant materials, to massage into the body or to inhale as a scent through burners.

Atomic and sub-atomic field
The atom is a basic unit of matter which consists of various sub-atomic particles: the electron, the proton and the neutron. The particles are, according to quantum theory, in a moving 'smear' in relation to each other, defined by probabilistic theory.

Aura
An aura is a field of radiation which is supposed to surround living people and objects, like the halo around the moon or a candle.

Ayurveda

Traditional medicine from the Indian sub-continent, based on an entire philosophy of life, allied with Hinduism and Buddhism, and involving a holistic view of health centred on energies, diet, exercise, and the fit of the individual within the universe. The name literally means 'life science' in Sanskrit.

Bioenergy

An approach linking electromagnetism to our understanding of the inter-active behaviour of cells in our bodies with surrounding electromagnetic fields.

Chakras

In Ayurveda, these are virtual places on the body where energy transfer from and to the body takes place. Seven of these energy 'wheels' have been described running consecutively along the body from the crown to the pelvic area, each with different names and functions.

Chaos theory

A division of mathematical physics, developed by Edward Lopez in 1963, which studies phenomena which cannot be predicted by conventional mathematics. Chaos theory is related to quantum physics through the notion of 'choice points' which determine randomicity. Every time more than one thing *could* happen, the eventuality that occurs splits off to create yet more possibilities and so on. The billions of possibilities thus formed creates an unpredictable 'chaos', hence the name.

Chinese therapeutic Wu Xing music

Music used in Traditional Chinese Medicine to balance disturbed energy in the major organs such as heart, spleen, lung, liver, and kidney.

Connectivity Hypothesis

The Connectivity Hypothesis, as part of an integral science of cosmos and consciousness has been developed by Ervin Laszlo, Hungarian philosopher of science, and Founder and President of the Club of Budapest. His hypothesis states how people's bodily energies are connected through elec-tromagnetic fields in space and time, within their own bodily selves as well as transpersonally with other people.

Crystal healing

A 'healing art' involving the laying of crystals and stones on the body.

Electromagnetic field

An area which consists of charged particles, which can be seen as the com-bination of an electric and magnetic field.

EPR Paradox (thought experiment)
A philosophical experiment carried out by Einstein, Podolsky, and Rosen (hence its name) in 1935 in quantum mechanics, challenging the relation between the observed values of physical quantities and their theory. The EPR paradox is a test of quantum theory, in that it helps us to assess the nature of pairing of characteristics of sub-atomic particles that ordinarily one might assume are independent. The experiment yields the conclusion that either observing one particle actually affects the behaviour of another or that quantum theory is incomplete and there is a hidden variable (in psychology, what we call a 'confound').

Healing touch
CAM practices which intend to heal a person by sending positive energy in the sense of thoughts over a distance, by concentrating on this person's name, image and so on in a positive, well-meaning way. The idea is that the degree to which these thoughts can be received depends on the relaxed and attentive state of this person, open for the energy to flow freely through the body field. In that sense the body field can be seen as one major variable resistance device as used in electronic apparatus to regulate the flow of current (e.g. volume control on a television). Hypotheses to explain this phenomenon can be found in quantum mechanics, more specifically described in, for example, Laszlo's connectivity hypothesis or Sheldrake's theory of morphological fields.

Heisenberg's uncertainty principle
Heisenberg, one of the fathers of quantum mechanics and Nobel Prize winner for Physics in 1932, explained that we cannot know the exact position and the exact velocity of an object at the same time, especially not for sub-atomic particles. This is not a fault in our measurement but rather a fundamental property of objects. If we know exactly where something is, we cannot know the speed it is travelling at, and vice versa.

Holism
The philosophy, prevalent in much of CAM, that it is important to assess and work with the whole person, rather than the specific disease or illness under treatment. It is essentially based on the notion that illnesses do not exist in isolation but are one part of the overall physical and mental system of the individual.

Hologram
A hologram is a three-dimensional image of an object obtained through the recorded reflection or transmission of light.

Homeopathy
A form of CAM developed by Samuel Hahnemann in 1796, based on the like-for-like theory as is used with vaccinations. Homeopathic medicine contains strong diluted substances.

Iatrogenesis
Adverse reactions resulting from medical (or CAM) treatments. Iatrogenic illness is that caused by treatments or the actions of health professionals.

Kirlian camera
A technical device in the form of contact photography, developed by Semyon Kirlian in 1939, in which a photogram can be made of a person who is in contact with a film on a metal plate which is charged with high-voltage, high-frequency electricity. Kirlian claims that the image he was studying might be compared with the human aura.

Kyungrak system
A theory developed by Bong Han Kim in Korea which reflects the structure of the human body as energy channels in a Kyung-rak system, through which the vital energy (Qi or Ki) runs through the body. It is posited that when the flow of the vital energy is blocked, health is lost, in a similar fashion as in Acupuncture.

Meditation
A form of mental concentration to stop the usual flow of thoughts, in order to clear one's mind and turn attention to a particular point of reference.

Meridians
Virtual channels as described in Traditional Chinese Medicine through which the qi or ki (life-giving and sustaining energy) flows into specific body organs.

Morphogenetic field
A group of cells, which responds to certain signals and interact with each other in order to form a coherent structure or organ, such as the lungs or the liver.

Morphic resonance
Morphic resonance is a term developed by the British Cambridge scholar Rupert Sheldrake to explain how interconnections between organisms work through 'thought' via 'morphogenetic fields'.

Morphogenetic singularity theory
This is a theory proposed by Charles Shang of the Emory University School of Medicine in Atlanta to explain the relationship between the meridian

system and embryogenesis, important for the understanding of the working of acupuncture, based on the singularity theory of mathematics.

Nadis
Channels of energy in the body connecting to the Chakras, according to Traditional Indian Medicine.

Photon
An elementary particle, with no mass, which forms the basic unit of light and all other forms of electromagnetic radiation. It has a wave/particle duality.

Psionic medicine
Psionic Medicine is an integrated medical system linking orthodox medicine, homoeopathy, energy medicine and radiesthesia, founded by the British physician George Laurence in 1960, who had become disabused with orthodox medicine's failure to make inroads into curing chronic diseases.

Quality Adjusted Life Years (QALYs)
A calculation to take into account both life expectancy and quality of the remaining life-years which is generally used to evaluate the cost effectiveness of healthcare interventions.

Quantum
An indivisible entity of a quantity as used in physics, which has the same units as the Planck constant.

Quantum mechanics
Quantum mechanics is an approach in physics to describe the reality at an atomic and subatomic level.

Radionics
This is a form of healing involving extra-sensory perception, can be conducted from afar, and involves an electronic instrument to aid the process. It is applied to animals and soil, in addition to human patients. Tailored healing energies are 'sent' to the recipient.

Reflexology
A form of CAM which works with foot or hand massaging in the belief that parts on these correspond with certain areas on the body.

Reiki
A Japanese CAM involving placing of hands above the body to regulate or redirect energies.

Remote healing
See Healing touch.

Rolfing
Known also as Structural Integration, this is a CAM involving manipulating tissues within the body, similar in some ways to certain aspects of physiotherapy.

Shiatsu
A form of finger-pressure massage originating from Japan, in order to stimulate the circulation of Ki through the body for health and well-being.

Therapeutic touch
A type of energy medicine whereby the therapists moves their hands over the patient's 'energy field', directing the flow of qi or prana to heal the patient.

Traditional Chinese Medicine (TCM)
A range of practices originating in China, which include acupuncture, Chinese herbal medicine, and Chinese therapeutic massage (tuina).

Telesomatic action
The belief that there are subtle interactions between the emotive and cognitive processes of individuals. Traditionally, telesomatic effects were produced by specially gifted natural healers, who would send what they claimed to be subtle forms of energy to their patients. 'Twin pain' and image transference between emotively closely linked individuals even when physically distant are examples of telesomatic action.

Wave/particle duality
All particles can take on the form of a wave and vice versa. Which of the two will appear is dependent on the choice of the observer, in the sense that the method of observation determines which is observed. This characteristic is one of the key achievements of quantum mechanics and has falsified earlier conceptions of the particles in Newtonian physics.

 # References

Ader, R. (1981) *Psychoneuroimmunology*. New York: Academic Press.

Ader, R. (2000) On the development of psychoneuroimmunology. *European Jounal of Pharmacy*, 405, 167–76.

Affleck, G., Tennen, H., Pfeiffer, C. and Fifield, J. (1987) Appraisals of control and predictability in adapting to a chronic disease. *Journal of Personality and Social Psychology*, 53(2), 273–9.

Ahles, T.A., Tope, D.M., Pinkson, B., Walch, S., Hann, D., Whedon, M., Dain, B., Weiss, J., Mills, L. and Silberfarb, P.M. (1999) Massage therapy for patients undergoing autologous bone marrow transplantation. *Journal of Pain and Symptom Management*, 18(3), 157–63.

Ahmad, M. (2005) Psychometric evaluation of cognitive appraisal of health scale with patients with prostate cancer. *Journal of Advanced Nursing*, 49, 78–86.

Ajzen, I. (1985) From intentions to actions: A theory of planned behavior, in J. Kuhl and J. Beckmann (eds), *Action control: From cognition to behavior*, (pp. 11–39). Berlin: Springer Verlag.

Ajzen, I. and Fishbein, M. (1980) *Understanding attitudes and predicting social behaviour*. New Jersey: Prentice-Hall.

Aldridge, D., Schmid, W., Kaeder, M., Schmidt, C. and Ostermann, T. (2005) Functionality or aesthetics? A pilot study of music therapy in the treatment of multiple sclerosis patients. *Complementary Therapies in Medicine*, 13(1), 25–33.

Allred, K.D. and Smith, T.W. (1989) The hardy personality: cognitive and physiological responses to evaluative threat. *Journal of Personality & Social Psychology*, 56(2), 257–66.

Almerud, S. and Petersson, K. (2003) Music therapy: a complementary treatment for mechanically ventilated intensive care patients. *Intensive and Critical Care Nursing*, 19, 20–1.

Alonso, Y. (2004) The biopsychosocial model in medical research: the evolution of the health concept over the last two decades. *Patient Education and Counseling*, 53(2), 239–44.

Anderson, B. (2002) Biobehavioural outcomes following psychological interventions for cancer patients. *Journal of Consulting and Clinical Psychology*, 70, 590–610.

Andrews, G. (2002) Private complementary medicine and older people: service use and user empowerment. *Ageing and Society*, 22(3), 343–68.

Angell, M. (1985) Disease as a reflection of the psyche. *New England Journal of Medicine*, 312, 1570–2.

Antoni, M., Baggett, L., Ironson, G., LaPerriere, A., August, S., Klimas, N., Schneiderman, N. and Fletcher, M. (1991) Cognitive-behavioral stress management intervention buffers distress responses and immunologic changes following notification of HIV-1 seropositivity. *Journal of Consulting and Clinical Psychology*, 59(6), 906–15.

Antonovsky A. (1979) *Health, stress and coping*. San Francisco, CA: Jossey-Bass.

Antonovsky A. (1987) *Unraveling the Mystery of Health: How People Manage Stress and Stay Well*. San Francisco, CA: Jossey-Bass.

Antonovsky A. (1993) The structure and properties of the sense of coherence scale. *Social Science & Medicine*, 36(6), 725–33.

Arasteh, A. and Sheikh, A. (1989) Sufism: the way to universal self, in A.A. Sheikh and K.S. Sheikh (eds), *Healing East & West: Ancient Wisdom and Modern Psychology* (pp. 146–80). New York: John Wiley & Sons.

Ashbury, F., Findlay, H., Reynolds, B. and McKerracher, K. (1998) A Canadian survey of cancer patients's experiences: are their needs being met? *Journal of Pain and Symptom Management*, 16(5), 298–306.

Astin, J.A. (1998) Why patients use alternative medicine: results of a national study. *Journal of the American Medical Association*, 279(19), 1548–53.

Astin, J.A., Marie, A., Pelletier, K., Hansen, E. and Haskell, W. (1998) A review of the incorporation of complementary and alternative medicine by mainstream physicians. *Archives of Internal Medicine*, 158(21), 2303–10.

Audi, R. (2004) *Epistemology: A Contemporary Introduction to the Theory of Knowledge*. London: Routledge.

Aujoulat, I., Marcolongo, R., Bonadiman, L. and Deccache, A. (2008) Reconsidering patient empowerment in chronic illness: a critique of models of self-efficacy and bodily control. *Social Science and Medicine*, 66, 1228–39.

Awasthi, P. and Mishra, R.C. (2007) Role of coping strategies and social support in perceived illness consequences and controllability among diabetic women. *Psychology Developing Societies*, 19(2), 179–97.

Bakal, D.A. (1999) *Minding the Body: Clinical Uses of Somatic Awareness*. New York: Guilford Press.

Bakal, D.A. (1992) *Psychology and Health*. New York: Springer.

Bakal, D.A., Steiert, M., Coll, P. and Schaefer, J. (2006) An experiential mind–body approach to the management of medically unexplained symptoms. *Medical Hypotheses*, 67(6), 1443–7.

Bakx, K. (1991) The 'eclipse' of folk medicine in western society. *Sociology of Health and Illness*, 13, 20–38.

Bale, T.L. (2006) Stress sensitivity and the development of affective disorders. *Hormones and Behavior*, 50(4), 529–33.

Balneaves, L., Kristjanson, L. and Tataryn, D. (1999) Beyond convention: describing complementary therapy use by women living with breast cancer. *Patient Education and Counselling*, 38, 143–53.

Baltrusch, H.J.F. and Walt, M. (1985) Cancer from a biobehavioural and social epidemiological perspective. *Social Science and Medicine*, 20(8), 789–94.

Banyard, P. (1999). *Controversies in Psychology*. London: Routledge.

Barnes, P., Powell-Griner, E., McFann, K. and Nahin, R. (2004) Complementary and alternative medicine use among adults: United States, 2002. *Adv Data*, 343, 1–19. PMID 15188733.

Barrett, B., Marchand, L., Scheder, J., Plane, M.B., Maberry R., Appelbaum D., Rakel D. and Rabago, D. (2003) Themes of holism, empowerment, access, and legitimacy define complementary, alternative, and integrative medicine in relation to conventional biomedicine. *Journal of Alternative and Complementary Medicine*, 9(6), 937–47.

Barry, C. (2002) *Alternative medicine users' and providers' views of health. Are they all the same?* Paper presented at the 9th Annual Symposium on Complementary Health Care, Exeter.

Bartz, R. (1999) Beyond the biopsychosocial model: new approaches to doctor–patient interactions. *The Journal of Family Practice*, 48(8), 601–7.

Beasley, M.K., Thompson, T. and Davidson, J.A. (2003) Resilience in response to life stress: the effects of coping style and cognitive hardiness. *Personality and Individual Differences*, 34, 819–29.

Beauchamp, T.L. and Childress, J.F. (2001) *Principles of Biomedical Ethics*. Oxford: Oxford University Press.

Beck, R., Daughtridge, R. and Sloane, P. (2002) Physician–patient communication in the primary care office: A systematic review. *JABFP*, 15(1), 25–38.

Becker, M. H. (1974) The Health Belief Model and Personal Health Behavior. *Health Education Monographs*, 2, 324–473.

Becker, R.O., Reichmanis, M., Marino, A.A. and Spadaro, J.A. (1976) Electrophysiological correlates of acupuncture points and meridians. *Psychoenergetic Systems*, 1(3), 105–12.

Beecher, H.K. (1955) The powerful placebo. *Journal of the American Medical Association*, 159(17), 1602–6.

Bennet, G. (1987) *The Wound and the Doctor: Healing, Technology and Power in Modern Medicine*. London: Secker & Warburg.

Bennett, P. (2000) *Introduction to Clinical Health Psychology*. Philadelphia, PA: Open University Press.

Bennett, P. and Murphy, S. (1997) *Psychology and Health Promotion*. Open University Press, Buckingham.

Bensing, J.M. and Verhaak, P.F.M. (2004) Communication in medical encounters, in A. Kaptein and J. Weinman (eds), *Health Psychology* (pp. 261–87). Malden, MA: Blackwell.

Benson, H., Beary, J.F. and Carol, M.P. (1974) The relaxation response. *Psychiatry*, 37, 37–45.

Benyamini, Y., Leventhal, E.A. and Leventhal, H. (1997) Attributions and health, in A. Baum, J. Newman, J. Weinman, R. West and C. McManus (eds), *Cambridge Handbook of Psychology, Health and Medicine*, pp. 72–7. Cambridge: Cambridge University Press.

Berger, J.A. and O'Brien, W.H. (1998) Effect of a cognitive-behavioral stress management intervention on salivary IgA, self-reported levels of stress, and physical health complaints in an undergraduate population. *International Journal of Rehabilitation & Health*, 4(3), 129–52.

Bertakis, K., Roter, D. and Putnam, S. (1991) The relationship of physician medical interview style to patient satisfaction. *Jounal of Family Practice*, 32, 175–81.

Berthelot, J.M., Maugers, Y., Abgrall, M. and Prost, A. (2001) Interindividual variations in beliefs about the placebo effect: a study in 300 rheumatology inpatients and 100 nurses. *Joint Bone Spine*, 68, 65–70.

Biley, F. (1992) Using music therapy in hospital settings. *Nursing Standard*, 6, 37–9.

Birkel, D.A. (2000) Hatha yoga: improved vital capacity of college students. *Alternative Therapies in Health and Medicine*, 6(6), 55–63.

Bishop, F., Yardley, L. and Lewith, G. (2006) Why do people use different forms of complementary medicine? Multivariate associations between treatment and illness beliefs and complementary medicine use. *Psychology and Health*, 21(5), 683–98.

Bishop, F., Yardley, L. and Lewith, G. (2007) A systematic review of beliefs involved in the use of complementary and alternative medicine. *Jounal of Health Psychology*, 12(6), 851–67.

Bishop, F.L. and Yardley, L. (2004) Constructing agency in treatment decisions: negotiating responsibility in cancer. *Health: An Interdisciplinary Journal for the Social Study of Health, Illness and Medicine*, 8(4), 465–82.

Bishop, G.D. (1993) Sense of coherence as a health resource in dealing with stress. *Psychologia* 36, 259–65.

Bittlinger, A. (1998) Der Individuationsprozess im Spiegel der Chakrensymbolik: Ein Beitrag C.G. Jungs zu einem 'westlichen' Verstandnis 'österliche' Symbole. *Analytisch Psychologie*, 29(4), 328–41.

Blaxter, M. (1990) *Health and Lifestyles*. London: Routledge.

BMA (1993) *Complementary Medicine: New Approaches to Good Practice*. London: BMA.

Bohm, D. (1973) Quantum theory as an indication of a new order in physics: implicit and explicit order in physical law. *Foundation of Physics*, 3, 139–68.

Bonso, E., Palomba, D., Perkovic, D. and Palatini, P. (2005) Effect of a biofeedback system using an auto-shaping method on blood pressure at rest and during stress in mild hypertension. *American Journal of Hypertension*, 18(5), 211.

Boon, H., MacPherson, H., Fleishman, S., Grimsgaard, S, Koithan, A., Norheim, A. and Walach, H. (2006) Evaluating complex healthcare systems: a critique of four approaches. *eCAM*, 1–7.

Boon, H., Stewart, M., Kennard, M., Gray, R., Sawka, C., Brown, J., McWilliam, C., Gavin, A., Baron, R. and Haines-Kamka, T. (2000) Use of complementary/alternative medicine by breast cancer survivors in Ontario: prevalence and perceptions. *Journal of Clinical Oncology*, 18(13), 2515–21.

Borg, O. and Shapiro, S. (1996) Personality type and student performance in principles of economics. *Journal of Economic Education*, 27, 3–25.

Borglin, G., Edberg, A. and Hallberg, I.R. (2005) The experience of quality of life among older people. *Journal of Ageing Studies*, 19, 201–20.

Borrell-Carrio, F., Suchman, A.L. and Epstein, R.M. (2004) The biopsychosocial model 25 years later: principles, practice and scientific inquiry. *Annals of Family Medicine*, 2(6), 576–82.

Botting, D. and Cook, R. (2000) Complementary medicine: knowledge, use and attitudes of doctors. *Complementary Therapies in Nursing and Midwifery*, 6, 41–7.

Bourgeault, I. (1996) Physicians' attitudes toward patients' use of alternative cancer therapies. *Canadian Medical Association Journal*, 15, 1679–85.

Bova, C., Burwick, T.N. and Quinones, M. (2008) Improving women's adjustment to HIV infection: results of the Positive Life Skills workshop project. *Journal of the Association of Nurses in AIDS Care*, 19(1), 58–65.

Bovbjerg, D. and Valdimarsdottir, H. (2001) Interventions for healthy individuals at familial risk for cancer: biobehavioral mechanisms for health benefits, in A. Baum and B. Anderson (eds), *Psychosocial Interventions for Cancer* (pp. 305–20). Washington, DC: American Psychological Association.

Bowie, J.V., Sydnor, K.D., Granot, M. and Pargament, K.L. (2004) Spirituality and coping among prostate cancer survivors. *Journal of Psychosocial Oncology*, 22(2), 41–56.

Bowles, N. (1995) Story telling: a search for meaning within nursing practice. *Nurse Education Today*, 15, 365–9.

Boylan, M. (2005) Massage enhances positive mood and reduces stress for spouses of cancer patients. *Australian Traditional-medicine Society*, 11(2), 81–2.

BPS (2007) Accreditation criteria MSc Health Psychology Programmes: first stage. Leicester: BPS Office.

Bradlow, J., Coulter, A. and Brookes, P. (1992) *Patterns of Referral*. Oxford: Health Services Research Unit.

Brazier, A., Mulkins, A. and Verhoef, M. (2006) Evaluating a yogic breathing and meditation intervention for individuals living with HIV/AIDS. *American Journal of Health Promotion*, 20, 192–5.

Brennan, B.A. (1988) *Hands of Light*. New York: Brennan Books.

Britten, N. (1994) Patients' ideas about medicines: a qualitative study in a general practice population. *Journal of General Practice*, 44, 465–8.

Brody, H. (1997) The doctor as therapeutic agent: a placebo effect research agenda, in A. Harrington (ed.), *The Placebo Effect: An Interdisciplinary Exploration* (pp. 77–92). Cambridge, MA: Harvard University Press.

Brody, H. (1999) The biopsychosocial model, patient centered care, and culturally sensitive practice. *The Journal of Family Practice*, 48(8), 585–7.

Broers S., Van Vliet K.P., Everaerd W., Le Cessie S. and Radder J.K. (2002) Modest contribution of psychosocial variables to hypoglycaemic awareness in Type 1 diabetes *Journal of Psychosomatic Research*, 52(2), 97–106.

Bronzaft, A.L. (2002) Noise pollution: a hazard to physical and mental well-being, in R.B. Bechtel and A. Churchman (eds), *Handbook of Environmental Psychology* (pp. 499–510). Hoboken, NJ: John Wiley & Sons.

Broom, A. (2005) Using qualitative interviews in CAM research: a guide to study design, data collection and data analysis. *Complementary Therapies in Medicine*, 13, 65–73.

Broom, A., Barnes, J. and Tovey, P. (2004) Introduction to the *Research Methods in CAM* series. *Complementary Therapies in Medicine*, 12, 126–30.

Brown, R.J. (2007) Introduction to the special issue on medically unexplained symptoms: background and future directions. *Clinical Psychology Review*, 27(7), 769–80.

Browne, G., Roberts, J., Weir, R., Gafni, A., Watt, S. and Byrne, C. (1994) The cost of poor adjustment to chronic illness: lessons from three studies. *Health and Social Care*, 2, 85–93.

Brownlee, S. and Dattilo, J. (2002) Therapeutic massage as a therapeutic recreation facilitation technique. *Therapeutic Recreation Journal*, 36(4), 369–81.

Brownlee, S., Leventhal, H. and Leventhal, E. (2000) Regulation, self-regulation, and construction of the self in the maintenance of the self, in M. Boekaerts and P. Pintrich (eds), *Handbook of Self-regulation* (pp. 369–416). London: Academic.

Bryant, L., Corbett, K. and Kutner, J. (2001) In their own words: a model of healthy aging. *Social Science and Medicine*, 53, 927–41.

Brydon-Miller, M. (2004) Using participatory action research to address health issues, in M. Murray (ed.), *Critical Health Psychology* (pp. 187–203). New York: Palgrave Macmillan.

Buber, M. (1922) *I and Thou*. Berlin: Schocken Verlag.

Buchanan, N. and Coulson, N. (2007) Acquisition of dental phobia: perceptions of online support group participation. *Health Psychology Review*, 1(1), 242.

Bugel, P., Groenier, K. and Roordink, M. (2001) Placebo effects of doctor behaviour. *Gedrag & Gezondheid: Tijdschrift voor Psychologie en Gezondheid*, 29(4), 228–40.

Burnett, K.M., Solterbeck, L.A. and Strapp, C.M. (2004) Scent and mood state following an anxiety-provoking task. *Psychological Reports*, 95(2), 707–22.

Burns, C. (1997) Comparative analysis of humor versus relaxation training for the enhancement of immunocompetence. *Dissertation Abstracts Internationals: Section B: The Sciences and Engineering*, 57(8-B), 5319–20.

Bury, M. (1982) Chronic illness as a biographical discription. *Sociology of Health and Illness*, 4, 167–82.

Busby, H. (1999) Alternative medicine/alternative knowledges: putting flesh on the bones (using traditional chinese approaches to healing), in U. Sharma (ed.), *Complementary and Alternative Medicines* (pp. 135–50). London: Free Association Books.

Callaghan, F.V. and Jordan, N. (2003) Postmodern values, attitudes and the use of complementary medicine. *Complementary Therapies in Medicine*, 11, 28–32.

Cambron, J.A., Dexheimer, J. and Coe, P. (2006) Changes in blood pressure after various forms of therapeutic massage: a preliminary study. *Journal of Alternative and Complementary Medicine*, 12(1), 65–70.

Campbell, C. (2004) Health psychology and community action, in M. Murray (ed.), *Critical Health Psychology* (pp. 203–30). New York: Palgrave Macmillan.

Campbell, C. and McGauley, G. (2005) Doctor–patient relationships in chronic illness: insights from forensic psychiatry. *British Medical Journal*, 330, 667–70.

Campbell, N., Murray, E., Darbyshire, J., Emery, J., Farmer, A., Griffiths, F., Guthrie, B., Lester, M., Wilson, P. and Kinmonth, A.L. (2007) Designing and evaluating complex interventions to improve health care. *British Medical Journal*, 334, 455–59.

Camus, A. (1942) *L'Etranger*. Paris: Gallimard.

Cannon, W. (1914) The emergency function of the adrenal medulla in pain and the major emotions. *American Journal of Physiology*, 33, 356–72.

Cannon, W. (1939) *The Wisdom of the Body*. New York: Norton Pubs.

Capra, F. (1990) *The Tao of Physics*. London: Flamingo.

Carey, S. (2000) Cultivating ethos through the body. *Human Studies*, 23, 23–42.

Carmody, J. and Ruth A. (2008) Relationships between mindfulness practice and levels of mindfulness, medical and psychological symptoms and well-being in a mindfulness-based stress reduction program. *Journal of Behavioral Medicine*, 31(1), 23–33.

Carney, R.M., Freedland, K.F., Eisen, S.A., Rich, M.W., Skala, J.A. and Jaffe, A.S. (1998) Adherence to a prophylactic medication regimen in patients with symptomatic versus asymptomatic ischemic heart disease. *Behavioral Medicine*, 24(1), 35–9.

Carroll, D., Bennett, P. and Smith, G. (1993) Socio-economic health inequalities: their origins and implications. *Psychology and Health*, 8(5), 295–316.

Carter, B. (2003) Methodological issues and complementary therapies: researching intangibles? *Complementary Therapies in Nursing and Midwifery*, 9, 133–9.

Cartwright, T. (2007) 'Getting on with life': the experiences of older people using complementary health care. *Social Science and Medicine*, 64(8), 1692–703.

Cartwright, T. and Torr, R. (2005) Making sense of illness: the experiences of users of complementary medicine. *Journal of Health Psychology*, 10(4), 555–68.

Cartwright, T., Porter, A. and Endean, N. (2009) Illness perceptions, coping and quality of life in alopecia sufferers. *British Journal of Dermatology*, 160, 1034–39.

Cassidy, C. (1998) Chinese medicine users in the United States. Part II: preferred aspects of care. *Journal of Alternative and Complementary Medicine*, 4, 189–202.

Cella, D.F. and Holland, J.C. (1988) Methodological considerations in studying the stress–illness connection in women with breast cancer, in C.L. Cooper (ed.), *Stress and Breast Cancer* (pp. 197–214). New York: John Wiley and Sons.

Chamberlain, K. (1997) Socio-economic health differentials: from structure to experience. *Journal of Health Psychology*, 2, 399–412.

Chamberlain, K. (2004) Qualitative research, reflexivity and contex. In M. Murray (ed.), *Critical Health Psychology* (pp. 83–101). New York: Palgrave.

Chamberlain, S. (1998) Yin, Yang and the six phases of QI: how they define health and disease. *American Journal of Acupuncture*, 26 (4), 281–303.

Charmaz, K. (1983) Loss of self: a fundamental form of suffering in the chronically ill. *Sociology of Health and Illness*, 5, 168–95.

Chatchawan, U., Thinkhamrop, B., Kharmwan, S., Knowles, J. and Eungpinichpong, W. (2005) Effectiveness of traditional Thai massage versus Swedish massage among patients with back pain associated with myofascial trigger points. *Journal of Bodywork and Movement Therapies*, 9, 298–309.

Chen, Y-H. (2006) The way of nature as a healing power, in P.T.P. Wong and L.C.J. Wong (eds) *Handbook of Multicultural Perspectives on Stress and Coping* (pp. 91–105). New York: Springer.

Cheug, C. and Kwan, A.Y. (2009) The erosion of filial piety by modernization in Chinese cities. *Ageing and Society*, 29(2), 179–98.

Chiavacci, D. (2005) Changing egalitarianism? Attitudes regarding income and gender: equality in contemporary Japan. *Japan Forum*, 17, 107–31.

Chui, Y.Y., Donoghue, J. and Chenoweth, L. (2005) Responses to advanced cancer: Chinese-Australians. *Journal of Advanced Nursing*, 52(5), 498–507.

Chun, C., Moos, R.H. and Cronkite, R.C. (2006) Culture: a fundamental contest for the stress and coping paradigm, in P.T.P. Wong and L.C.J. Wong (eds), *Handbook of Multicultural Perspectives on Stress and Coping* (pp. 29–55). New York: Springer.

Claridge, G. (1970) *Drugs and Human Behaviour*. London: Allen Lane.

Clark, P.E. and Clark M.J. (1985) Therapeutic touch: is there a scientific basis for the practice? in D. Stalker and C. Glymour (eds), *Examining Holistic Medicine* (pp. 287–96). Amherst, NY: Prometheus.

Clow, A. (2001) Behavioural conditioning of the immune system, in D. Peters (ed.), *Understanding the Placebo Effect in Complementary Medicine: Theory, Practice and Research* (pp. 51–66). London: Churchill Livingstone.

Clow, A., Lambert, S., Evans, P., Hucklebridge, F. and Higuchi K. (2003) An investigation into asymmetrical cortical regulation of salivary S-IgA in conscious man using transcranial magnetic stimulation. *International Journal of Psychophysiology*, 47, 57–64.

Cocilovo, A. (1999) Colored light therapy: overview of its history, theory, recent developments and clinical applications combined with acupuncture. *American Journal of Acupuncture*, 27(1–2), 71–83.

Cohen, F., Kearney, K.A., Zegans, L.S., Kemeny, M.E., Neuhaus, J.M. and Stites, D.P. (1999) Differential immune system changes with acute and persistent stress for optimists vs pessimists. *Brain, Behavior, and Immunity*, 13(2), 155–74.

Cohen, M. (2005) Challenges and future directions for integrative medicine in clinical practice: 'integrative', 'complementary' and 'alternative' medicine. *Evidence Based Integral Medicine*, 2(3), 117–22.

Cohen, M., Tripp-Reimer, T., Smith, C., Sorofman, B. and Lively, S. (1994) Explanatory models of diabetes: patient–practitioner variation. *Social Science and Medicine*, 38(1), 59–66.

Cohen, M.A. and Alfonso, C.A. (1997) A comprehensive approach to sexual history-taking using the biopsychosocial model. *International Journal of Mental Health*, 26(1), 3–14.

Cohen, S. and Herbert, T. (1996) Health psychology: psychological factors and physical disease from the perspective of human psychoneuroimmunology. *Annual Review of Psychology*, 47, 113–42.

Coleman, A. (2008) Iyengar yoga as a treatment for secondary traumatic stress in mental health professionals. *Dissertation Abstracts International: Section B: The Sciences and Engineering*, 69(1-B), 669.

Colquhoun D. (2007) Should NICE evaluate complementary and alternative medicine? *British Medical Journal*, 334, 507.

Conner, L. (2004) Relief, risk and renewal: mixed therapy regiments in Australia. *Social Science and Medicine*, 59(8), 1695–705.

Conrad, P. (1985) The meaning of medications: another look at compliance. *Social Science and Medicine*, 20(1), 29–37.

Consortium of Academic Health Centers for Integrative Medicine (2004) www.ahc.umn.edu/cahcim/about/home.html accessed on 31st August 2008.

Conway, S. and Hockey, J. (1998) Resisting the 'mask' of old age? The social meaning of lay health beliefs in later life. *Ageing and Society*, 18(4), 469–94.

Cooke, M., Holzhauser, K.J., Mark, D. and Cathy, F. (2007) The effect of aromatherapy massage with music on the stress and anxiety levels of emergency nurses: comparison between summer and winter. *Journal of Clinical Nursing*, 16(9), 1695–703.

Corner, J. and Harewood, J. (2004) Exploring the use of complementary and alternative medicine by people with cancer. *Nursing Times Research*, 9(2), 101–9.

Costa, P.T. Jr., Terracciano, A. and McCrae, R.R. (2001) Gender differences in personality traits across cultures: robust and surprising findings. *Journal of Personality and Social Psychology*, 81(2), 322–31.

Coulter, A. (1999) Paternalism or partnership? Patients have grown up – and there's no going back. *British Medical Journal*, 319, 19–20.

Coward, R. (1989) *The Whole Truth: The Myth of Alternative Medicine*. London: Faber & Faber.

Croke, M. and Dass Bourne, R. (1999) A review of recent research studies on the efficacy of esogetic colorpuncture therapy: a wholistic acu-light system. *American Journal of Acupuncture*, 27(1–2), 85–94.

Cropley, M. and Steptoe, A. (2005) Social support, life events and physical symptoms: a prospective study of chronic and recent life stress in men and women. *Psychology, Health and Medicine*, 10(4), 317–25.

Crossley, M. (2000) *Rethinking Health Psychology*. Maidenhead: Open University Press.

Crossley, M.L. (1999) Stories of illness and trauma survival: liberation or repression. *Social Science and Medicine*, 48, 1685–95.

Crossman, J. and Mackenzie, F.J. (2005) The Randomized Controlled Trial (RCT): gold standard, or merely standard? *Perspectives in Biology and Medicine*, 48(4), 516–34.

Crotty, M. (1998) *The Foundations of Social Research: Meaning and Perspective in the Research Process*. London: Sage.

Cruess, S., Antoni, M., McGregor, B., Kilbourn, K., Boyers, A., Alferi, S., Carver, C. and Kumar, M. (2000) Cognitive-behavioral stress management reduces serum cortisol by enhancing benefit finding among women being treated for early stage breast cancer. *Psychosomatic Medicine*, 62(3), 304–8.

Cruess, S., Antoni, M., Kilbourn, K., Ironson, G., Klimas, N., Fletcher, M., Baum, A. and Schneiderman, N. (2000) Optimism, distress, and immunologic status in HIV-infected gay men following Hurricane Andrew. *International Journal of Behavioral Medicine*, 7(2), 160–82.

Curtis R., Groarke, A., Coughlan, R. and Gsel, A. (2004) The influence of disease severity, perceived stress, social support and coping in patients with chronic illness: a one year follow-up. *Psychology, Health and Medicine*, 9, 456–82.

Curtis, P. and Gaylord, S. (2005) Safety issues in the interaction of conventional, complementary, and alternative health care. *Complementary Health Practice Review*, 10(1), 3–31.

Dahlsgaard, K., Peterson, C. and Seligman, M.E.P. (2005) Shared virtue: the convergence of valued human strengths across culture and history. *Review of General Psychology*, 9, 203–13.

Dancy, J. (1985) *An Introduction to Contemporary Epistemology*. Oxford: Basil Blackwell.

Danoff-Burg, S. and Revenson, T. (2005) Benefit-finding among patients with rheumatoid arthritis: positive effects on interpersonal relationships. *Journal of Behavioural Medicine*, 28(1), 91–103.

Darras, J.C. (1977) Thermografie et acupuncture. *Le Menuel*, 37, 273.

Daveson, B. and Skewes, K. (2002) A philosophical inquiry into the role of rhythm in music therapy. *The Arts in Psychotherapy*, 29, 265–70.

Davidson, L. (2005) Recovery, self management and the expert patient: changing the culture of mental health from a UK perspective. *Journal of Mental Health*, 14, 25–35.

De Craen, A.J.M., Lampe-Schoenmaeckers, A.J.E.M. and Kleijnen, J. (2001) Non-specific factors in randomised clinical trials: some methodological considerations, in D. Peters (ed.), *Understanding the Placebo Effect in Complementary Medicine: Theory, Practice and Research* (pp. 179–88). London: Churchill Livingstone.

De Fruyt, F., McCrae, R.R., Szirmák, Z., and Nagy, J. (2004) The Five-Factor personality inventory as a measure of the Five-Factor Model: Belgian, American, and Hungarian comparisons with the NEO-PI-R. *Assessment*, 11, 207–15.

de Vernejoul, P. (1985) Etude des meridiens d'acupuncture par les traceurs radioactifs. (Study of the acupuncture meridians with radioactive tracers). *Bulletin of the Academy of National Medicine*, 169, 1071–5.

de Vernejoul, P. Albarede, P., Darras, J.C., Beguin, C., Cazalaa, J.B., Daury, G. and de Vernejoul, J. (1984) Approche isotopique de la visualisation des meridians d'acupuncture. (Isotopic approach to the visualization of acupuncture meridians). *Aggressologie*, 25(10), 1107–11.

Deary, I.J. and Frier, B.M. (1995) Personality, stress and diabetes, in C.D. Spielberger and I.G. Sarason (eds), *Stress and Emotion: Anxiety, Anger, and Curiosity*, vol. 15, (pp. 33–49). Washington, DC: Taylor & Francis.

Delgado, C. (2007) Sense of coherence, spirituality, stress and quality of life in chronic illness. *Journal of Nursing Scholarship*, 39(3), 229–34.

DeLoach Walworth, D. (2005) Procedural-support music therapy in the health care setting: a cost-effectiveness analysis. *Journal of Pediatric Nursing*, 20(4), 276–84.

Demarco, A. and Clarke, N. (2001) An interview with Alison Demarco and Nichol Clarke: light and colour therapy explained. *Complementary Therapies in Nursing & Midwifery*, 7, 95–103.

Denollet, J. (1991) Negative affectivity and repressive coping: pervasive influence on self-reported mood, health, and coronary-prone behavior. *Psychosomatic Medicine*, 53 (5), 538–56.

Department of Health (2001) *Government Response to the House of Lords Select Committee on Science and Technology's Report on Complementary and Alternative Medicine*. Norwich: Her Majesty's Stationery Office.

Di Blasi, Z. and Kleijnen, J. (2003) Context effects: powerful therapies or methodological bias? *Evaluation and the Health Professions*, 26(2), 166–79.

Dolbier, C.L., Smith, S.E. and Steinhardt, M.A. (2007) Hardiness and support at work as predictors of job stress and job satisfaction. *American Journal of Health Behavior*, 31(4), 423–33.

Donaldson, L. (2003) Expert patients usher in a new era of opportunity for the NHS. *British Medical Journal*, 326, 1279–80.

Donovan, J.L. and Blake, D.R. (1992) Patient non-compliance: deviance or reasoned decision-making? *Social Science and Medicine*, 34(5), 507–13.

Dossey, L. (1997) The forces of healing: reflections on energy, consciousness and the beef stroganoff principle. *Alternative Therapies*, 3(5), 139–68.

Drolet, M. (ed.) (2004) *The Postmodernism Reader*. New York: Routledge.

Dunfield, J.F. (1996) Consumer perceptions of health care quality and the utilization of non-conventional therapy. *Social Science and Medicine*, 43(2), 149–61.

Dunn, K.S. and Horgas, A.L. (2000) The prevalence of prayer as a spiritual self-care modality in elders. *Journal of Holistic Nursing*, 18, 337–51.

Easthope, G., Tranter, B. and Gill, G. (2000) General practitioners' attitudes towards complementary therapies. *Social Science and Medicine*, 51, 1555–61.

Eastwood, C. (2006) *Endometriosis: Power and Modernity*, Unpublished PhD thesis. Middlesbrough: University of Teesside.

Eberhardt, J., van Wersch, A., van Schaik, P. and Cann, P. (2006) Information, social support and anxiety before gastrointestinal endoscopy. *British Journal of Health Psychology*, 11, 551–9.

Edwards, J. (2005) Possibilities and problems for evidence-based practice in music therapy. *Arts in Psychotherapy*, 32(4), 293–301.

Einstein, A., Podolsky, B. and Rosen, N. (1935) Can quantum-mechanical description of physical reality be considered complete? *Physics Review*, 47, 777–80.

Eisenberg, D., Davis, R., Ettner, S., Appel, S., Willery, S., Van Rompay, M. and Kessler, R. (1998) Trends in alternative medicine use in the United States, 1990–1997. *Journal of the American Medical Association*, 280, 1569–1575.

Eisenberg, D.M., Kessler, R. and Foster, C. (1993) Unconventional medicine in the United States: prevalence, costs and patterns of use. *New England Journal of Medicine*, 328, 246–52.

Elkin, T.D., Jensen, S.A., McNeil, L., Gilbert, M.E., Pullen, J. and McComb, L. (2007) Religiosity and coping in mothers of children diagnosed with cancer: an exploratory analysis. *Journal of Pediatric Oncology Nursing*, 24(5), 274–8.

Ellis, A. (1957) Rational psychotherapy and individual psychology. *Journal of Individual Psychology*, 13, 38–44.

Engel, G. (1977) The need for a new medical model: a challenge for biomedicine. *Science*, 196, 129–36.

Engels, G. (1977) The need for a new medical model: a challenge for biomedicine. *Science*, 196, 129–36.

Epes-Brown, J. (1989) Becoming part of it, in D.M. Dooling and P. Jordan-Smith (eds), *I Became Part of It: Sacred Dimensions in Native American Life* (pp. 9–20). San Francisco, CA: Harper.

Epstein, R.M. and Borrell-Carrio, F. (2005) The biopsychosocial model: exploring six impossible things. *Families, Systems and Health*, 23(4), 426–31.

Erikson, H., Olff, M., Murison, R. and Ursin, H. (1999) The time dimension in stress response: relevance for survival and health. *Psychiatry Research*, 85(1), 39–50.

Ernst E. (1995) Bitter pills of nature: safety issues in complementary medicine. *Journal of Biomechanics*, 28(5), 237–8.

Ernst, E. (2000) The role of complementary and alternative medicine in cancer. *The Lancet Oncology*, 1, 176–80.

Ernst, E. (2001) Towards a scientific understanding of placebo effects, in D. Peters (ed.), *Understanding the Placebo Effect in Complementary Medicine: Theory, Practice and Research* (pp. 17–30). London: Churchill Livingstone.

Ernst, E. and Cassileth, B. (1998) The prevalence of complementary/alternative medicine in cancer: a systematic review. *Cancer*, 83(4), 777–82.

Ernst, E. and Resch, K.L. (1995) The concept of the perceived and true placebo effect. *British Medical Journal*, 311, 551–3.

Ernst, E. and Stevinson, C. (2004) Complementary and alternative medicine in patients with cancer, in R. Moore and D. Spiegel (eds) *Cancer, Culture and Communication*. New York: Plenum.

Ernst, E. and White, A. (2000) The BBC survey of complementary medicine use in the UK. *Complementary Therapies in Medicine*, 8, 32–6.

Ernst, E., Resch, K. and White, A. (1995) Complementary medicine: what physicians think of it – a meta-analysis. *Archives of Internal Medicine*, 155(22), 2405–8.

Ettorre, E. (2005) Gender, older female bodies and autoethnography: finding my feminist voice by telling my illness story. *Women's Studies International Forum*, 28, 535–46.

Evans, P., Hucklebridge, F. and Clow, A. (2000) *Mind, Immunity and Health: The Science of Psychoneuroimmunology*. London: Free Association Books.

Ezzo, J., Streitberger, K. and Schneider, A. (2006) Cochrane systematic reviews examine P6 acupuncture-point stimulation for nausea and vomiting. *Journal of Alternative Complementary Medicine*, 12(5), 489–95.

Fallon, J. (2008) Yoga as an intervention for stress reduction and enhanced wellbeing in African American athletes. *Dissertation Abstracts International: Section B: The Sciences and Engineering*, 69(3-B), 1951.

Fallowfield, L. (1990) *The Quality of Life: The Missing Measurement in Health Care*. London: Souvenir Press.

Farr, L.E. (1967) Medical consequences of environmental home noises. *Journal of the American Medical Association*, 202(3), 171–4.

Faull, K. (2005) A pilotsyudy of the comparative effectiveness of two water-based treatments for fibromyalgia syndrome: Watsu and Aix massage. *Journal of Bodyworks and Movement Therapies*, 9, 202–10.

Fellowes, D., Barnes, K. and Wilkinson, S. (2004) Aromatherapy and massage for symptom relief in patients with cancer. *Cochrane Database System Review*, 3, CD002287.

Fenwick, P. (2001) Psychoneuroimmunology: the mind–brain connection, in D. Peters (ed.), *Understanding the Placebo Effect in Complementary Medicine: Theory, Practice and Research* (pp. 215–26). London: Churchill Livingstone.

Ferguson, E. and Cox, T. (1997) The functional dimensions of coping scale: theory, reliability and validity. *British Journal of Health Psychology*, 2, 109–29.

Fernros, L., Furhoff, A. and Wändell, P.E. (2008) Improving quality of life using compound mind–body therapies: evaluation of a course intervention with body movement and breath therapy, guided imagery, chakra experiencing and mindfulness meditation. *Quality of Life Research: An International Journal of Quality of Life Aspects of Treatment, Care & Rehabilitation*, 17(3), 367–76.

Festinger, L. (1957) *A Theory of Cognitive Dissonance*. Stanford, CT: Stanford University Press.

Feyerabend, P.K. (1981) *Realism, Rationalism and Scientific Method*. Cambridge: Cambridge University Press.

Field, T. (2000) *Touch Therapy*. London: Churchill Livingstone.

Field, T. (2003) *Touch*. Cambridge, MA: MIT Press.

Field, T., Diego, M. and Hernandez-Reif, M. (2007) Massage therapy research. *Developmental Review*, 27(1), 75–89.

Finn, O.J. (2001) Assessing the important effector mechanisms in the immune response against cancer, in A. Baum and B. Anderson (eds), *Psychosocial Interventions for Cancer* (pp. 175–91). Washington, DC: American Psychological Association.

Flynn, D., van Schaik, P. and van Wersch, A. (2004) A comparison of multi-item Likert and Visual Analogue Scales for the assessment of transactionally defined coping function. *The European Journal of Psychological Assessment*, 20(1), 49–59.

Folkman, S. and Moskowitz, J.T. (2004) Coping: pitfalls and promise. *Annual Review of Psychology*, 55, 745–74.

Folkman, S. and Lazarus, R.S. (1980) An analysis of coping in a middle-aged community sample. *Journal of Health and Social Behaviour*, 21, 219–39.

Folkman, S., Lazarus, R.S., Gruen, R.J. and DeLongis, A. (1986) Appraisal, coping, health status, and psychological symptoms. *Journal of Personality and Social Psychology*, 50(3), 571–9.

Forjuoh, S.N., Rascoe, T.G., Symm, B. and Edwards, J.C. (2003) Teaching medical students complementary and alternative medicine using evidence-based principles. *Journal of Alternative and Complementary Medicine*, 9(3), 429–39.

Forshaw, M. (2002) *Essential Health Psychology*. London: Arnold.

Foucault, M. (1976) *The Birth of the Clinic*. London: Routledge.

Fox, N. (1999) *Beyond Health. Postmodernism and Embodiment*. London: Free Association Books.

Franck, L., Chantler, C. and Dixon, M. (2007) Should NICE evaluate complementary and alternative medicine? *British Medical Journal*, 334, 506.

Frank, A. (1991) *At the Will of the Body: Reflections on Illness*. Boston, MA: Houghton Mifflin.

Frank, A. (1995) *The Wounded Storyteller: Body, Illness and Ethics*. Chicago, IL: The University of Chicago Press.

Frank, J.D. (1984) *Persuasion and Healing: A Comparative Study of Psychotherapy*. Baltimore, MD: Johns Hopkins University Press.

Frank, L.S., Frank, J.L., March, D., Makari-Judson, G., Barham, R.B. and Mertens, W.C. (2007) Does therapeutic touch ease the discomfort or distress of patients undergoing stereotactic core breast biopsy? A randomized clinical trial. *Pain Medicine*, 8(5), 419–24.

Fredrickson. (2005) The broaden-and-build theory of positive emotions, in F. Huppert, N. Baylis and B. Keverne (eds), *The Science of Well-being*. Oxford: Oxford University Press.

French, D., Maissi, E. and Marteau, T. (2005) The purpose of attributing cause: beliefs abut the causes of myocardial infarction. *Social Science and Medicine*, 60(7), 1411–21.

Freud, S. (1901) The psychopathology of everyday life, in J. Strachley (ed.), *The Standard Edition of the Complete Works of Sigmund Freud (Vol.3)*. London: Hogarth Press.

Freud, S. (1911) Formulations on the two principles of mental functioning. In J. Strachley (ed.), *The Standard Edition of the Complete Works of Sigmund Freud (Vol.3)*. London: Hogarth Press.

Friedman, M. and Rosenman, R.H. (1974) *Type A Behavior and Your Heart*. New York: Knopf.

Fulder, S. (1996) *Handbook of Alternative and Complementary Medicine*. London: Vermillion.

Fulder, S. (2005) Remembering the holistic view. *Journal of Alternative and Complementary Medicine*, 11(5), 775–6.

Furnham, A. and Beard, R. (1995) Health, just world beliefs and coping style preferences in patients of complementary and orthodox medicine. *Social Science and Medicine*, 40(10), 1425–2.

Furnham, A. and Bhagrath, R. (1993) A comparison of health beliefs and behaviours of clients of orthodox and complementary medicine. *Complementary Therapies in Medicine*, 32, 237–46.

Furnham, A. and Forey, J. (1994) The attitudes, behaviours, and beliefs of patients of traditional vs complementary (alternative) medicine. *Journal of Clinical Psychology*, 50, 458–69.

Furnham, A. and Kirkcaldy, B. (1996) The medical beliefs and behaviours of orthodox and complementary medicine clients. *British Journal of Clinical Psychology*, 35, 49–62.

Furnham, A. and Lovett, J. (2001) Predicting use of complementary medicine: a test of the theories of reasoned action and planned behaviour. *Journal of Applied Social Psychology*, 31(12), 2588–620.

Furnham, A. and Smith, C. (1988) Choosing alternative medicine: a comparison of the beliefs of patients visiting a general practitioner and a homeopath. *Social Science and Medicine*, 26, 685–9.

Furnham, A., Vincent, C. and Wood, R. (1995) The health beliefs and behaviours of three groups of complementary medicine and a general practice group of patients. *Journal of Alternative and Complementary Medicine*, 1, 347–59.

Gøtzschke, P.C. (1994) Is there logic in the placebo? *The Lancet*, 344, 925–6.

Gaab, J., Sonderegger, L., Scherrer, S. and Ehlert, U. (2006) Psychoneuroendocrine effects of cognitive-behavioral stress management in a naturalistic setting: a randomized controlled trial. *Psychoneuroimmunology*, 31(4), 428–38.

Gagne, D. and Toye, R.C. (1994) The effects of therapeutic touch and relaxation therapy in reducing anxiety. *Archives of Psychiatric Nursing*, 8(3), 184–9.

Galantino, M.L. (2004) The impact of modified hatha yoga on chronic low back pain: a pilot study. *Alternative Therapies in Health and Medicine*, 10(2), 56–9.

Gallegos, E. (2002) Animal imagery, the chakra system, and psychotherapy, in A. Sheikh (ed.), *Handbook of Therapeutic Imagery Techniques* (pp. 98–114). New York: Baywood.

Gallo, F. (2002) *Energy Psychology in Psychotherapy: A Comprehensive Sourcebook*. New York: Norton & Co.

Garhammer, M. (2002) Pace of life and enjoyment of life. *Journal of Happiness Studies*, 3(3), 217–56.

Garland, E. (2007) The meaning of mindfulness: a second-order cybernetics of stress, metacognition, and coping. *Complementary Health Practice Review*, 12(1), 15–30.

Gatchel, R. (2004) Comorbidity of chronic pain and mental health disorders: the biopsychosocial perspective. *American Psychologist*, 59(8), 795–805.

Gedney, J.J., Glover, T.L. and Fillingim, R.B. (2004) Sensory and affective pain discrimination after inhalation of essential oils. *Psychosomatic Medicine*, 66(4), 599–606.

Geller, G. and Francomano C.A. (2005) Complementary medicine and genetic medicine: polar disciplines or dynamic partners? *Journal of Alternative and Complementary Medicine*, 11(2), 343–7.

Gerber, R. (2001) *Vibrational Medicine*. Rochester, VT: Bear & Company.

Gergen, K.J. (1985) The social constructionist movement in modern psychology. *American Psychologist*, 40, 266–75.

Gettier, E. (1963) Is justified true belief knowledge? *Analysis*, 23, 121–3.

Geyer, S. (1997) Some conceptual considerations on the sense of coherence. *Social Science and Medicine*, 44, 1771–9.

Gilbert, D.G., Stunkard, M.E., Jensen, R.A., Detwiler, F.R.J. and Martinko, J.M. (1996) Effects of exam stress on mood, cortisol, and immune functioning: influences of neuroticism and smoker–non-smoker status. *Personality and Individual Differences*, 21(2), 235–46.

Gilchrist, R. and Mikulas, W. (1993) A chakra-based model of group development. *Journal for Specialists in Group Work*, 18(3), 141–50.

Giltay, E.J., Kamphuis, M.H., Kalmijn, S., Zitman, F.G. and Kromhout, D. (2006) Dispositional optimism and the risk of cardiovascular death: the Zutphen Elderly Study. *Archives of Internal Medicine*, 166(4), 431–6.

Giorgi, A. (1995) Phenomenological psychology, in J. Smith, R. Harré and L. van Langehove (eds), *Rethinking Psychology* (pp. 24–43). London: Sage.

Glaser, R. and Kiecolt-Glaser, J.K. (2005) Stress-induced immune dysfunction: implications for health, *Nature Reviews Immunology*, 5, 10–18.

Glinder, J. and Compas, B. (1999) Self-blame attributions in women with newly diagnosed breast cancer: a prospective study of psychological adjustment. *Health Psychology*, 18(5), 475–81.

Godoy-Izquierdo, D., Lopez-Chicheri, I., Lopez-Torrecillas, F., Velez, M. and Godoy, J. (2007) Contents of lay illness models dimensions for physical and mental diseases and implications for health professionals. *Patient Education and Counseling*, 67(1–2), 196–213.

Goel, N., Kim, H. and Lao, R.P. (2005) An olfactory stimulus modifies nighttime sleep in young men and women. *Chronobiology International*, 22(5), 889–904.

Goldman, A.I. (1992) *Liaisons: Philosophy Meets the Cognitive and Social Sciences*. Cambridge, MA: MIT Press.

Goodenough, B., Kamel, L., Champion, G.D., Laubreaux, L., Nicholas, M.K., Zigler, J.B. and McInterney, M. (1997) An investigation of the placebo effect and age-related factors in the report of needle pain from venipuncture in children. *Pain*, 72, 383–91.

Goodfellow, L.M. (2003) The effects of therapeutic back massage on psychophysiologic variables and immune function in spouses of patients with cancer. *Nursing Research*, 52(5), 318–28.

Gordon, A., Merenstein, J.H., D'Amico, F. and Hudgens, D. (1998) The effects of therapeutic touch on patients with osteoarthritis of the knee. *The Journal of Family Practice*, 47(4), 271–7.

Gøtzschke, P.C. (1994). Is there Logic in the Placebo? *The Lancet*, 344, 925–6.

Gould, A. and MacPherson, H. (2001) Patient perspectives on outcomes after treatment with acupuncture. *The Journal of Alternative and Complementary Medicine*, 7(3), 261–8.

Gould, S.J. (1992) Perceived affective symptoms: a new approach to affect patterning and response. *Imagination, Cognition and Personality*, 12(3), 249–71.

Graham, H. (1999) *Complementary Therapies in Context: The Psychology of Healing*. London: Jessica Kingsley.

Grant, S. & Langan-Fox, J. (2007) Personality and the occupational stressor-strain relationship: the role of the big five. *Journal of Occupational Health Psychology*, 12, 20–33.

Greaves, D. (2002) Reflections on a new medical cosmology. *Journal of Medical Ethics*, 28(2), 81–5.

Greenberg, L.W., Jewett, L.S., Gluck, R.S., Champion, L.A.A., Leiken, S.F., Altieri, M.F. et al. (1984) Giving information for a life-threatening diagnosis: Parents and oncologists' perceptions. *American Journal of Diabetes Care*, 138, 649–53.

Greene, M., Adelman, R., Friedman, E. and Charon, R. (1994) Older patient satisfaction with communication during an initial medical encounter. *Social Science and Medicine*, 38, 1279–88.

Greenfield, S.M., Innes, M.A., Allan, T.F. and Wearn, A. (2002) First year medical students' perceptions and use of complementary and alternative medicine. *Complementary Therapies in Medicine*, 10(1), 27–32.

Greer, S., Morris, T. and Pettingale K.W. (1979) Psychological response to breast cancer: effect on outcome. *The Lancet*, 8146, 785–7.

Greer, S. and Watson, M. (1987) Mental adjustment to cancer: its measurement and prognostic importance. *Cancer surveys*, 6(3), 439–53.

Griffiths, C., Foster, G., Ramsay, J., Eldridge, S. and Taylor, S. (2007). How effective are expert patient (lay led) education programmes for chronic disease? *British Medical Journal*, 334, 1254–6.

Gruzelier, J., Levy, J., Williams, J. and Henderson, D. (2001) Self-hypnosis and exam stress: comparing immune and relaxation-related imagery for influences on immunity, health and mood. *Contemporary Hypnosis*, 18(2), 73–86.

Gumbel, D. (1997) Die Bedeutung der Sinne in der Therapie. *Erfahrungsheilkunde,* 46(1), 2–8.

Gura, S. (2007) Yoga for stress reduction and injury prevention at work, in A. Monat, R. Lazarus and G. Reevy (eds), *The Praeger Handbook on Stress and Coping (vol. 2).* (pp. 489–95). Westport, CT: Praeger/Greenwood.

Gustavsson-Lilius, M., Julkunen, J., Keskivaara P. and Hietanen P. (2007) Sense of coherence and distress in cancer patients and their partners. *Psychooncology,* 16(12), 1100–10.

Haack, S. (2003) *Defending Science within Reason: Between Scientism and Cynicism.* New York: Prometheus.

Haddy, R. and Clover, R. (2001) The biological processes in psychological stress. *Families, Systems and Health,* 19(3), 291–302.

Hagger, M. and Orbell, S. (2003) A meta-analytic review of the common-sense model of illness representations. *Psychology and Health,* 18(2), 141–84.

Hahn, E.G., Brinkhaus, B., Joos, S., Lindner, M., Kohnen, R., Witt, C. and Willich, S.N. (2005) Integration of complementary and alternative medicine into German medical school curricula: contradictions between the opinions of decision makers and the status quo. *Forschende Komplementarmedizin und Klassische Naturheilkunde* 12(3), 139–43.

Hampson, S. (1997) Illness representations and the self-management of diabetes, in K. Petrie and J. Weinman (eds), *Perceptions of Health and Illness.* Amsterdam: Harwood.

Hampson, S.E. (1992) *The Construction of Personality: An Introduction.* London: Routledge.

Harari, S.S. (2003) What's the matter – your energy or your matter? An exploratory study examining body–mind–spirit correlates of Tibetans and Caucasian-Americans for multicultural holistic health practice intake. *Dissertation Abstracts International: Section B: The Sciences and Engineering,* 64(6B), 2920.

Harré, R. (1995) Discursive psychology, in J. Smith, R. Harré and L. van Langehove (eds), *Rethinking Psychology* (pp. 143–60). London: Sage.

Harré, R. (1998) *The Singular Self: An Introduction to the Psychology of Personhood.* London: Sage.

Harrington, A. (1997) *The Placebo Effect.* Cambridge, MA: Harvard University Press.

Harvey, P.G. (1988) *Health Psychology.* London: Longman.

Hasson, D., Arnetz, B., Jelveus, L. and Edelstam, B. (2004) A randomized clinical trial of the treatment effects of massage compared to relaxation tape recordings on diffuse long-term pain. *Psychotherapy and Psychosomatics,* 73(1), 17–24.

Haug, M. and Lavin, B. (1983) *Consumerism in Medicine: Challenging Physician Authority.* Beverly Hills, CA: Sage.

Hawkins, J. (2001) How can we optimize non-specific effects, in D. Peters (ed.), *Understanding the Placebo Effect in Complementary Medicine: Theory, Practice and Research* (pp. 69–88). London: Churchill Livingstone.

Haynes, R.B. (1999) A warning to complementary medicine practitioners: get empirical or else. *British Medical Journal,* 319, 1632.

Haywood, K., Marshall, S. and Fitzpatrick, R. (2006) Patient participation in the consultation process: a structured review. *Patient Education and Counselling, In press.*

He, D., Hostmark, A.T., Veiersted, K.B. and Medbo, J.I. (2005) Effect of intensive acupuncture on pain-related social and psychological variables for women with chronic neck and shoulder pain: an RCT with six month and three year follow up. *Acupuncture in Medicine*, 23(2), 52–61.

Heelas, P. (1996) The *New Age Movement: Religion, Culture and Society in the Age of Postmodernity*. London: Blackwell.

Heijmans, M. (1998) Coping and adaptive outcome in chronic fatigue syndrome: importance of illness cognitions. *Journal of Psychosomatic Research*, 45, 39–51.

Heijmans, M. (1999) The role of patients' illness representations in coping and functioning with Addison's disease. *British Journal of Health Psychology*, 4, 137–49.

Heinrich, K.T. (1992) Create a tradition: teach nurses to share stories. *Journal of Nurse Education*, 31(3), 141–3.

Heller, M.A. and Schiff, W. (eds) (1991) *The Psychology of Touch*. Hillsdale, NJ: Lawrence Erlbaum Associates.

Helman, C.G. (2001) Placebos and nocebos: the cultural construction of belief, in D. Peters (ed.), *Understanding the Placebo Effect in Complementary Medicine: Theory, Practice and Research* (pp. 3–16). London: Churchill Livingstone.

Herberman, R.B. (2002) Stress, natural killer cells, and cancer, in H.G. Koenig and H.J. Cohen (eds), *The Link between Religion and Health: Psychoneuroimmunology and the Faith Factor* (pp. 69–84). New York: Oxford University Press.

Heron, J. (2001) The placebo effect and a participatory world view, in D. Peters (ed.), *Understanding the Placebo Effect in Complementary Medicine: Theory, Practice and Research* (pp. 189–212). London: Churchill Livingstone.

Herzlich, C. (1973) *Health and Illness: A Social Psychological Approach*. London: Academic Press.

Higginson, I. and Carr, A. (2001) Using quality of life measures in the clinical setting. *British Medical Journal*, 322, 1297–300.

Hilsden, R.J. and Verhoef, M.J. (1999) Complementary therapies: evaluating their effectiveness in cancer. *Patient Education and Counselling*, 38, 101–8.

Hirschkorn, K. and Bourgeault, I. (2005) Conceptualising mainstream health care providers' behaviours in relation to complementary and alternative medicine. *Social Science and Medicine*, 61, 157–70.

Hobfoll, S.E. & Schroder, K.E.E. (2001) Distinguishing between passive and active prosocial coping: bridging inner-city women's mental health and AIDS risk behavior. *Journal of Social and Personal Relationships*, 18(2), 201–17.

Hodges, D. and Scofield, T. (1995) The healing effect: complementary medicine's unifying principle? *Network*, 58, 3–8.

Hofstede, G. (2001) *Culture's Consequences: Comparing Values, Behaviors, Institutions and Organizations Across Nations*. Thousand Oaks, CA: Sage.

Holahan, C.J. and Moos, R. (1985) Life stress and health: personality, coping, and family support in stress resistance. *Journal of Personality and Social Psychology*, 51, 389–95.

Holmes, T.H. and Rahe, R.H. (1967) Holmes-Rahe life changes scale. *Journal of Psychosomatic Research*, 11, 213–18.

Horne, R. (1997) Representations of medication and treatment: advances in theory and measurement, in K.J. Petrie and J. Weinman (eds), *Perceptions of Health and Illness*. Amsterdam: Harwood.

Horne, R. (1999) Patients' beliefs about treatment: the hidden determinant of treatment outcome? *Journal of Psychosomatic Research*, 47(6), 491–5.

Horne, R., Weinman, J. and Hankins, M. (1999) The beliefs about medication questionnaire: the development and evaluation of a new method for assessing the cognitive representation of medication. *Psychology and Health*, 14, 1–24.

Hornung, J. (1994) Was ist ein Placebo? Die Bedeutung einer korrekten Definition für die klische Forschung. *Fortschritte der Komplementärmedizin*, 1, 160–5.

House, J.S. (1981) *Work Stress and Social Support*. Reading, MA: Addison-Wesley.

Hover-Kramer, D. (2002) Incorporating biofield and chakra concepts into energy psychotherapy, in F. Gallo (ed.), *Energy Psychology in Psychotherapy: A Comprehensive Sourcebook* (pp. 135–51). New York: Norton & Co.

Hoyle, R. (ed.) (1995) *Structural Equation Modeling: Concepts, Issues, and Applications* (pp. 56–75). Thousand Oaks, CA: Sage.

Hsu, F.L.K. (1971) Psychosocial homeostasis and Jen: Conceptual tools for advancing psychological anthropology. *American Anthropologist*, 73, 23–44.

Hughes, B.M. (2007) Social support in ordinary life and laboratory measures of cardiovascular reactivity: gender differences in habituation-sensitization. *Annals of Behavioral Medicine*, 34(2), 166–76.

Hunt, H.T. (1985) Relations between the phenomena of religious mysticism (altered states of consciousness) and the psychology of thought: a cognitive psychology of state of consciousness and the necessity of subjective states for cognitive theory. *Perceptual and Motor Skills*, 61(3), 911–61.

Huppert, F., Baylis, N. and Keverne, B. (2005) *The Science of Well-being*. Oxford: Oxford University Press.

Hyland, M.E., Geraghty, A.W.A., Joy, O.E.T. and Turner, S.I. (2006) Spirituality predicts outcome independently of expectancy following flower essence self-treatment. *Journal of Psychosomatic Research*, 60, 53–8.

Idou, H. (2001) A study of meridian-meridian point effect by using photo signals. *Journal of International Society of Life Information Science*, 19(2), 381–5.

Ilmberger, J., Heuberger, E., Mahrhofer, C., Dessovic, H., Kowarik, D. and Buchbauer, G. (2001) The influence of essential oils on human attention. I: alertness. *Chemical Senses*, 26(3), 239–45.

Ingham, R. and van Zessen, G. (1997) Towards an alternative model of sexual behaviour: from individual properties to interactional processes. in L. van Camphoudt, M. Cohen, G. Guizzardi and D. Hausser (eds), *Sexual Interactions and HIV Risk: New Conceptual Perspectives in European Research*. London: Taylor & Francis.

Irinson, G., Antoni, M., Schneiderman, N., Chesney, M., O'Cleirigh, C., Balbin, E., Greenwood, D., Lutgendorf, S., LaPerriere, A., Klimas, N. and Fletcher, M. (2002) Coping: interventions for optimal disease management, in M. Chesney and M. Antoni (eds), *Innovative Approaches to Health Psychology: Prevention and Treatment Lessons from AIDS* (pp. 167–95). Washington, DC: American Psychological Association.

Irwin, M. (1991) Cellular immune changes in stress and depression: role of corticotrophin-releasing factor and endogenous opioid peptides, in S. Risch (ed.), *Central Nervous System Peptide Mechanisms in Stress and Depression* (pp. 105–28). Washington, DC: American Psychiatric Association.

Irwin, M., Olmstead, R. and Motivala, S.J. (2008) Improving sleep quality in older adults with moderate sleep complaints: a randomized controlled trial of Tai Chi Chih. *Journal of Sleep and Sleep Disorders Research*, 31(7), 1001–8.

Iwasaki, Y. and Bartlett J. (2006) Stress-coping among Aboriginal Individuals with diabetes in an urban Canadian city: from woundedness to resilience. *Journal of Aboriginal Health*, 1, 15–25.

Jacobs, S. (1989) A philosophy of energy. *Holistic Medicine*, 4, 95–111.

Jacobson, E. (1938) *Progressive Relaxation*. Chicago, IL: University of Chicago Press.

Jacobson, E. (1978) *You Must Relax*. New York: McGraw-Hill.

James, W. (1890/1950) *Principles of Psychology Vol. I and II*. New York: Dover.

James, W. (1897/1956) *The Will to Believe and Other Essays in Popular Philosophy*. New York: Dover.

James, W. (1902/1982) *The Varieties of Religious Experience*. London: Penguin.

James, W. (1907/1982) *Pragmatism*. Indianapolis, IN: Hackett.

Janz, N. K. and Becker, M. H. (1984) The Health Belief Model: A Decade Later. *Health Education Quarterly*, 11, 1–47.

Jessel-Kenyon, J., Pfeffier, L. and Brenton, M.A. (1998) Statistical comparison of repeatability in three commonly used bioelectrical devices: Kirlian photography, the segmental electrogram, and the AMI of Motoyama. *Acupuncture in Medicine*, 16(1), 40–2.

Jing, H. (2007) What Confucianism can contribute to psychological counseling. *Acta Psychologica Sinica*, 39(2), 371–80.

Johnson, F. (1985) The western concept of self, in A.J. Marsella, G. DeVos and F.L.K. Hsu (eds), *Culture and Self: Asian and Western Perspectives* (pp. 91–138). London: Tavistock.

Johnson, G. and Helman, C. (2004) Remedy or cure? Lay beliefs about over-the-counter medicines for coughs and colds, *British Journal of General Practice*, 54, 98–102.

Jonas, W.B. (1997) Safety in complementary medicine, in E. Ernst (ed.), *Complementary Medicine: An Objective Appraisal* (pp. 126–50). Oxford: Butterworth-Heinemann.

Jung, C.G. (1965/1982) *The Development of Personality*. London: Routledge.

Jung, C.G. (1969) *On the Nature of the Psyche*. London: Routledge.

Jung, C.G. (1976) Psychological commentary on Kundalini Yoga. *Annual*, Spring. 1–31.

Kabat-Zinn, J. (1994) *Wherever You Go, There You Are*. London: Piatkus.

Kabat-Zinn, J. (2003) Mindfulness-based interventions in context: past, present and future. *Clinical Psychology: Science and Practice*, 10, 44–56.

Kabat-Zinn, J., Lipworth, L. and Burney, R. (1985) The clinical use of mindfulness meditation for the self-regulation of chronic pain. *Journal of Behavioural Medicine*, 8, 162–90.

Kahn, J.H., Hessling, R.M. and Russell, D.W. (2003) Social support, health, and well-being among the elderly: what is the role of negative affectivity? *Personality and Individual Differences*, 35, 5–17.

Kahn, M. (2008) Type-D personality, occupational stress and mental health: links and outcomes. *Social Science International*, 24(1), 57–65.

Kahneman, D., Diener, E. and Schwartz, N. (1999) *Well-being: The Foundations of Hedonic Psychology*. New York: Russel Sage Foundation.

Kaptchuk, T.J. (1996) Complementary medicine: efficacy beyond the placebo effect. *Complementary Therapies in Medicine*, 4(2), 142–3.

Kaptchuk, T.J. (2000) *The Web That Has No Weaver: Understanding Chinese Medicine*. Chicago, IL: Contemporary Books.

Kaptchuk, T.J., Edwards, R.A. and Eisenberg, D.M. (1997) Complementary medicine: efficacy beyond the placebo effect, in E. Ernst (ed.), *Complementary Medicine: An Objective Appraisal* (pp. 42–71). Oxford: Butterworth-Heinemann.

Karademas, E.C. and Kalantzi-Azizi, A. (2004) The stress process, self-efficacy expectations, and psychological health. *Personality and Individual Differences*, 37(5), 1033–3.

Kardum, I. and Krapic, N. (2001) Personality traits, stressful life events, and coping styles in early adolescence. *Personality and Individual Differences*, 30(3), 503–15.

Karlins, M. and Andrews, L.M. (1972) *Biofeedback: Turning on the Power of Your Mind*. Aylesbury: Hazel Watson & Viney.

Kayser, K., Watson, L. and Andrade, J. (2007) Cancer as a 'we-disease': examining the process of coping from a relational perspective. *Families, Systems, and Health*, 25(4), 404–18.

Keefe, F.J., Affleck, G., Lefebvre, J., Underwood, L., Caldwell, D.S., Drew, J., Egert, J., Gibson, J. and Pargament, K. (2003) Living with rheumatoid arthritis: the role of daily spirituality and daily religious and spiritual coping. *The Journal of Pain*, 2(2), 101–10.

Kelner, M. and Wellman, B. (1997) Health care and consumer choice: medical and alternative therapies. *Social Science and Medicine*, 45(2), 203–12.

Kelner, M. and Wellman, B. (2001) The therapeutic relationships of older adults: comparing medical and alternative patients. *Health and Canadian Society*, 6(1), 87–109.

Kelner, M. and Wellman, B. (2003) Complementary and alternative medicine: how do we know if it works? *HealthcarePapers*, 3(5), 10–28.

Kennedy, A., Rogers, A. and Bower, P. (2007) Support for self care for patients with chronic diseases. *British Medical Journal*, 335, 968–70.

Kennedy, P., Taylor, N.M. and Duff, J. (2005) Characteristics predicting effective outcomes after coping effectiveness training. *Journal of Clinical Psychology in Medical Settings*, 12(1), 93–8.

Kenyon, J.D. (1989) *Forbidden Science: From Ancient Technologies to Free Energy*. Rochester, VT: Bear & Company Publishers.

Kerr, C.E., Wasserman, R. and Moore, C.I. (2007) Cortical dynamics as a therapeutic mechanism for touch healing. *Journal of Alternative and Complementary Medicine*, 13(1), 59–66.

Kido, M. and Sato, T. (2001) Measurement of biophysical and mental effects due to remote Qi healing. *Journal of International Society of Life Information Science*, 119(1), 200–4.

Kiecolt-Glaser J.K., Page, G.G., Marucha, P.T., MacCallum, R.C. and Glaser R. (1998) Psychological influences on on immune function. *Psychosometic Medicine*, 60, 479–83.

Kiecolt-Glaser, J.K., Fisher, L.D., Ogrocki, P., Stout, J.C., Speicher, C.E. and Glaser, R. (1987) Marital quality, marital disruption, and immune function. *Psychosomatic Medicine*, 49(1), 13–34.

Kiecolt-Glaser, J.K., McGuire, L., Robles, T. and Glaser, R. (2002) Psychoneuroimmunology: psychological influences on immune function and health. *Journal of Consulting and Clinical Psychology*, 70, 537–47.

Kienle, G.S. (2005) Is there a rationale for pluralistic evaluation models? Limitations of Randomized Controlled Clinical Trials. *Zeitschrift für Artzliche Fortbildung und Qualitätssicherung*, 99(4), 289–94.

Kienle, G.S. and Kiene, H. (1998) The placebo effect: a scientific critique. *Complementary Therapies in Medicine*, 6, 14–24.

Kienle, G.S. and Kiene, H. (2001) A critical reanalysis of the concept, magnitude and existence of placebo effects, in D. Peters (ed.), *Understanding the Placebo Effect in Complementary Medicine: Theory, Practice and Research* (pp. 31–51). London: Churchill Livingstone.

Kim, B.H. (1964) *On the Kyungrak System*. Pyongyang: Foreign Languages Publishing House.

King, K. (2005) Why is discrimination stressful? The mediating role of cognitive appraisal. *Cultural Diversity and Ethnic Minority Psychology*, 11(3), 202–12.

Kirkcaldy, B.D., Furnham, A. and Cooper, C.L. (1999) The relationship between Type A, internality–externality, emotional distress and perceived health. *Personality and Individual Differences*, 26, 223–5.

Kirkham, R. (1984) 'Does the Gettier problem rest on a mistake?' *Mind*, 93, 501–13.

Kirsch, I., Frankel, A. and Steven, V. (1977) Self-guided imagery vs systematic desensitization: a preliminary test. *Psychological Reports*, 40(3), 904–6.

Kirscht, J.P. (1988) The Health Belief Model and prediction of health actions, in D.S. Gochman (eds.) *Health Behavior: Emerging Research Perspectives (13)*. New York: Plenum Press.

Klaassen, D.W., McDonald, M.J. and James, S. (2006) Advance in the study of religious and spiritual coping, in P.T.P. Wong and L.C.J. Wong (eds), *Handbook of Multicultural Perspectives on Stress and Coping* (pp. 105–32). New York: Springer.

Klag, S. and Bradley G. (2004) The role of hardiness in stress and illness: an exploration of the effect of negative affectivity and gender. *British Journal of Health Psychology*, 9(2), 137–61.

Kleinman, A. (1980) *Patients and Healers in the Context of Culture*. Berkeley, CA: University of California Press.

Kleinman, A. (1988) *The Illness Narratives: Suffering, Healing and the Human Condition*. New York: Basic Books.

Kobasa, S. (1979) Stressful life events, personality, and health: an inquiry into hardiness. *Personality and Social Psychology*, 37, 1–11.

Koenig, H.G., McCullough, M.E. and Larson D.B. (2001) *Handbook of Religion and Health*. New York: Oxford University Press.

Kohler, B. (1997) Die Möglichkeiten der neuen bipolaren Farbtherapie bei umweltbedingten Erkrankungen. *Erfahrungsheilkunde*, 46(1), 18–21.

Komiya, M., Takeuchi, T. and Harada, E. (2006) Lemon oil vapor causes an anti-stress effect via modulating the 5-HT and DA activities in mice. *Behavioural Brain Research*, 172(2), 240–9.

Kostanski, M. and Hassed, C. (2008) Mindfulness as a concept and a process. *Australian Psychologist*, 43(1), 15–21.

Kressin, N.R., Spiro, A., III and Skinner, K.M. (2000) Negative affectivity and health-related quality of life. *Medical Care*, 38(8), 858–67.

Krieger, D. (1979) *Therapeutic Touch: How to Use Your Hands to Help and to Heal*. Englewood Cliffs, NJ: Prentice-Hall.

Kryter, K.D. (1994) *The Handbook of Hearing and the Effects of Noise: Physiology, Psychology, and Public Health*. San Diego, CA: Academic Press.

Kutlenios, R.M. (1987) Healing mind and body: a holistic perspective. *Journal of Gerontological Nursing*, 13(12), 9–13.

Lan, C., Lai, J.S. and Chen, S.Y. (2002) Tai Chi Chuan: an ancient wisdom on exercise and health promotion. *Sports Medicine*, 32(4), 217–24.

Lancer, K.M. (2007) Immune function and psychological distress in familial dementia caregivers: A controlled trial of a cognitive-behavioral intervention.

Dissertation Abstracts International: Section B: The Sciences and Engineering, 68(3-B), 1931.

Laszlo, E. (2003) *The Connectivity Hypothesis: Foundations of an Integral Science of Quantum, Cosmos, Life and Consciousness*. Albany, NY: State of New York University Press.

Lau, R. and Hartman, K. (1983) Common sense representations of common illnesses. *Health Psychology*, 2, 167–86.

Lau, R.R. (1982) Origins of health locus of control beliefs. *Journal of Personality and Social Psychology*, 42(2), 322–34.

Laungani, P. (1995a) Stress in eastern and western cultures, in C.D. Spielberger, I.G., Sarason, J.M.T., Brebner, E. Greengless and P. Laungani (eds), *Stress and Emotion: Anxiety, Anger and Curiosity* (pp. 265–80). Philadelphia, PA: Taylor & Francis.

Laungani, P. (1995b) *Understanding Cross-cultural Psychology*. London: Sage.

Lawrence, G.H. (1976) Use of biofeedback for performance enhancement in stress environments, in I.G. Sarason and C.D. Spielberger (eds), *Stress and Anxiety*. Oxford: Hemisphere.

Lazarus R. and Folkman, S. (1984) *Stress, Appraisal, and Coping*. New York: Springer.

Lazarus, R.S. and Folkman, S. (1984) *Stress, Appraisal, and Coping*. New York: Springer.

Lee, D., Meehan, R., Robinson, C. and Smith, M.L. (1995) Psychosocial correlates of immune responsiveness and illness episodes in US Air Force Academy cadets undergoing Basic Cadet Training. *Journal of Psychosomatic Research*, 39(4), 445–57.

Lee, H. (1998) Yin and yang-can they promote environmental health to benefit patients? *Journal of Interpersonal Care*, 12(4), 411–18.

Lefcourt, H.M. and Thomas, S. (1998) Humor and stress revisited; in W. Ruch (ed.), *The sense of Humor: Explorations of a Personality Characteristic* (pp. 179–202). Berlin: Walter de Gruyter.

Legge, J. (1888) *Confucius and Confucianism, Taoism, Christianity and Other Religions*. London: Hodder and Stoughton.

Lehrner, J., Eckersberger, C., Walla, P., Potsch, G. and Deecke, L. (2000) Ambient odor of orange in a dental office reduces anxiety and improves mood in female patients. *Physiology and Behavior*, 71(1–2), 83–6.

Lehrner, J., Marwinski, G., Lehr, S., Johren, P. and Deecke, L. (2005) Ambient odors of orange and lavender reduce anxiety and improve mood in a dental office. *Physiology and Behavior*, 86(1–2), 92–5.

Leventhal, H. (1986) Symptom reading: A focus on process, in S. McHugh and T.M. Vallis (eds), *Illness Behaviour: A Multidisciplinary Model* (pp. 219–37). Plenum: New York.

Leventhal, H. and Diefenbach, M. (1991) The active side of illness cognition, in J.A. Skelton and R.T. Croyle (eds), *Mental Representations in Health and Illness*. New York: Springer.

Leventhal, H., Brissette, I. and Leventhal, E.A. (2003) The common-sense model of self-regulation of health and illness, in L.D. Cameron and H. Leventhal (eds), *The Self-regulation of Health and Illness Behaviour* (pp. 42–65). London: Routledge.

Leventhal, H., Meyer, D., Nerenz, D.R. (1980) The common sense representation of illness danger, in S. Rachman (ed.), *Contributions to Medical Psychology* (pp. 17–30). New York: Pergamon Press.

Leventhal, H., Nerenz, D. and Steele, D. (1984) Illness representations and coping with health threats, in A. Baum, S. Taylor and J. Singer (eds), *Handbook of Psychology and Health: Social Psychological Aspects of Health*, vol. IV, Mahwah, NJ: Erlbaum.

Levinas, E. (1961) *Totalité et Infini*. The Hague: Martinus Nijhoff.

Levinas, E. (1968) La substitution. *Revue Philosophique de Louvain*, 66, 487–508.

Levinas, E. (1971) *Totalité et Infini*. The Hague: Martinus Nijhoff.

Levinas, E. (1972) *Humanism de l'autre homme*. Paris: Fata Morgana.

Levinas, E. (1974) *Autrement qu'être ou au-delà de l'essence*. The Hague: Martinus Nijhoff.

Levinas, E. (1979) *Le Temps et l'Autre*. Paris: Fata Morgana.

Lewith, G. (1996) Cancer. *Complementary Therapies in Medicine*, 4, 242–6.

Lewith, G., Broomfield, J. and Prescott, P. (2002) Complementary cancer care in Southampton: a survey of staff and patients. *Complementary Therapies in Medicine*, 10, 100–6.

Lewith, G., Hyland, M. and Gray, S. (2001) Attitudes to and use of complementary medicine among physicians in the United Kingdom. *Complementary Therapies in Medicine*, 9, 167–72.

Lewith, G.T. and Chan, J. (2002) An exploratory qualitative study to investigate how patients evaluate complementary and conventional medicine. *Complementary Therapies in Medicine*, 10(2), 69–77.

Lewith, G.T., Godrey, A.D. and Prescott, P. (2005) A single-blinded, randomized pilot study evaluating the aroma of lvandula augustifolia as a treatment for mild insomnia. *Journal of Alternative and Complementary Medicine*. 11(4), 631–7.

Li, F., Harmer, P., Mack, K.A., Sleet, D., Fisher, K., Kohn, M., Millet, L., Xu, J., Yang, T., Sutton, B. and Tompkins, Y. (2008) Tai chi: moving for better balance: development of a community-based falls prevention program. *Journal of Physical Activity and Health*, 5(3), 445–55.

Li, J.X., Hong, Y. and Chan, K.M. (2001) Tai chi: physiological characteristics and beneficial effects on health. *British Journal of Sports Medicine*, 35(3), 148–56.

Lindsay, P.H. and Norman, D.A. (1977) *Human Information Processing*. New York: Academic Press.

Loewe, R., Schwartzman, J., Freeman, J., Quinn, L. and Zuckerman, S. (1998) Doctor talk and diabetes: towards an analysis of the clinical construction of chronic illness. *Social Science and Medicine*, 47(9), 1267–76.

Luff, D. and Thomas, K.J. (2000) 'Getting somewhere', feeling cared for: patients' perspectives on complementary therapies in the NHS. *Complementary Therapies in Medicine*, 8(4), 253–9.

Lumley, M., Rowland, L., Torosian, T., Bank, A., Ketterer, M. and Pickard, S. (2000) Decreased health care use among patients with silent myocardial ischemia: support for a generalized rather than cardiac-specific silence. *Journal of Psychosomatic Research*, 48(4–5), 479–84.

Lupton, D. (1997) Consumerism, reflexivity and the medical encounter. *Social Science and Medicine*, 45, 373–81.

Lutgendorf, S. and Costanzo, E.S. (2003) Psychoneuroimmunology and health psychology: an integrative model. *Brain, Behaviour and Immunity*, 17(4), 225–32.

Lyke, J.A. (2009) Insight, but not self-reflection, is related to subjective well-being. *Personality and Individual Differences*, 46(1), 66–70.

Lyles, A. (2005) Editorial comment: evidence gaps in complementary and alternative medicine use. *Clinical Therapeutics*, 27, 1832–3.

Lyons, A. and Chamberlain, K. (2006) *Health Psychology: A Critical Introduction.* Cambridge: Cambridge University Press.

MacLachlan, M. (2004) *Embodiment: Clinical, Critical and Cultural Perspectives on Health.* Maidenhead: Open University Press.

MacPherson, H., Thomas, K., Armstrong, B., de Valois, B., Relton, C., Mullinger, B., White, A., Flower, A. and Scheid, V. (2008) Developing research strategies in complementary and alternative medicine. *Complementary Therapies in Medicine,* 16, 359–62.

McArthur, D. (2003) The radiant heart: healing the heart, healing the soul and birthing radiant babies. *Journal of Prenatal and Perinatal Psychology and Health,* 17(4), 333–4.

McCain, N.L., Gray, D., Elswick, R., Robins, J., Tuck, I., Walter, J., Rausch, S., Ketchum, J. and MacKinney, A. (2008) A randomized clinical trial of alternative stress management interventions in persons with HIV infection. *Journal of Consulting and Clinical Psychology,* 76(3), 431–41.

McCain, N.L., Gray, D., Walter, J. and Robins, J. (2005) Implementing a comprehensive approach to the study of health dynamics using the psychoneuroimmunology paradigm. *Advances in Nursing Science,* 28(4), 320–32.

McCormick, R. and Wong, P.T.P. (2006) Adjustment and coping in aboriginal people, in P.T.P. Wong and L.C.J. Wong (eds), *Handbook of Multicultural Perspectives on Stress and Coping* (pp. 515–35). New York: Springer.

McCrae, J.D. and Lumley, M.A. (1998) Health status in sickle cell disease: examining the roles of pain coping strategies, somatic awareness, and negative affectivity. *Journal of Behavioural Medicine,* 21, 35–55

McCrae, R.R. and Costa, P.T. (1990) *Personality in Adulthood.* New York: The Guildford Press.

McCutcheon, M. (2002) *The Final Theory.* Sydney: Universal.

McIntyre, S., Hunt, K. and Sweeting, H. (1996) Gender differences in health: are things really as simple as they seem? *Social Science and Medicine,* 42(4), 617–24.

McKay, S. and Bonner, F. (1999) Telling stories: breast cancer pathographies in Australian women's magazines. *Women's Studies International Forum,* 22(5), 563–71.

McLaren, N. (1998) A critical review of the biopsychosocial model. *Australian and New Zealand Journal of Psychiatry,* 32, 8692.

McLaren, N. (2002) The myth of the biopsychosocial model. *Australian and New Zealand Journal of Psychiatry,* 36, 701.

McMahon, S.D. and Jason, L.A. (2000) Social support in a worksite smoking intervention: a test of theoretical models. *Behavior Modification,* 24(2), 184–201.

McSweeney, B. (2002) Hofstede's 'Model of National Cultural Differences and Consequences: A Triumph of Faith - A Failure of Analysis, *Human Relations*', 55(1), 89–118.

McTaggert, L. (2001) *The Field: The Quest for the Secret Force of the Universe.* London: HarperCollins.

Maddi, S.R. (1999) The personality construct of hardiness, I: effect on experiencing, coping, and strain. *Consulting Psychology Journal,* 51, 83–94.

Maddi, S.R. (2002) The story of hardiness: twenty years of theorising, research, and practice. *Consulting Psychology Journal,* 54, 173–85.

Maddi, S.R. (2006) Hardiness: the courage to grow from stresses. *The Journal of Positive Psychology,* 1(3), 160–8.

Madsen, M.V., Gøtzsche, P.C. and Hróbjartsson, A. (2009) Acupuncture treatment for pain: systematic review of randomised clinical trials with acupuncture, placebo acupuncture, and no acupuncture groups. *British Medical Journal*, 338, a3115.

Malarkey, W.B. and Mills, P.J. (2007) Endocrinology: the active partner in PNI research. *Brain, Behavior, and Immunity*, 21(2), 161–8.

Maltby, J. and Day, L. (2003) Religious orientation, religious coping and appraisals of stress: assessing cognitive factors in the relationship between religiosity and psychological well-being. *Personality and Individual Differences*, 34, 1209–24.

Marian, F., Widmer, M., Herren, S., Donges, A. and Busato, A. (2006) Physicians philosophy of care: a comparison of complementary and conventional medicine. *Forschende Komplementarmedizin und Klassische Naturheilkunde*, 13(2), 70–7.

Marks, D. (1996) Health psychology in context. *Journal of Health Psychology*, 1(1), 7–21.

Marks, D. (2002) Freedom, responsibility and power: contrasting approaches to health psychology. *Journal of Health Psychology*, 5(3), 5–19.

Marks, D.F. (2000) *The Psychology of the Psychic*. New York: Prometheus Books.

Marks, D.F., Murray, M., Evans, B. and Willig, C. (2000) *Health Psychology: Theory, Research and Practice*. London: Sage.

Marmot, M. (2001) Inequalities in health. *New England Journal of Medicine*, 345, 183–203.

Marsella, A.J., DeVos, G. and Hsu, F.L.K. (eds) (1985) *Culture and Self: Asian and Western Perspectives*. London: Tavistock.

Martin, G.N. (1996) Olfactory remediation: current evidence and possible applications. *Social Science and Medicine*, 43, 63–70.

Maslow, A.H. (1954/1987) *Motivation and Personality*. New York: Harper and Row.

Mason, K. (2001) *The Radionics Handbook*. London: Piatkus.

Mason, S., Tovey, P. and Long, A.F. (2002) Evaluating complementary medicine: methodological challenges of randomised controlled trials. *British Medical Journal*, 325, 832–4.

Matarazzo, J.D. (1982) Behavioral health challenge to academic, scientific and professional psychology. *American Psychologist*, 37(1), 1–14.

Mayr, E. (1998) *This Is Biology: The Science of the Living World*. Cambridge, MA: Harvard University Press.

Mead, G.H. (1934) *Mind, Self, and Society*. Chicago, IL: University of Chicago Press.

Meichenbaum, D.M. and Cameron, R. (1983) Stress inoculation training: toward a general paradigm for training coping skills, in D.M. Meichenbaum and M.E. Jaremko (eds), *Stress Reduction and Prevention* (pp. 115–54). New York: Plenum.

Melzack, R. and Wall, P.D. (1965) Pain mechanisms: a new theory. *Science*, 150, 171–9.

Meyer, D., Leventhal, H. and Gutman, M. (1985) Common-sense models of illness: the example of hypertension. *Health Psychology*, 4(2), 115–35.

Milgrom, L.R. (2005) Are Randomized Controlled Trials (RCTs) redundant for testing the efficacy of homeopathy? A critique of RCT methodology based on entanglement theory. *Journal of Complementary and Alternative Medicine*, 11(5), 831–8.

Miller, G.E., Cohen, S. and Ritchey, A.K. (2002) Chronic psychological stress and the regulation of pro-inflammatory cytokines: a glucocorticoid-resistance model. *Health Psychology*, 21(6), 531–41.

Miller, S.M. (1987) Monitoring and blunting: validation of a questionnaire to assess styles of information seeking under threat. *Journal of Personality and Social Psychology*, 52(2), 345–53.

Milligan, C. (2006) Yoga for stress management program as a complementary alternative counseling resource in a university counseling center. *Journal of College Counseling*, 9(2), 181–7.

Mills, S.Y. (2001) The House of Lords report on complementary medicine: a summary. *Complementary Therapies in Medicine* 9(1), 34–9.

Mirza Tahir, A.H. (1998) *Revelation, Rationality, Knowledge and Truth*. Surrey: Islam International Publications.

Mischel, W. (1968) *Personality and Assessment*. New York: Wiley.

Mischel, W. (1969) Community and change in personality. *American Psychologists*, 24, 1012–18.

Mischler, E. (1984) *The Discourse of Medicine: The Dialectics of Medical Interviews*. Norwood, NJ: Ablex.

Moos, R.H. (2002) The mystery of human context and coping: an unraveling of clues. *American Journal of Community Psychology*, 30(1), 67–88.

Morrin, M. and Ratneshwar, S. (2000) The impact of ambient scent on evaluation, attention, memory for familiar and unfamiliar brands. *Journal of Business Research*, 49(2), 157–65.

Moss, M., Cook, J., Wesnes, K. and Duckett, P. (2003) Aromas of rosemary and lavender essential oils differentially affect cognition and mood in healthy adults. *International Journal of Neuroscience*, 113(1), 15–38.

Moss, M., Howard, R., Wilkinson, L. and Wenses, K. (2006) Expectancy and the aroma of Roman chamomile influence mood and cognition in healthy volunteers. *The International Journal of Aromatherapy*, 16, 63–73.

Moss-Morris, R., Petrie, K. and Weinman, J. (1996) Functioning in chronic fatigue syndrome: do illness perceptions play a regulatory role? *British Journal of Health Psychology*, 1, 15–25.

Motoyama, H. and Brown, R. (1978) *Science and Evolution of Consciousness: Chakras, Ki, and Psi*. Brookline, MA: Autumn Press.

Much, N. (1995) Cultural psychology, in J.A. Smith, R. Harré and L.V. Langenhove (eds), *Rethinking Psychology* (pp. 97–121). London: Sage.

Muir, B. (1998) A critical review of the biopsychosocial model. *Australian and New Zealand Journal of Psychiatry*, 32(1), 93–4.

Murray, J. and Shepherd, S. (1993) Alternative or additional medicine? An exploratory study in general practice. *Social Science and Medicine*, 37(8), 983–8.

Murray, M. (ed.) (2004) *Critical Health Psychology*. New York: Palgrave Macmillan.

Murray, M. and Campbell, C. (2003) Living in a material world: reflecting on some assumptions of health psychology. *Journal of Health Psychology*, 8(2), 231–6.

National Institute for Clinical Excellence (NICE) (2004) *Guidance on Cancer Services: Improving Supportive and Palliative Care for Adults with Cancer – The Manual*. London: NICE.

Nielsen, A.M. and Hansson, K. (2007) Associations between adolescents' health, stress and sense of coherence. *Stress and Health*, 23, 331–41.

Noble, L.M. (1998) Doctor–patient communication and adherence to treatment, in L. Myers and K. Midence (eds), *Adherence to Treatment in Medical Conditions*. Amsterdam: Harwood.

Nordenstrom, B. (1983) *Biologically Closed Electric Circuits: Clinical, Experimental and Theoretical Evidence for an Additional Circulatory System*. Stockholm: Nordic.

Norheim, A.J. and Fønnebø, V. (2002) Attitudes to the contribution of placebo in acupuncture: a survey. *Complementary Therapies in Medicine*, 10, 202–9.

Norman, P. and Bennett, P. (1996) Health locus of control, in M. Conner and P. Norman (eds), *Predicting Health Behaviour* (pp. 62–94). Buckingham: Open University Press.

Nowack, K.M. (1986) Type A, hardiness, and psychological distress. *Journal of Behavioral Medicine*, 9(6), 537–48.

Nowack, K.M. (1991) Psychosocial predictors of health status. *Work and Stress*, 5(2), 117–31.

Nunes, D., Rodriguez, A.L., da Silva Hoffman, F., Luz, C., Filho, A., Muller, M. and Bauer, M. (2007) Relaxation and guided imagery program in patients with breast cancer undergoing radiotherapy is not associated with neuroimmunomodulatory effects. *Journal of Psychosomatic Rsearch*, 63(3), 647–65.

Oakley, A. (1984) *The Captured Womb: A History of the Medical Care of Pregnant Women*. Oxford: Blackwell.

Oberbaum M., Vithoulkas, G. and van Haselen, R. (2003) Clinical trials of classical homeopathy: reflections on appropriate research designs. *Journal of Alternative and Complementary Medicine*, 9(1), 105–111.

Oberbaum, M., Singer, S.R. and Frass, M. (2005) Editorial: homeopathic research after the *Lancet* meta-analysis – a moment for introspection. *Complementary Therapies in Medicine*, 13, 303–5.

O'Connor, D.B. and Shimizu, M. (2002) Sense of personal control, stress and coping style: a cross-cultural study. *Stress and Health*, 18(4), 173–83.

Ogden, J. (1996) *Health Psychology*. Maidenhead: Open University Press.

Oliver, J. and Brough, P. (2002) Cognitive appraisal, negative affectivity and psychological well-being. *New Zealand Journal of Psychology*, 31, 2–7.

Ong, L.M., de Haes, J.C., Hoos, A.M. and Lammes, F.B. (1995) Doctor–patient communication: a review of the literature. *Social Science and Medicine*, 40, 903–18.

Owen, D., Lewith, G. and Stephens, C. (2001) Can doctors respond to patients' increasing interest in complementary and alternative medicine? *British Medical Journal*, 322, 154–8.

Pak, S.T. (1998) Color therapy. *Journal of Naturopathic Medicine*, 8(1), 68–76.

Pakenham, K.I. (2005) Benefit finding in multiple sclerosis and associations with positive and negative outcomes. *Health Psychology*, 24, 123–32.

Pakenham, K.I. (2006) Investigation of the coping antecedents to positive outcomes and distress in multiple sclerosis (MS). *Psychology and Health*, 21(5), 633–49.

Pakenham, K.I., Goodwin, V. and MacMillan, J. (2004) Adaptation to being at-risk for Huntington's Disease and the availability of genetic testing: application of a stress and coping model. *Psychology Health and Medicine*, 9, 380–97.

Pakenham, K.I., Smith, A. and Rattan, S. (2007) Application of a stress and coping model to antenatal depressive symptomatology. *Psychology, Health and Medicine*, 12(3), 266–77.

Palsane, M.N. and Lam, D.J. (1996) Stress and coping from traditional Indian and Chinese perspectives. *Psychology and Developing Societies*, 8, 29–53.

Pargament, K.I., Koenig, H.G. and Perez, L.M. (2000) The many methods of religious coping: development and initial validation of the RCOPE. *Journal of Clinical Psychology*, 56(4), 519–43.

Pariente, J., White, P., Frackowiak, R.S.J. and Lewith, G. (2005) Expectancy and belief modulate the neuronal substrates of pain treated by acupuncture. *NeuroImage*, 25, 1161–7.

Park, C.L. (2006) The roles of religiousness and religious coping in stress-related growth. *Archives of the Psychology of Religion*, 28, 287–302.

Park, C.L., Edmondson, D., Fenster, J.R. and Blank, T.O. (2008) Positive and negative health behavior changes in cancer survivors: a stress and coping perspective. *Journal of Health Psychology*, 13, 1198–206.

Parker, I. (1997) Discursive psychology, in D. Fox and I. Prilleltensky (eds), *Critical Psychology: An Introduction* (pp. 284–98). London: Sage.

Parks, F.M. (2007) Working with narratives: coping strategies in African American folk beliefs and traditional healing practices. *Journal of Human Behavior in the Social Environment*, 15(1), 135–47.

Parsons, T. (1978) *Action Theory and the Human Condition.* New York: Free Press.

Paterson, C. (2004) Chinese medicine acupuncture as a complex intervention: a holistic model. *Journal of Alternative and Complementary Medicine*, 10(5), 791–801.

Paterson, C. (2007) NICE on CAM: appraisals of specific treatments are needed. *British Medical Journal*, 334(7594), 600.

Paterson, C. and Britten, N. (2003) Chinese medicine acupuncture for people with chronic illness: combining qualitative and quantitative outcome assessment. *Journal of Alternative and Complementary Medicine*, 9, 671–81.

Pawluch, D., Cain, R. and Gillett, J. (2000) Lay constructions of HIV and complementary therapy use. *Social Science and Medicine*, 51(2), 251–64.

Perkin, M., Pearcy, R. and Fraser, J. (1994) A comparison of the attitudes shown by general practitioners, hospital doctors and medical students towards alternative medicine. *Journal of the Royal Society of Medicine*, 87(9), 523–5.

Perry, N. and Perry, E. (2006) Aromatherapy in the management of psychiatric disorders: clinical and neuropharmacological perspectives. *CNS Drugs*, 20(4), 257–80.

Perry, T.E., Davis-Maye, D. and Onolemhemhen, D.N. (2007) Faith, spirituality, fatalism and hope: Ghanaian women coping in the face of HIV/AIDS. *Journal of HIV/AIDS & Social Services*, 6(4), 37–58.

Peters, D. (1998) Is complementary medicine holistic? in A. Vickers (ed.), *Examining Complementary Medicine* (pp. 138–46). Cheltenham: Stanley Thornes.

Peters, D. (2001) *Understanding the Placebo effect in Complementary Medicine: Theory, Practice and Research.* London: Churchill Livingstone.

Peters, D. (ed.) (2001) *Understanding the Placebo Effect in Complementary Medicine: Theory, Practice and Research.* London: Churchill Livingstone.

Petrie, K.J. and Revenson, T. (2005) Editorial: new psychological interventions in chronic illness: towards examining mechanisms of action and improved targeting. *Journal of Health Psychology*, 10(2), 179–84.

Petrie, K.J., Cameron, L., Ellis, C., Buick, D. and Weinman, J. (2002) Changing illness perceptions after myocardial infarction: an early intervention randomized controlled trial. *Psychosomatic Medicine*, 64, 580–6.

Petry, J.J. (2000) Surgery and complementary therapies: a review. *Alternative Therapies in Health and Medicine*, 6(5), 64–74.

Pietroni, P. (1987) Holistic medicine: new lessons to be learned. *Practitioner*, 231(1437), 1386–90.

Pietroni, P. (1997) Is complementary medicine holistic? *Complementary Therapies in Nursing and Midwifery*, 3(1), 9–11.

Plews-Ogan, M., Owens, J.E., Goodman, M., Wolfe, P. and Schorling, J. (2005) A pilot study evaluating mindfulness-based stress reduction and massage for the management of chronic pain. *Journal of General Internal Medicine*, 20(12), 1136–8.

Plotkin, H. (2004) *Evolutionary Thought in Psychology: A Brief History*. Oxford: Blackwell.

Plotnikoff, N.P., Faith, R.E., Murgo, A.J. and Good, R.A. (eds) (2007) *Cytokines: Stress and Immunity*. Cleveland, OH: CRC Press/Taylor & Francis.

Popp, F.A. (1998) *Electromagnetic Bio-information*. Munich: Urban & Scharzenberg.

Porter, R. (1997) *The Greatest Benefit to Mankind: A Medical History of Humanity from Antiquity to the Present*. London: HarperCollins.

Post-White, J. (1998) The role of sense of coherence in mediating the effects of mental imagery on immune function, cancer outcome, and quality of life, in H. McCubbin, E. Thompson, A. Thompson and J. Former (eds), *Stress, Coping, and Health in Families: Sense of Coherence and Resiliency* (pp. 279–91). Thousand Oaks, CA: Sage.

Potter, J., Stringer, P. and Wetherell, M. (1984) *Social Texts and Contexts: Literature and Social Psychology*. London: Routledge & Kegan Paul.

Pound, P., Britten, N., Morgan, M., Yardley, L., Pope, C., Daker-White, G. and Campbell, R. (2005) Resisting medicines: a synthesis of qualitative studies of medicine taking. *Social Science and Medicine*, 61, 133–55.

Prilleltensky, I. and Prilleltensky, O. (2003) Towards a critical health psychology practice. *Journal of Health Psychology*, 8(2), 197–210.

Prince, M., Harwood, R., Thomas, A. and Mann, A. (1998) A prospective population based cohort study of the effects of disablement and social milieu on the onset and maintenance of late life depression. *Psychological Medicine*, 28, 337–50.

Prochaska, J. O. & DiClemente, C.C. (1986) Toward a comprehensive model of change, in W. R. Miller and N. Heather (eds), *Addictive Behaviors: Processes of Change* (pp. 3–27). New York: Plenum Press.

Puustinen, R., Leiman, M. and Viljanen, A.M. (2003) Medicine and the humanities: theoretical and methodological issues. *Medical Humanity*, 29, 77–80.

Quinn, J.F. (1984) Therapeutic touch as energy exchange: testing the theory. *Advances in Nursing Science*, 2, 42–9.

Radley, A. (1994) *Making sense of illness: the social psychology of health and disease*. London: Sage.

Rampes, H., Sharples, F., Maragh, S. and Fisher, P. (1997) Introducing complementary medicine into the medical curriculum. *Journal of Royal Society Medicine*, 90(1), 19–22.

Rampes, H., Sharples, F., Maragh, S. and Fisher, P. (1998) Introducing complementary medicine into the medical curriculum. *Biomedical Therapy*, 16(2), 197–200.

Rao, P.V. and Motoyama, T. (1993) The apparatus for measuring the functioning of the meridians and their corresponding internal organs (AMI): a reliability study. *Journal of Indian Psychology*, 11(1–2), 32–7.

Ratcliffe, J., Thomas, K., MacPherson, H. and Brazier, J. (2006) A randomised controlled trial of acupuncture for persistent low back pain: a cost effective analysis. *British Medical Journal*, doi:10.1136/bmj.38932.806134.7C.

Raub, J.A. (2002) Psychophysiologic effects of hatha yoga on musculoskeletal and cardiopulmonary function: a literature review. *Journal of Alternative and Complementary Medicine*, 8(6), 797–812.

Rees, L. (2001) Integrated medicine imbues orthodox medicine with the values of complementary medicine. *British Medical Journal*, 322, 119–20.

Reich, W. (1961) *Selected Writings*. New York: Farrar, Strauss and Giroux.

Reich, W. (1973) *The Function of the Orgasm*. New York: Touchstone.

Reichmanis, M., Marino, A.A. and Becker, R.O. (1975) Electrical correlates of acupuncture points. *IFEE Transactions on Bio-medical Engineering*, 22(6), 533–5.

Reilly, D. (1983) Young doctors' views on alternative medicine. *British Medical Journal*, 287(6388), 337–9.

Reilly, D. (2001) Some reflections on creating therapeutic consultations, in D. Peters (ed.), *Understanding the Placebo Effect in Complementary Medicine: Theory, Practice and Research* (pp. 89–110). London: Churchill Livingstone.

Rhodewalt, F., Hays, R.B., Chemers, M.M. and Wysocki, J. (1984) Type A behavior, perceived stress, and illness: a person-situation analysis. *Personality and Social Psychology Bulletin*, 10, 149–59.

Richardson, J. (2001) Intersubjectivity and the therapeutic relationship, in D. Peters (ed.), *Understanding the Placebo Effect in Complementary Medicine: Theory, Practice and Research* (pp. 131–46). London: Churchill Livingstone.

Richardson, J. (2004) What patients expect from complementary medicine: a qualitative study. *American Journal of Public Health*, 94(6), 1049–53.

Richardson, M., Sanders, T., Palmer, J., Greisinger, A. and Singletary, S. (2000) Complementary/alternative medicine use in a comprehensive cancer centre and the implications for oncology. *Journal of Clinical Oncology*, 18(13), 2505–14.

Rieber, R.W. and Robinson, D.V. (2001) *Wilhelm Wundt in History*. New York: Springer.

Riesman, D., Denney, R. and Glazer, N. (1953) *The lonely crowd: a study of the changing American character*. New Haven, CT: Yale University Press.

Ritenbaugh, C., Verhoef, M., Fleishman, S., Boon, H. and Leis, A. (2003) Whole systems research: a discipline for studying complementary and alternative medicine. *Alternative Therapies in Health and Medicine*, 9(4), 32–6.

Robins, J. L.W. (2000) Psychoneuroimmunology and healing touch in HIV disease. *Dissertation Abstracts International: Section B: The Sciences and Engineering*, 61(B): 196.

Robinson, A. and McGrail, M. (2004) Disclosure of CAM use to medical practitioners: a review of qualitative and quantitative studies. *Complementary Therapies in Medicine*, 12, 90–8.

Robinson, F., Matthews, H. and Witek-Janusek, L. (2000) Stress reduction and HIV disease: a review of intervention studies using a psychoneuroimmunological framework. *Journal of the Association of Nurses in AIDS Care*, 11(2), 87–96.

Roesch, S. and Weiner, B. (2001) A meta-analytic review of coping with illness: do causal attributions matter? *Journal of Psychosomatic Research*, 50(4), 205–19.

Rogers, C.R. (1959) A theory of therapy, personality and interpersonal relationships as developed in the client-centred framework, in S. Koch (ed.), *Psychology: A Study of a Science*, vol.3 (pp. 184–256). New York: McGraw-Hill.

Rogers, M. (1990) Nursing science of unitary, irreducible, human beings: update, in E. Barrett (ed.), *Visions of Rogers' Science Based Nursing* (pp. 46–59). New York: National League for Nursing.

Rogers, R. W. (1983) Cognitive and physiological processes in fear appeals and attitude change: a revised theory of protection motivation, in J. T. Cacioppo and R. E. Petty (eds.) *Social Psychophysiology: A sourcebook* (pp. 153–76). New York: The Guildford Press.

Roney-Dougal, S.M. (1999) On a possible psychophysiology of the Yogic chakra system. *Journal of Indian Psychology*, 17(2), 18–40.

Rosenberg, A. (1980) *Sociobiology and the Preemption of Social Science*. London: The Johns Hopkins University Press.

Rosenstock, I. M. (1966) Why People Use Health Services. *Milbank Memorial Fund Quarterly*, 44, 94–124.

Rotter, J. (1966) Generalised expectancies for internal versus external locus of control of reinforcement. *Psychological Monographs*, 80(1), 1–28.

Sadler, J.Z. and Hulgus, Y.F. (1992) Clinical problem solving and the biopsycho-social model. *American Journal of Psychiatry*, 149(10), 1315–23.

Salmon, P. and Hall, G. (2003) Patient empowerment and control: a psychological discourse in the service of medicine. *Social Science and Medicine*, 57, 1969–80.

Salovey, P. and Rothman, A. J. (2003) *The social psychology of health*. Philadelphia, PA: Psychology Press.

Saper R.B. (2004) Prevalence and patterns of adult yoga use in the United States: results of a national survey. *Alternative Therapies in Health and Medicine*, 10(2), 44–9.

Sarafino, E.P. (1998) *Health Psychology: Biopsychosocial Interactions*. New York: John Wiley.

Sarojjakool, S. (2006) *When Sickness Heals: The Place of Religious Beliefs in Health Care*. West Conhohocken, PA: Templeton Foundation Press.

Savage, R. and Armstrong, D. (1990) Effects of a general practitioner's consulting style on patients' satisfaction: a controlled study. *British Medical Journal*, 6758, 968–70.

Say, R.E. and Thomson, R. (2003) The importance of patient preferences in treatment decisions: challenges for doctors. *British Medical Journal*, 327, 542–5.

Scambler, A., Scambler, G. and Craig, D. (1981) Kinship and friendship networks and women's demands for primary care. *Journal of the Royal College of General Practitioners*, 26, 746–50.

Schachter, S & Singer, J.E. (1962) Cognitive, social and physiological determinants of emotional state. *Psychological Review*, 69, 379–99.

Schaeffer, R. (2000a) Yoga notebook: tension headache relief. *Natural Health*, 30(6), 44–5.

Schaeffer R. (2000b) Ease lower back pain. *Natural Health*, 30(7), 44–5.

Scheier, M.F. and Carver, C.S. (1987) Dispositional optimism and physical well-being: the influence of generalized outcome expectancies on health. *Journal of Personality*, 55, 169–210.

Scheier, M.F. and Carver, C.S. (1988) A model of behavioural self-regulation: trans-lating intention into action, in L. Berkowitz (ed.), *Advances in Experimental Psych-ology* (Vol 21, pp. 303–6). New York: Academic Press.

Scheier, M.F., Matthews, K.A., Owens, J., Magovern, G., Lefebvre, R., Abbott, R.A. and Carver, C. (1989) Dispositional optimism and recovery from coronary artery bypass surgery: the beneficial effects on physical and psychological well-being. *Journal of Personality and Social Psychology*, 57(6), 1024–40.

Schickler, P. (2005) Achieving health or achieving wellbeing? *Health and Social Care*, 4(4), 217–27.

Schmied, L.A. and Lawler, K.A. (1986) Hardiness, Type A behavior, and the stress–illness relationship in working women. *Journal of Personality and Social Psychology*, 47, 156–63.

Schneider, K. (2005) A qualitative and quantitative validation study of the assessment of the chakras through qualitative responses. *Dissertation Abstracts International: Section B: The Sciences and Engineering*, 65(9-B), 4876.

Schneiderman, N. (1999) Behavioral medicine and the management of HIV/AIDS. *International Journal of Behavioral Medicine*, 6(1), 3–12.

Schneiderman, N., Antoni, M., Ironson, G. and Lapierre, A. (1992) Applied psychological science and HIV-1 spectrum disease. *Applied and Preventive Psychology*, 1(2), 67–82.

Schnittker, J. (2005) Chronic illness and depressive symptoms in later life. *Social Science and Medicine*, 60, 13–23.

Schwartz, G.E. and Schloss, E.P. (2006) World hypotheses and the evolution of integrative medicine: combining categorical diagnoses and cause–effect interventions with whole systems research and nonvisualization (seemingly 'impossible') healing. *Explore: The Journal of Science and Healing*, 2(6), 509–14.

Schwartzer, R. (1992) *Self-efficacy: Thought control action*. Washington, DC: Hemisphere.

Schwartzer, R. and Knoll, N. (2003) Positive coping mastering demands and searching for meaning, in S.J. Lopez and C.R. Snyder (eds), *Positive Psychological Assessment: A Handbook of Models and Measures* (pp. 393–409). Washington, DC: American Psychological Association.

Schweizer, K. and Dobrich, P. (2003) Self-reported health, appraisal, coping, and stress in teachers. *Psychology Science*, 45, 92–105.

Scott, C.M., Verhoef, M.J. and Hilsden, R.J. (2003) Inflammatory bowel disease patients' decisions to use complementary therapies: links to existing models of care. *Complementary Therapies in Medicine*, 11(1), 22–7.

Scott, J., Kearney, N., Hummerston, S. and Molassiotis, A. (2005) Use of complementary and alternative medicine in patients with cancer: a UK survey. *European Journal of Oncology Nursing*, 9, 131–7.

Scott-Sheldon, L.A.J., Kalichman, S.C., Carey, M.P. and Fielder, R. (2008) Stress management in adults with HIV/AIDS: a meta-analysis. *Health Psychology*, 27, 129–39.

Scully, J.A., Tosi, H. and Banning, K. (2000) Life event checklists: revisiting the social readjustment rating scale after 30 years. *Educational and Psychological Measurement*, 60(6), 864–76.

Searle, A. and Murphy, S. (2000) Representations of illness: their relationship with an understanding of and adherence to homeopathic treatment. *Psychology, Health and Medicine*, 5, 179–91.

Segerstrom, S.C. (2005) Optimism and immunity: do positive thoughts always lead to positive effects? *Brain, Behavior, and Immunity*, 19(3), 195–200.

Segerstrom, S.C. (2007) Stress, energy, and immunity: an ecological view. *Current Directions in Psychological Science*, 16, 326–30.

Segerstrom, S.C. (2008) Social networks and immunosuppression during stress: relationship conflict or energy conservation? *Brain, Behavior, and Immunity*, 22, 279–84.

Selye, H. (1936) A syndrome produced by diverse nocuous agents. *Nature*, 138, 32.

Selye, H. (1950) *The Physiology and Pathology of Exposure to Stress*. Oxford: Acta.

Selye, H. and Fortier, C. (1950) Adaptive reaction to stress. *Psychosomatic Medicine*, 12, 149–57.

Sephton, S. (2007) The definition and measurement of chronic stress, and the effects of chronic stress on the cytotoxic activity of natural killer cells. *Dissertation Abstracts Internationals: Section B: The Sciences and Engineering*, 56(11-B), 6450.

Shang, C. (2000) The past, present and future of meridian system research. *Clinical Acupuncture and Oriental Medicine*, 1(2), 115–24.

Shang, C. (2001) Emerging paradigms in mind–body medicine. *Journal of Alternative and Complementary Medicine*, 7(1), 83–91.

Shankar, K. and Liao, L.P. (2004) Traditional systems of medicine. *Physical Medicine and Rehabilitation Clinics of North America*, 15(4), 725–47.

Sharloo, M., Kaptein, A., Weinman, J., Hazes, J., Willems, L., Bergman, W. and Rooijmans, H. (1998) Illness perceptions, coping and functioning in patients with rheumatoid arthritis, chronic obstructive pulmonary disease and psoriasis. *Journal of Psychosomatic Research*, 44(5), 573–85.

Sharma, U. (1994) The Equation of responsibility: the patient practitioner relationship in complementary medicine, in U. Sharma and S. Budd (eds), *The Healing Bond: Therapeutic Responsibility and the Patient Practitioner Relationship*. London: Routledge.

Sharma, U. (2000) Medical pluralism and the future of CAM, in M. Kelner, B. Wellman, B. Pescosolido and M. Saks (eds), *Complementary and Alternative Medicine: Challenge and Change* (pp. 211–22). Australia: Harwood.

Sharma, U. (2001) Using alternative therapies: marginal medicine and central concerns, in B. Davey, A. Gray and C. Seale (eds), *Health and Disease: A Reader* (3rd edn, pp. 102–8). Buckingham: Open University Press.

Sharma, U.M. (1992) *Complementary Medicine Today: Practitioners and Patients*. London: Routledge.

Sharpe, L. and Curran, L. (2006) Understanding the process of adjustment to chronic disease. *Social Science and Medicine*, 62, 1153–66.

Shekelle, P.S, Woolf, S.H., Eccles, M. and Grimshaw, J. (1999) Clinical guidelines: developing guidelines. *British Medical Journal*, 318, 593–6

Sheldrake, R. (1988) *The Presence of Past: Morphic Resonance and the Habits of Nature*. London: Collins.

Shiloh, S. and Orgler-Shoob, M. (2006) Monitoring: a dual-function coping style. *Journal of Personality*, 74(2), 457–78.

Shotter, J. (1984) *Social Accountability and Selfhood*. Oxford: Basil Blackwell.

Siapush, M. (1998) Postmodern values, dissatisfaction with conventional medicine and popularity of complementary therapies. *Journal of Sociology*, 34, 58–70.

Siapush, M. (1999) Postmodern attitudes about health: a population-based exploratory study. *Complementary Therapies in Medicine*, 7, 164–9.

Sidman, M. (1960) *Tactics of Scientific Research*. New York: Basic Books.

Simpson, S.H., Eurich, D.T., Majumdar, S.R., Padwal, R.S., Tsuyuki, R.T., Varney, J. and Johnson, J.A. (2006). A meta-analysis of the association between adherence to drug therapy and mortality. *British Medical Journal*, *333(7557)*, 15, doi:10.1136/bmj.38875.675486.55.

Sirois, F.M. and Gick, M.L. (2002) An investigation of the health beliefs and motivations of complementary medicine clients. *Social Science and Medicine*, 55(6), 1025–37.

Sjösten, N., Vaapio, S. and Kivelä, S.-L. (2008) The effects of fall prevention trials on depressive symptoms and fear of falling among the aged: a systematic review. *Aging and Mental Health*, 12(1), 30–46.

Skinner, B.F. (1953) *Science and Human Behaviour*. New York: Macmillan.

Skinner, B.F. (1984) What are the scope and limits of radical behaviorist theory? *Behavioral and Brain Sciences*, 7, 721–4.

Smith, J.A. (2008). Effects of yoga on stress among college students in a post-Katrina population. *Dissertation Abstracts International: Section B: The Sciences and Engineering*, 68(11-B), 7678.

Smith, J. and Osborn, M. (2003) Interpretative phenomenological analysis, in J. Smith (ed.), *Qualitative Psychology* (pp. 51–81). London: Sage.

Smith, J., Harré, R. and van Langehove, L. (eds) (1995) *Rethinking Psychology*. London: Sage.

Smith, K.L. (2006) Appreciation of holistic nursing. *Journal of Holistic Nursing*, 24(2), 139.

Sodergren, S., Hyland, M., Singh, S. and Sewell, L. (2002) The effect of rehabilitation on positive interpretations of health. *Psychology and Health*, 17(6), 753–60.

Song, C. (2001) Anxiety and the immune system: the modulation of benzodiazepines. *Stress and Health*, 17(3), 129–31.

Sparber, A., Bauer, L., Curt, G., Eisenberg, D., Levin, T., Parks, S., Steinberg, S. and Wootton, J. (2000) Use of complementary medicine by adult patients participating in cancer clinical trials. *Oncology Nursing Forum*, 27(4), 129–36.

Spence, J. and Olson, M. (1997) Quantitative research on therapeutic touch: an integrative review of the literature 1985–1995. *Scandinavian Journal of Caring Sciences*, 11(3), 183–90.

Spiegel, D., Bloom, J. and Kraemer, H. (1989) Effects of psychosocial treatment on survival of patients with metatastic breast cancer. *The Lancet*, 298, 291–3.

St Claire, L. (2003) *Rival Truths: Common Sense and Social Psychological Explanations in Health and Illness*. Hove: Psychology Press.

Störig, H. (1979) *Geschiedenis van de Filosofie*. Utrecht: Het Spectrum.

Stainton Rogers, W. (1991) *Explaining Health and Illness: An Exploration of Diversity*. Hemel Hemstead: Wheatsheaf.

Stainton Rogers, W. (1996) Critical approaches to health psychology. *Journal of Health Psychology*, 1, 65–77.

Stam, H. (2000) Theorizing health and illness: functionalism, subjectivity, and reflexivity. *Journal of Health Psychology*, 5(3), 273–83.

Stam, H.J. (2004) A sound mind in a sound body: a critical historical analysis of health psychology, in M. Murray (ed.), *Critical Health Psychology* (pp. 15–31). New York: Palgrave Macmillan.

Stanton, A. and Revenson, T. (2005) Progress and promise in research on adaptation to chronic illness, in H. Friedman and R. Silver (eds), *The Oxford Handbook of Health Psychology*. Oxford: Oxford University Press.

Stefano, G.B., Fricchione, G.L., Slingsby, B.T. and Benson, H. (2001) The placebo effect and relaxation response: neural processes and their coupling to constitutive nitric oxide. *Brain Research Reviews*, 35, 1–19.

Steptoe, A. and Hamer, M. (2007) Psychosocial determinants of the stress response, in M. Al'Absi, (ed.), *Stress and Addiction: Biological and Psychological Mechanisms* (pp. 211–25). San Diego, CA: Elsevier Academic Press.

Steptoe, A., Wright, C., Kunz-Ebrecht, S.R. and Iliffe, S. (2006) Dispositional optimism and health behaviour in community-dwelling older people: associations with healthy ageing. *British Journal of Health Psychology*, 11(1), 71–84.

Strang, S. and Strang, P. (2001) Spiritual thoughts, coping and 'sense of coherence' in brain tumour patients and their spouses. *Palliative Medicine*, 15(2), 127–34.

Strauss, A.L. and Corbin, J.A. (1990) *Basics of Qualitative Research: Grounded Theory Procedures and Techniques*. London: Sage.

Stroebe, M.S., Schut, H.A.W. and Stroebe, W. (2007) The health consequences of bereavement: a review. *The Lancet*, 370, 1960–73.

Suarez, T. and Reese, F. (2000) Coping, psychological adjustment, and complementary and alternative medicine use in persons living with HIV and AIDS. *Psychology and Health*, 15(5), 635–49.

Sulmasy, D.P. (2002) A biopsychosocialspiritual model for the care of patients at the end of life. *Gerontologist*, 42, 24–33.

Suls, J. and Sanders, G.S. (1988) Type A behavior as a general risk factor for physical disorder. *Journal of Behavioral Medicine*, 11, 201–26.

Sun, E., Wei, L., Roberts, A., Liu, C. and Shi, Y. (2007) Chronic stress induces death of lymphocytes, in N. Plotnikoff, R. Faith, A. Murgo and R. Good (eds), *Cytokines: Stress and Immunity* (pp. 157–69). Cleveland, OH: CRC Press.

Sun, W., Dosch, M., Gilmore, G.D., Pemberton, W. and Scarseth, T. (1996) Effects of a Tai Chi Chuan program on Hmong American older adults. *Educational Gerontology*, 22(2), 161–7.

Sveinsdottir, H., Gunnarsdottir, H. and Fririksdottir, H. (2007) Self-assessed occupational health and working environment of female nurses, cabin crew and teachers. *Scandinavian Journal of Caring Sciences*, 21(2), 262–73.

Szondy, M. (2004) Optimism and immune functions. *Mentalhigiene es Pszichoszomatika*, 5(4), 301–20. (Abstract only)

Taine, H. (1871), *On Intelligence*. London: L. Reeve and Co.

Tarakeshwar, N., Vanderwerker, L.C., Paulk, E., Pearce, M.J., Kasl, S.V. and Prigerson, H.G. (2006) Religious coping is associated with the quality of life of patients with advanced cancer. *Journal of Palliative Medicine*, 9(3), 646–57.

Tavares, M. (2003) *National Guidelines for the Use of Complementary Therapies in Supportive and Palliative Care*. London: NCHSPCS/PoWFIH.

Taylor, S., Lichtman, R. and Wood, J. (1984) Attributions, beliefs about control, and adjustment to breast cancer. *Journal of Personality and Social Psychology*, 46(3), 489–502.

Taylor-Piliae, R.E., Haskell, W.L., Waters, C.M. and Froelicher, E.S. (2006) Change in perceived psychosocial status following a 12-week Tai Chi exercise programme. *Journal of Advanced Nursing*, 54(3), 313–29.

Tennen, H., Affleck, G., Allen, P., McGrade, B., and Ratzan, S. (1984) Causal attributions and coping with insulin dependent diabetes. *Basic and Applied Social Psychology*, 5, 131–42.

Thayer, R.E. (1989) *The Biopsychology of Mood and Arousal*. New York: Oxford University Press.

Thayer, R.E. (1996) *The Origin of Everyday Moods*. New York: Oxford University Press.

Thomas, K. and Coleman, P. (2004) Use of complementary or alternative medicine in a general population in Great Britain: results from the National Omnibus survey. *Journal of Public Health*, 26(2), 152–7.

Thomas, K., Fall, M. and Nicholl, J. (2001) Access to complementary medicine via general practice. *British Journal of General Practice*, 51, 25–30.

Thomas, K., MacPherson, H., Thorpe, L., Brazier, J., Fitter, M., Campbell, M., Roman, M., Walters, S. and Nicholl, J. (2006) Randomised controlled trial of a short course of traditional acupuncture compared with the usual care for persistent non-specific low back pain. *British Medical Journal*, doi:10.1136/bmj.38878.907361.7C.

Thomas, K., Nicholl, J. and Coleman, P. (2001). Use and expenditure on complementary medicine in England: a population based survey. *Complementary Therapies in Medicine*, 9, 2–11.

Thomas, S.P. (1986) A descriptive profile of type B personality. *Journal of Nursing Scholarship*, 18(1), 4–7.

Thompson, S., Armstrong, W. and Thomas, C. (1998) Illusions of control, underestimations, and accuracy: a control heuristic explanation. *Psychological Bulletin*, 123, 143–61.

Thorne, S., Paterson, B., Russell, C. and Schultz, A. (2002) Complementary/alternative medicine in chronic illness as informed self-care decision making. *International Journal of Nursing Studies*, 39(7), 671–83.

Thorne, S.E. (1999) The science of meaning in chronic illness. *International Journal of Nursing Studies*, 36, 397–404.

Thorne, S.E., Nyhlin, K.T. and Paterson, B.L. (2000) Attitudes toward patient expertise in chronic illness. *International Journal of Nursing Studies*, 37, 303–11.

Thornton, L.M., Andersen, B.L., Crespin, T.R. and Carson, W.E. (2007) Individual trajectories in stress covary with immunity during recovery from cancer diagnosis and treatments. *Brain, Behavior, and Immunity*, 21(2), 185–94.

Tiller, W. (1979) Creating a new functional model of body healing energies. *Journal of Holistic Health*, 4, 102–14.

Tomakowsky, J., Lumley, M.A., Markowitz, N. and Frank, C. (2001) Optimistic explanatory style and dispositional optimism in HIV-infected men. *Journal of Psychosomatic Research*, 51(4), 577–87.

Toneatto, T. and Nguyen, L. (2007) Does mindfulness meditation improve anxiety and mood symptoms? A review of the controlled research. *The Canadian Journal of Psychiatry*, 52(4), 260–6.

Tosevski, D.L. and Milovancevic, M.P. (2006) Stressful life events and physical health. *Current Opinion in Psychiatry*, 19(21), 84–9.

Trevelyan, J. (1996) A true complement? *Nursing Times*, 92(5), 42–3.

Truant, T. and Bottorff, J. (1999) Decision making related to complementary therapies: a process of regaining control. *Patient Education and Counselling*, 38, 131–42.

Trull, T.J. and Geary, D.C. (1997) Comparison of the big-five factor structure across samples of Chinese and American adults. *Journal of Personality Assessment*, 69(2), 324–41.

Trumpington, M. (1987) Alternative medicines and therapies and the DHSS. *Journal of Royal Society of Medicine*, 80, 336–8.

Turnquist, D., Harvey, J. and Anderson, B. (1988) Attributions and adjustment to life-threatening illness. *British Journal of Clinical Psychology*, 27, 55–65.

Tweed, R.G. and Conway, L.G. (2006) Coping strategies and culturally influenced beliefs about the world, in P.T.P. Wong and L.C.J. Wong (eds), *Handbook of Multicultural Perspectives on Stress and Coping* (pp. 133–55). New York: Springer.

van Dongen, E. (2004) Touch, the forgotten sense. *Contemporary Psychology: APA Review of Books*, 49(1), 69–70.

van Haselen, R. and Luedtke, R. (2008) Editorial: research in homeopathy – from confusion to disillusion or resolution? *Complementary Therapies in Medicine*, 16, 59–60.

van Vegchel, N., de Jonge, J., Bosma, H. and Schaufeli, W. (2005) Reviewing the effort-reward imbalance model: drawing up the balance of 45 empirical studies. *Social Science and Medicine*, 60(5), 1117–31.

van Vliet, K. Willemsen, E.M., Radder, J.K., Lemkes, H.H.P.J and Jacobi, C.E. (1997) Symptom perception and hypoglycemia unawareness in IDDM patients. *Gedrag and Gezondheid: Tijdschrift voor Psychologie en Gezondheid*, 25(1), 22–32.

van Wersch, A. (2007). Avoiding surgical removal of gallbladder stones: a study of information and social support of self treatment methods through the internet. Paper presented at the 5th *Biennial Conference of the Society of Critical Health Psychology*, Boston (USA), 18 July.

van Wersch, A. and Eccles, M. (1999) Patient involvement in evidence based medicine in relation to clinical guidelines, in M. Gabbay (ed.), *The Handbook of Evidence Based Medicine for Primary Care* (pp. 91–105). London: Royal Society of Medicine.

van Wersch, A. and Eccles, M. (2001) Involving patients in the development of evidence based clinical guidelines: practical experiences from the North of England evidence based guideline development programme. *Quality in Health Care*, 10, 10–16.

van Wersch, A. de Boer, M.F., van der Does, E., de Jong, P. Knegt, P. Meeuwis, C.A., Stringer, P. and Pruyn, J.F. (1997) Continuity of information in head and neck cancer care: evaluation of a logbook. *Patient Education and Counseling*, 31, 223–6.

van Wersch, A. Turnbull, T. and Watson, R. (2003) General practitioner's attitudes to complementary medicine. *Complementary Therapies in Medicine*, 11(3), 200.

van Wersch, A., Bonnema, J., Pruyn, J., Wiggers, T., Prinsen, B. and van Geel, A. (1997) Continuity of information for breast-cancer patients: the development, use and evaluation of a multidisciplinary protocol. *Patient Education and Counseling*, 30 (2), 175–86.

van Wijk, E.P.A. Ackerman, J. and van Wijk, R. (2005) Effect of meditation on ultraweak photon emission from hands and forehead. *Forschende Komplementärmedizin – Klassische Naturheilkunde*, 12, 107–12.

van Wijk, E.P.A. Koch, H., Bosman, S. and van Wijk, R. (2006) Anatomic characterisation of human ultra-weak photon emission in practitioners of transcedental meditation and control subjects. *The Journal of Alternative and Complementary Medicine*, 12(1), 31–8.

van Wijk, R. and van Wijk, E.P.A. (2005) An introduction to human biophoton emission. *Forschende Komplementärmedizin – Klassische Naturheilkunde*, 12, 77–83.

van Zuuren, F.J. and Dooper, R. (1999) Coping style and self-reported health promotion and disease detection behaviour. *British Journal of Health Psychology*, 4, 81–9.

Verbrugge, C. and Ascione, F. (1989) Exploring the iceberg: common symptoms and how people care for them. *Medical Care*, 25, 539–69.

Verhoef, M., Mulkins, A. and Boon, H. (2005) Integrative health care: how can we determine whether patients benefit? *Jounal of Alternative and Complementary Medicine*, 11(Supplement 1), S-57–65.

Verhoef, M.J., Lewith, G., Ritenbaugh, C., Boon, H., Fleishman, S. and Leis, A. (2005) Complementary and alternative medicine whole systems research: beyond identification of inadequacies of the RCT. *Complementary Therapies in Medicine*, 13(3), 206–12.

Vickers, A. (2000) Recent advances in complementary medicine. *British Medical Journal*, 321, 683–6.

Vickers, A. (ed.) (1998) *Examining Complementary Medicine*. Cheltenham: Stanley Thornes.

Vilhjalmsson, R. (1998) Direct and indirect effects of chronic physical conditions on depression: a preliminary investigation. *Social Science and Medicine*, 47(5), 603–11.

Villemure, C. and Bushnell, M.C. (2002) Cognitive modulation of pain: how do attention and emotion influence pain processing? *Pain*, 95, 195–99.

Vincent, C. and Furnham, A. (1996) Why do patients turn to complementary medicine? An empirical study. *British Journal of Clinical Psychology*, 35, 37–48.

Vincent, C. and Furnham, A. (1997) *Complementary Medicine: A Research Perspective*. Chichester: John Wiley.

Visser, M. (2006) Orientatieweekend antroposofische geneeskunde succes. (Orientation weekend anthroposophical medicine successful). Retrieved: //httm. www.zonmw.nl. 2nd October 2006.

Von Korff, M., Glasgow, R. and Sharpe, M. (2002) Organising care for chronic illness. *British Medical Journal*, 325, 92–4.

Wadee, A., Kuschke, R., Kometz, S. and Berk, M. (2001) Personality factors, stress and immunity. *Stress and Health: Journal of the International Society for the Investigation of Stress*, 17(1), 25–40.

Wahner-Roedler, D.L., Elkin P.L., Vincent, A., Loehrer, L.L., Schilling, T.D. and Bauer, B.A. (2005) Development of a complementary and alternative medicine programme at an academic medical centre. *Evidence Based Integrated Medicine*, 2(1), 9–12.

Walach, H. (2005) Generalized entanglement: a new theoretical model for understanding the effects of complementary and alternative medicine. *Journal of Alternative and Complementary Medicine*, 11(3), 549–59.

Walji, R. and Boon, H. (2006) Redefining the Randomized Trial in the context of acupuncture research. *Complementary Therapies in Clinical Practice*, 12(2), 91–6.

Watson, D., Clark, L.A. and Tellegen, A. (1988) Development and validation of brief measures of positive and negative affect: the PANAS scales. *Journal of Personality and Social Psychology*, 54(6), 1063–70.

Watson, J.B. (1913) Psychology as the behaviorist views it. *Psychological Review*, 20, 158–77.

Watt J. (1988) *Talking Health: Conventional and Complementary Approaches*. London: The Royal Society of Medicine.

Watt, S., Roberts, J., Browne, G. and Gafni, A. (1997) Age, adjustment, and costs: a study of chronic illnesses. *Social Science and Medicine*, 44(10), 1483–90.

Weiger, W., Smith, M., Boon, H., Richardson, M., Kaptchuk, T. and Eisenberg, D. (2002) Advising patients who seek complementary and alternative medical therapies for cancer. *Annals of Internal Medicine*, 137(11), 889–905.

Weiner, B. (1982) An attributionally-based theory of motivation and emotion: Focus, range, and issues, in N.T. Feather (ed.), *Expectancy, incentive, and action*, (pp.163–206). Hillsdale, N J: Erlbaum.

Wellard, S. (1998) Constructions of chronic illness. *International Journal of Nursing Studies*, 35, 49–55.

Wertheimer, A. and Santella, T. (2003) Medication compliance research: still so far to go. *Journal of Applied Research*, 3(3), 1–11.

Westerman, N. (2006) *Bio-energie: De potentie van niet-reguliere geneeskunde (Bio-energy: the potential of non-regulated medicine)*. Dordrecht: Rathega publishers.

Wetzel M.S., Eisenberg, D.M. and Kaptchuk, T.J. (1998) Courses involving complementary and alternative medicine at US medical schools. *Journal of the American Medical Association*, 280(9), 784–7.

White, A. (1998). Complementary medicine treatment of cancer: a survey of provision. *Complementary Therapies in Medicine*, 6, 10–13.

White, A. (2003) Is integrated medicine respectable? *Complementary Therapies in Medicine*, 11, 140–1.

White, A., Resch, K. and Ernst, E. (1997) Complementary medicine: use and attitudes among GPs. *Family Practice*, 14(4), 302–6.

Whitehead, L. (2006) Quest, chaos and restitution: living with chronic fatigue syndrome/myalgic encephalomyelitis. *Social Science and Medicine*, 62, 2236–45.

Wilkinson, R. (1996) *Unhealthy Societies*. London: Routledge.

Wilkinson, S. (2004) Feminist contributions to critical health psychology, in M. Murray (ed.), *Critical Health Psychology* (pp. 83–101). New York: Palgrave Macmillan.

Williams, G. (1984) The genesis of chronic illness: narrative reconstruction. *Sociology of Health and Illness*, 6(2), 175–200.

Williams, K. (2006) Mindfulness-Based Stress Reduction (MBSR) in a Worksite Wellness Program, in R. Baer (ed.), *Mindfulness-based Treatment Approaches: Clinician's Guide to Evidence Base and Applications* (pp. 361–76). San Diego, CA: Elsevier Academic Press.

Williams, P., Holmbeck, G.N. and Greenley, R.N. (2002) Adolescent health psychology. *Journal of Consulting and Clinical Psychology*, 70(3), 828–42.

Williams, S., Weinman, J., Dale, J. and Newman, S. (1995) Patient expectations: what do primary care patients want from the GP and how far does meeting expectations affect patient satisfaction? *Family Practice*, 12(20), 193–201.

Williamson, A., Fletcher, P. and Dawson, K. (2003) Complementary and alternative medicine: use in an older population. *Journal of Gerontology and Nursing*, 29(5), 20–8.

Willig, C. (2004) Discourse analysis and health psychology, in M. Murray (ed.), *Critical Health Psychology* (pp. 155–71). New York: Palgrave Macmillan.

Willison, K. and Andrews, G. (2004) Complementary medicine and older people: past research and future directions. *Complementary Therapies in Nursing and Midwifery*, 10, 80–91.

Willison, K.D. (2006). Integrating Swedish massage therapy with primary health care initiatives as part of a holistic nursing approach. *Complementary Therapies in Medicine*, 14(4), 254–260.

Wilson, P. (2001) A policy analysis of the expert patient in the United Kingdom: self-care as an expression of pastoral power? *Health and Social Care in the Community*, 9, 134–42.

Wilson, P., Kendall, S. and Brooks, F. (2007) The Expert Patients Programme: a paradox of patient empowerment and medical dominance. *Health and Social Care in the Community*, 15(5), 426–38.

Wilson, S.M. and Miles, M.S. (2001) Spirituality in African-American mothers coping with a seriously ill infant. *Journal of the Society of Pediatric Nurses*, 6(3), 116–22.

Wilson, T., Buck, D. and Ham, C. (2005) Rising to the challenge: will the NHS support people with long term conditions? *British Medical Journal*, 330, 657–61.

Withers, R. (2001) Psychoanalysis, complementary medicine and the placebo, in D. Peters (ed.), *Understanding the Placebo Effect in Complementary Medicine* (pp. 111–31). London: Churchill Livingstone.

Winnick, T.A. (2005) From quackery to 'complementary' medicine: the American medical profession confronts alternative therapies. *Social Problems*, 52, 38–61.

Wong, C.M. (2002) Post-traumatic stress disorder: advances in psychoneuroimmunology. *Psychiatric Clinics of North America*, 25(2), 369–83.

Wong, C.M. and Yehuda, R. (2002) Sex differences in posttraumatic stress disorder, in F. Lewis-Hall, T. Williams, J. Panetta and J. Herrera (eds), *Psychiatric Illness in Women: Emerging Treatments and Research* (pp. 57–96). Arlington, VA: American Psychological Publishing.

Wong, H., Lopez-Nahas, V., and Molassiotis, A. (2001) The effects of music therapy on anxiety in ventilator dependent patients. *Heart and Lung*, 30, 378–87.

Wong, P.T.P. and McDonald, M. (2002) Tragic optimism and personal meaning in counselling victims of abuse. *Pastoral Sciences*, 20, 231–49.

Wong, P.T.P. and Sproule, C.F. (1984) Attributional analysis of locus of control and the Trent Attribution Profile (TAP), in H.M. Lefcourt (ed.), *Research with Locus of Control Constructs* (pp. 309–60). New York: Academic Press.

Wong, P.T.P. and Ujimoto, K. (1998) The elderly Asial Americans: their stress, coping and wellbeing, in L.C. Lee and N.W. Zane (eds), *Handbook of Asian American Psychology* (pp. 165–209). Thousand Oaks, CA: Sage.

Wong, P.T.P. and Wong, L.C.J. (2006) *Handbook of Multicultural Perspectives on Stress and Coping*. New York: Springer.

Wood, C. (1998) Subtle energy and the vital force in complementary medicine, in A. Vickers (ed.), *Examining Complementary Medicine* (pp. 113–24). Cheltenham: Stanley Thornes.

World Health Organization (WHO) (2003) *The World Health Report 2003: Shaping the Future*. Geneva: WHO.

Worwood, V.A. (1995) *The fragrant mind. Aromatherapy for personality, mind, mood and emotion*. London: Transworld Publishers Limited.

Wright, S. G. and Sayre-Adams, J. (2001) Healing and Therapeutic Touch: is it all in the mind? in D. Peters (ed.), *Understanding the Placebo Effect in Complementary Medicine* (pp. 165–87). London: Churchill Livingstone.

Wu, H.C. (2006) The effect of work on people with severe mental illness in Taiwan using a stress-social support model: an exploratory study. *International Journal of Rehabilitation Research*, 29(2), 145–50.

Wu, H.S., Wu, S.C., Lin, J.G. and Lin, L.C. (2004) Effectiveness of acupressure in improving dyspnoea in chronic obstructive pulmonary disease. *Journal of Advanced Nursing*, 45(3), 252–9.

Yardley, L., Sharples, K., Beech, S. and Lewith, G. (2001) Developing a dynamic model of treatment perceptions. *Journal of Health Psychology*, 6(3), 269–82.

Yueping, Z. Jianhong, M. and Lianying, Z. (2004) The relationship between sense of coherence and stressors. *Psychological Science*, 27(4), 964–66.

Zeitlin D., Keller, S.E., Shiflett, S.C., Schleifer, S.J. and Bartlett, J.A. (2000) Immunological effects of massage therapy during acute academic stress. *Psychiatric Medicine*, 62(1), 83–4.

Zimmerman, M.A., Ramirez-Valles, J., Zapert, K.M. and Maton, K.I. (2000) A longitudinal study of stress-buffering effects for urban African-American male adolescent problem behaviors and mental health. *Journal of Community Psychology*. 28(1), 17–33.

Zohar, D. (1990) *The Quantum Self*. London: Bloomsbury Publishers.

Zollman C. and Vickers, A. (1999) What is complementary medicine? *British Medical Journal*, 319(7211), 693–6.

Index